A Grim Almanac of

Kent

W.H. Johnson

British Library Cataloguing in Publication Data
A catalogue record for this book is available from the British Library.

ISBN 978-0-7509-4948-4

Typeset in 10.5/12.5pt Photina.
Typesetting and origination by The History Press.
Printed and bound in England by Ashford Colour Press Ltd.

The Grim Almanacs are from an original idea by Neil R. Storey.

Meet the author at www.johnniejohnson.co.uk

Acknowledgements

I am very grateful to all who have helped me with this book. A fellow writer, Neil R. Storey, has again generously permitted me to use pictures from his archive. As on previous occasions, the Sussex historian Peter Longstaff-Tyrrell has answered my pleas for help as has Paul Williams whose Murder Files service has been the source of many of the items in the book.

The journalist and historian Frank Chapman has most kindly permitted me to reproduce pictures from his *Book of Tonbridge* and Geoff Copus and Brian Woodgate allowed me to use the photograph of the Baltic Sawmills at Tunbridge Wells. And up in Argyllshire, Prison Governor Gavin Dick agreed to my using some illustrations from the Inverary Gaol website. As always I am grateful to my old friend David Orchard of Edenbridge, and to the ever-helpful John Endicott, curator of the excellent Kent Police Museum.

The museums and library services of Kent have, as ever, been helpful. May I therefore thank, in no particular order: Karen Tayler (Tunbridge Wells); Sally Rowe (Canterbury); Gill Everest (Tonbridge); Sarah Frampton (Deal); and particularly Susan Rogers (Maidstone St Faith's).

Outside of the county, Jenny O'Keefe at Greenwich Heritage Centre and Shelley Morrow of Hastings Reference Library have hunted out material, as have the staff of Bromley Library.

But perhaps my greatest thanks ought to go to all the long-gone journalists who have furnished such dramatic and full accounts of past events, both minor and major, and to the contributors, most of them amateur, to the now sadly defunct *Bygone Kent* magazine whose volumes are a rich mine for all who seek information on this county's past.

Not least, my thanks go to my wife Anne for her sorely tried patience and for her invaluable commentary on every item in the book. As a consequence of her input there are fewer infelicities of language, fewer gross solecisms and less unnecessary verbiage.

For any whose copyright I may have failed to acknowledge or even wrongly attributed, may I apologise in advance. Working through so much material does present occasional problems which I hope have for the most part been overcome. And lastly, may I express my apologies to those who deserve to be mentioned but whom, out of carelessness, I have omitted to mention.

Once more, to each and all, named and unnamed, my grateful thanks for all of your help.

CONTENTS

Introduction

Isuppose that digging into Kent's past – and I have included all those areas of the old county which now are subsumed within Greater London – ought to reveal something, ought to give new insights into our own situation. But this book makes no high-sounding claims. It is a record of criminality and vice, of wretched living conditions and blind fate which lead to the most appalling consequences. It offers simply what the title proposes: it is an almanac and it is certainly grim. The murderous, respectable Stauntons are here jostling for villainy with George Joseph Smith of 'Brides in the Bath' notoriety and Sydney Fox, the ex-jailbird and con man, who did away with his mother in a Margate hotel. And you will discover the original Great Train Robbers in these pages, subtler by far than those who stole the limelight in 1957. Here are petty thieves and highwaymen and all manner of ruthless men and women.

There are graphic accounts of the wretchedness of the poor and the squalor they lived in. Take, for example, conditions at Maidstone's Paradise Row – was ever a place less well named? There is lawlessness here, sometimes frightening, sometimes understandable; and harsh sentences handed down to hapless small-time thieves and even young boys and girls. Nor do the entries of the first half of the twentieth century suggest that better living conditions had raised the aspirations of many, had made them kinder or more considerate.

Mercifully, there are no longer any public spectacles at the gallows or indeed at the stake. At one time people turned up in their thousands to watch these obscene rites. Ten thousand came to watch 14-year-old John Any Bird Bell hang at Maidstone. We have to ask why they came: to enjoy the occasion, to offer support or to learn a lesson? Sadly, the first option seems most likely. Perhaps, despite what we read and hear and see today, we might have made some progress.

I have included extracts from official reports, newspapers, magazines and letters which give some savour of the concerns of the 200 years covered in this book. But most interesting is how the newspapers once reported catastrophes with a frankness that even the brashest tabloid of today would shun. Yet the idea of newspaper sales promoted through shock was not in the minds of any of the editors. They knew their readers did not wish to be spared the awful details of some or other calamity but they express a righteous anger and horror at the wickedness of criminals and some kind of awe at cataclysmic events. It is then for their sometimes startling intensity that I have quoted frequently from the earlier newspapers. The newspaper columns from the early twentieth century onwards are milk and water compared to the strong brews of the past. Nevertheless, despite its dour promise, there is room in these pages for acts of kindness, undoubted courage and honourable behaviour in the face of the disasters and dangers which spring from the most awful occasions.

So, as you consider your fellow man, dear reader, you may find yourself hovering somewhere in a web of uncertainty, swinging from optimistic illusion to deepest despair about the past and the people who inhabited it. But it should always be remembered that the darkest deeds are carried out by a minority and that the darkest times most always pass.

W.H. Johnson, 2008

JANUARY

William Calcraft, Britain's longest serving executioner, hanged more than 400 people in a career spanning forty-five years from 1825. Some hanged by the inept Calcraft, who often used too short a rope, failed to die immediately from a broken neck and instead slowly strangled. On such occasions, he was known to jump on the back of the struggling wretch in an attempt to cut short the death agonies. Calcraft officiated at the execution of Stephen Forwood, the last man to be publicly executed at Maidstone. Apparently not deeply interested in his gruesome trade, Calcraft preferred his garden, his rabbits and his pony. He was said to be particularly fond of children.
(Courtesy of the Neil R. Storey Archive)

1 JANUARY 1856

In front of a large crowd, Dedea Redanies (26) was executed on top of the porter's lodge at Maidstone Gaol. He appeared little concerned, approaching the scaffold with 'a cheerful step'. Once there, he called out: 'In a few moments I shall be in the arms of my dear Caroline. I care not for death.'

Redanies had murdered 21-year-old Caroline Back along with her younger sister, Maria, one Sunday morning in August. Perhaps she was having doubts about marrying the Serb mercenary, now a member of the British-Swiss Legion, enlisted to fight alongside the British against the Russians in the Crimea. Recently, Redanies had had doubts about her faithfulness and had become obsessively jealous. And so, on the day before he committed his double murder, he bought himself a knife with a 4-inch blade.

It was arranged that on this August Sunday the soldier and the two girls would set off before dawn to walk the 10 miles from the Backs' house in Albion Place, Dover, along the cliff-top path to Folkestone. When at about seven o'clock they passed the Royal Oak, east of Capel-le-Ferne, the ostler thought they seemed very happy. But the bodies of Caroline and Maria were discovered only two hours later at Steddy Hole, a desolate spot, today called The Warren. They were both dead from deep stab wounds to the chest.

British-Swiss legionnaire uniform.

Soldiers of the Foreign Legion at Shorncliffe camp, *c.* 1855.

Maidstone Gaol.

But where was Redanies? The next day he was first spotted at Barham Down. Later he called at a shop in Lower Hardres where he bought writing paper and wrote two letters. In the afternoon, a policeman approached him near Milton Chapel, outside Canterbury. The soldier took out a knife and stabbed himself.

Redanies recovered slowly in St Augustine's Gaol in Canterbury. He wrote letters to the Back family, expressing his sorrow, and these suggest that he was insane. Nevertheless, he was sentenced to hang. He said that he looked forward to being reunited with Caroline and her sister. Another letter to the Backs, to be opened after his death, read: 'We are above with our Father again . . . I greet you with my dear Caroline and Maria . . . It was signed: 'Caroline Back. Dedea Redanies, Maria Back.'

And so to that last scene and the words of a contemporary ballad:

> The dismal bell is tolling, for the scaffold I must prepare.
> I trust in heaven my soul shall rest and meet dear Caroline there.
> Now, all young men, take warning from this sad fate of mine.
> To the memory of Maria Back and lovely Caroline.

2 JANUARY 1795

The *Maidstone Journal* reported the problems of the poor in two towns during a severe winter: 'A committee of the principal inhabitants of this parish [Chatham] have undertaken to open subscriptions and to make a collection for the relief of the industrious poor at this inclement season in order to supply them with necessary food; and particularly in the article of bread which is at such an exorbitant price that poor families cannot, but with the greatest difficulty, obtain that staff of life.'

And from Maidstone on the same date comes the following:

In addition to the many charitable donations so liberally conferred upon the poor in these parts at this inclement season, on Friday last Sir Charles Style gave 100 stone of beef and the Reverend Mr Style a large quantity of bread to the poor.

At a time like the present when through the severity of the weather and the high price of provisions, where the poor are humbly obliged to look up to the rich for relief, the parishes of Egerton and Boughton Malherbe have found a kind and benevolent benefactor in Sir Horace Mann, Baronet, whose heart and hand are ever open and ready to relieve the distressed.

3 JANUARY 1846

At Rochester Quarter Sessions, Mary Ann Vigo (13) was tried on a charge of putting three-year-old Sarah Gold into a tub of boiling tea. The child was so severely scalded that the skin fell from the soles of her feet. After six weeks the wounds were just beginning to heal. The surgeon to the North Aylesford Workhouse, where both children were inmates, had examined Sarah and said that she would be a cripple for life. Mary Ann was sentenced to one year's imprisonment in Maidstone Gaol.

4 JANUARY 1841

At the inquiry before magistrates at Rochester into the charges against James Miles, Master of the Hoo Union Workhouse, several witnesses gave accounts of beatings of boys and girls.

The *Maidstone Journal* reported that Martha Davies, an inmate of the workhouse since its opening in 1836, was an orphan. She did not know how old she was (in fact, she was born in 1832). She had been beaten on the naked buttocks by the Master.

Frances Roberts said that she had stayed at the workhouse for five months until the preceding May. She told magistrates: 'I have seen Eliza Screese flogged. The Master told her to lay herself upon the table in the hall and directed me to hold her down. I was not able because I was near my confinement. I don't know how many stripes for I turned away and knelt on the coal box. If I had not, I should have fainted away. I saw Screese punished twice since by the Master who made her take her clothes off down to her waist. I have also seen Mary Paste once flogged in the laundry by the Master. Mary Paste was then 14 years of age. She was flogged with a rod on her naked back, her clothes being removed down to the waist. Her chemise was bloody when she went about her work. I saw little Jemmy Davis flogged with a stick by the Master. He was then turned two years. I afterwards on the same evening saw great gashes on his thigh. He carried the marks for a month afterwards.'

Ruth Bills, an epileptic who, during a fit had fallen into the fire, was described as being 'horribly disfigured by a burn, having lost an eye and part of her face.' She had been in the workhouse for four years. She told the court: 'I have seen Sarah Barnes flogged twice by the Master. The Master pulled up her clothes and beat her on the lower part of her person.'

Mary Lowes, an inmate for about eight months, remembered Eliza Screese being beaten. She told magistrates: 'Mary Paste and I had to hold her down. The Master called me to hold her and I begged him to excuse me because I had children of my own. He said, "Don't let us have any of your damned nonsense or I'll serve you the same."'

Miles was dismissed from his post but there was no prosecution.

5 JANUARY 1815

What journalists of the nineteenth century would typically describe as 'a melancholy accident' occurred at Whitstable. Robert Newing, out fishing with his 16-year-old son, accidentally fell overboard. The boy immediately threw out a rope which Mr Newing managed to tie round his body. But all attempts by the son to effect a rescue failed as he had insufficient strength to haul his father into the boat. After being dragged for nearly 2 miles, Mr Newing was drowned. He left a wife and nine children.

6 JANUARY 1808

The *Maidstone Journal* reported that: 'On the 6th instant was committed to the House of Correction, Maidstone, aged 89, Dinah Shadgate, formerly an errand-woman from Otham to Maidstone, but late a pauper in Coxheath workhouse, charged with abusing, assaulting, and putting in bodily fear, the Master and Mistress of the said workhouse, for which indecorous behaviour she was ordered to be kept to hard labour for one calendar month.'

7 JANUARY 1902

Twenty-year-old Harold Apted was charged with the murder of Frances O'Rourke. The 7-year-old girl's body had been found in a pond at Vauxhall, although her death resulted from a cut throat. The clasp knife with which Frances was killed was entangled in her hair. Prior to her death she had been stripped and raped. Earlier in the day, New Year's Eve, she had been sent on an errand by her father to Tunbridge Wells and was on her way home when Apted offered her a lift in his wagon. Witnesses swore to have seen the wagon near the crime scene and two other witnesses claimed to recognise the knife as one that Apted had borrowed to cut up rabbits. Blood in the wagon and on Apted's clothing was presented as further proof of his guilt, although he claimed that it came from calves which he had taken to slaughterhouses in Tunbridge Wells.

The accused, Harold Apted. *(Kent and Sussex Courier)*

The victim, Frances O'Rourke. *(Kent and Sussex Courier)*

Found guilty, Apted confessed to the murder. He was hanged at Maidstone on 18 March.

Vauxhall Lane. *(Kent and Sussex Courier)*

The Vauxhall Inn, where the body was taken for the inquest. *(Kent and Sussex Courier)*

8 JANUARY 1859

The *South Eastern Gazette* gave details of an inquest held at the Ship Inn, Canterbury, into the death of Joseph Bolton, a prisoner in St Augustine's Gaol: 'The jury viewed the body of the dead man and the machinery of the treadmill where the accident happened. Bolton was oiling the machinery of one of the wheels which was not in motion. When the lid of the oil-can fell off and rolled under the machine, Bolton knelt down to find it. Unthinkingly, he

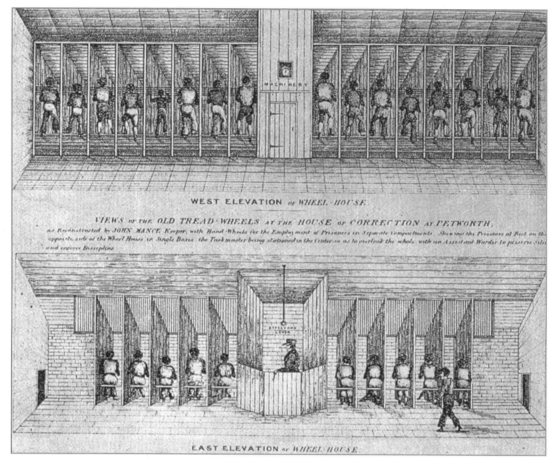

The treadmill at Petworth, Sussex, similar to that at St Augustine's, Canterbury.

placed his head between the spokes of the wheel which was in motion. His head was immediately crushed between the wheel and the upright post which supported it and was nearly severed from the body. Thomas Kent, the turnkey, ran to the Pump House and reversed the machinery and the body was released.'

Kent explained to the court that Bolton had been a prisoner for fifteen months and for the last nine months had been in the habit of oiling the machinery. The jury returned a verdict of 'accidental death' and made a recommendation that in future both wheels of the treadmill should be stopped while the machinery was being oiled.

9 JANUARY 1773
An extract from a letter of this date from a correspondent in Rochester appeared in the *Sussex Weekly Advertiser*:

Last night, about five o'clock, as some boys were playing in a field near this place, they were alarmed by hearing a groan, and being desirous to know what it was, they made their way towards a hedge hard by, which they got over, and hearing the groans still continue, one of them perceived something white in a pond near adjoining, to which they immediately proceeded, where, on taking a large bundle out of the water with a long stick, they found it contained a female child about 5 years of age, with her hands and feet tied together, and wrapped in a sheet. As the child was not quite dead, all possible means were taken to save her life, but she expired in half an hour after. The murderers have made their escape, but it is hoped that no pains will be spared to bring such atrocious offenders to condign punishment.

10 JANUARY 1866

At the Quarter Sessions it was resolved that, in view of the serious foot and mouth outbreak from 15 January to 1 March, no cow, heifer, bullock, ox, calf, sheep, goat or swine should be moved to any market, fair or parish or to any place whatsoever for the purpose of exhibition or sale. At the same time none of these animals were to be allowed to pass along or across any highway or public road in the county and an application was to be made to the Home Secretary to increase the police force temporarily by up to thirty constables. The court drew the attention of the Home Secretary not only to the inadequate existing provisions relating to sheep, swine and other animals but also to the transit of skins, hides, hoofs, offal and manure. Furthermore, the view was that all movement of live cattle by railway ought to be stopped as soon as possible.

11 JANUARY 1866

Stephen Forwood was the last man to be publicly executed at Maidstone Gaol. On a bitterly cold morning with the snow falling thickly, the crowd numbered no more than 1,500, unusually small for such an occasion. His executioner was the infamous William Calcraft.

According to the *Maidstone and Kentish Journal*, 'the scaffold was hung round with black cloth to such a height that when the drop fell, only just the top of the convict's head was visible to the crowd. The body, after hanging an hour, was cut down and a cast of the head taken. In the afternoon the body was buried within the precincts of the gaol.'

The crime horrified the nation. Forwood's common-law wife, presumably tired of his feckless ways, had decided to take their three boys with her to Australia. But Forwood had found the boys, aged 6, 8 and 10, and poisoned them. After the murders, Forwood made his way to Ramsgate where he shot his wife, whom he had left eight years earlier, and their 8-year-old daughter.

Forwood, who in recent years had called himself Ernest Southey, was a baker by trade but had tried to make a living as a professional billiards player and gambler. He also sent begging letters to wealthy people, but nothing he did seemed

William Calcraft at work.

to succeed and in his last weeks he was practically destitute. There is every reason to believe that another judge might have declared him criminally insane and at least spared him the gallows.

12 JANUARY 1945

Twenty soldiers were killed and another twenty-five injured in an explosion at an unidentified military camp in Kent. Men from fifty-two regiments were taking courses at the camp and about sixty were attending a lecture in a Nissen hut when the accident occurred. A sergeant had been demonstrating the working of an anti-personnel mine. It exploded when he was taking out the detonator, instantly killing him and fifteen others. Others died on the way to hospital. A dozen men were blinded.

13 JANUARY 1759

The *Maidstone Journal* reported a hold-up: 'ROBBED – last Wednesday evening, Dr Nash of Sevenoaks was stopped in a Post-Chariot in the New Road between Newington Butts and Kent Street Road, by a single Highwayman, well mounted, who robbed him of his Purse and about five Pounds in Money, then took Leave of him in a very genteel Manner.'

14 JANUARY 1887

At Maidstone Assizes James Dawkins was charged with the murder of George Challen, in Trenley Wood near Canterbury. A secondary charge of being out poaching with arms was brought against James Dawkins, Richard Terry, Henry Curtis and Henry Dawkins who all pleaded guilty to the offence. But all of Dawkins' companions acted as prosecution witnesses. Grant, the first of the poachers to offer assistance to the police, faced no charges although he, like James Dawkins, had carried a shotgun.

    The court heard how, on the night of 6 December, George Challen, a gamekeeper on the Elmbridge Estate, and accompanied by his son Benjamin and a lad named Boys, were

in the wood on the lookout for poachers. Shortly before midnight they heard a shot and went towards the sound. Hearing men coming towards them, they hid behind bushes until two of the poachers were almost upon them. At this point George Challen stepped forward and attempted to catch hold of James Dawkins, who stepped back a pace, at which point his gun went off. 'Oh, Ben, I am shot,' he called out and fell to the ground with a gunshot wound to his leg.

A poaching affray. (*Courtesy of the Neil R. Storey Archive*)

Benjamin then made a move towards Dawkins, who first appeared to raise his gun to his shoulder but then turned and ran away. Henry Curtis, his companion, also turned tail, but as he did so he slipped and fell to the ground, giving Boys the chance to hit him with a stick. Curtis struggled to his feet and ran off to join Dawkins and the rest of the gang. In the course of their flight, the poachers hid their two guns and a pheasant in a hedge where they were found later by police.

Challen's death two days after the skirmish led to the possibility of severe prison terms for all of the party. Small wonder perhaps that they lined up to act as prosecution witnesses. In any event, Dawkins seems not to have attempted to deny what was so easy to prove. He admitted a shot from his gun had killed Challen but claimed that it was an accident and that he bitterly regretted it. The jury accepted his plea and found him not guilty of murder.

On a second charge, all four poachers admitted to being armed by night for the purpose of poaching. James Dawkins, recognised as a confirmed poacher, received five years' penal servitude. Henry Dawkins, Richard Terry and Henry Curtis were each sentenced to six months' imprisonment with hard labour.

15 JANUARY 1862

The *Maidstone and Kentish Journal* noted that Robert Thomas Palin was charged with burgling a house in Fremantle, Australia. He had threatened to blow out the brains of the owner, Mrs Harding, if she made any noise. After the judge had passed sentence of death, the prisoner replied that he was not the first innocent man to die and that he could die but once. A few days later he was hanged.

'It may be remembered,' says the *Journal*, 'that Palin was tried at the Maidstone Spring Assizes in 1854 for the murder of a woman at Cudham.' He was acquitted on that charge but was apprehended immediately after the trial on a charge of burglary committed near Bristol for which offence he was transported for life.

16 JANUARY 1904

Owing to severe weather the Maidstone Soup Kitchen was open every Tuesday, Thursday and Saturday for the benefit of the poor and unemployed. The recently published report indicated that in similar circumstances the previous winter, the kitchen opened for three months, during which time 18,836 people were given soup and bread. Of these, 297 people paid a penny each time, the rest being served without charge. The dining hall was crowded each day with men, women and children. Others carried their soup home.

Funds were raised by benefit concerts given by the Alexandra Minstrels, the Friendly Society and the Corporation Band. The funds were further increased by the Cabmen's Dinner, the Idlers' Cork Club, the Robinson Lodge Freemasons, and the Table Tennis Association.

17 JANUARY 1837

The *Kent Herald* reported on the conduct of the schoolmistress of the Eastry Poor Law Union towards a poor infant named Redman, which excited intense feelings of disgust and indignation: 'It is attested from various sources that this woman actually administered to the child what would be too nauseating to describe or even to mention. An inquiry into all the circumstances of the case took place on Tuesday, before a bench of magistrates assembled at the Union. The fact was substantially proved, and the woman was sentenced to pay a fine of £5. Being unable to pay, she was immediately taken into custody.'

18 JANUARY 1832

It was some time after midnight when the thieves completed their night's work. They had used a ladder to climb up to the entrance of Mrs Ann Rudd's pigeon-house at Detling. Once inside, they had stuffed up the pigeon-holes with straw and had then killed nearly 300 birds which they crammed into bags. In the early hours they concealed their plunder in a nearby sandpit. On the gang's return to Maidstone, some of the birds were sold locally and they arranged to take the rest to London. Within days, all of the pigeons had been sold at Leadenhall Market. Mrs Rugg was determined not to let matters lapse and she eventually traced some of the pigeons' purchasers in London. Other purchasers in Tonbridge, quite innocent of any wrongdoing, came forward with further evidence. At Maidstone Assizes two men, John Glover (24) and Daniel Selby (17), were found guilty of theft.

19 JANUARY 1935

Leonard Brigstock, a 33-year-old stoker Petty Officer of HMS *Arethusa*, then in Chatham Dockyard, was incensed that Chief Petty Officer Hubert Deggan had charged him with three relatively minor breaches of naval discipline. It being Saturday, Brigstock went into Chatham where he had some drinks, although witnesses would say that he was still sober when he returned to the ship. He went to Deggan's mess and found the CPO lying in his bunk. He cut Deggan's throat so violently that the head was almost severed. Brigstock then went to another mess, carrying a bloody razor, and spoke to another PO 'Here, Ted,' he said, 'I've cut that CPO's throat.'

When charged, Brigstock said, 'I did not know what I was doing . . . I did not do it maliciously. Not so far as I know.'

At his trial later in the month two of Brigstock's brothers, both constables in the Metropolitan Police, gave evidence of his strange behaviour, but the senior medical officer of Brixton Prison, called by the prosecution, said he had kept Brigstock under observation and he could find no evidence that he was insane when he committed the murder. Brigstock was hanged at Wandsworth on 2 April.

20 JANUARY 1881

John Slater Nye of Marden called on Mr Payne, a Tonbridge jeweller, telling him that he would like to take away a selection of jewellery for a lady to select from. He left the shop with rings, bracelets and watches worth £11,000 at today's value. But Payne had no initial worries. He thought he knew Nye well enough and had no doubts about his probity. Nevertheless, after some weeks, he became uneasy and wrote to Nye asking him to settle his account. Nye visited him a second time and this time left with jewellery worth £7,000.

As the weeks went by, Payne's anxieties returned. He saw Nye again and was promised half of the account before Christmas. But there was no payment, and finally the police were called and Nye was arrested.

At the Assizes, the jury learnt that Nye had pledged all of the articles and he was found guilty of stealing. It must have been a difficult decision for the jury to make. After all, John Slater Nye was the curate of Marden.

21 JANUARY 1891

A rapid thaw caused considerable flooding in the county. A huge volume of water flowed down the Stour Valley and Canterbury was seriously affected on its southern and south-western boundaries. The danger was to some degree averted in the lower part of the city by the opening of the mill sluices. Low-lying houses on the Ashford road were severely affected and the old Roman road through the city from Dover became a canal down which the torrent swept. From the county cricket ground down into the city, the roadway was flooded and the centre of the city was converted into a lake.

In the country areas of East Kent there were devastating floods. The early morning boat train on the London, Chatham and Dover Railway was delayed for about an hour due to a landslip on the line between Canterbury and Faversham, and traffic on the Elham Valley line between Canterbury and Folkestone was interrupted due to a flooded tunnel. At Cheriton a landslip demolished a hillside cottage in which two adults and a child were killed. At Walmer and Deal a violent hailstorm caused damage.

22 JANUARY 1773

Residents of Maidstone had only to visit Mr Walker – there was no further precise address – or Mr Pike at Ashford had they any doubts about the efficacy of Dr Flugger's Drops. Newspapers throughout the country advertised the doctor's exceptional cures. In the following, taken from the *Sussex Weekly Advertiser*, a mother testified:

To Dr FLUGGER in Prescot Street, Goodman's Fields,
Author of the Lignorum Antiscorbutic Drops.

Sir,
I return you my most grateful thanks for the cure of my son, a child about six years of age, who was for a considerable time afflicted with a most shocking King's Evil [tuberculosis], on both sides of his neck, in which he had several ulcers, from which run a most violent matter, and he was in so bad a state of health that his life was miserable: I tried everything that could be thought of for his relief, but all in vain, when hearing of the great cures performed by your Drops, I gave him some, by which he is now perfectly cured of a complaint which was thought incurable: in gratitude for so great a cure, and for the benefit of the afflicted, I give you my free consent to publish this, and any person calling at my house in Swallows Garden, Rosemary Lane, may see the child. As witness my hand.

The above letter from Mrs Mary Mills was sworn at the Mansion House before the mayor but there must be some doubts about a medicine which claimed to 'perfectly cure the most inveterate scurvy, leprosy, pimpled face of ever so long standing. Likewise the evil fistula, piles, old obstinate sores or ulcers; and is a sovereign remedy in all disorders rising from the foulness of blood incident to the fair sex; and may be taken by persons of the most delicate constitutions in any season or climate, without the least inconvenience or hindrance of business; and hath this particular quality, different from most other medicines, that it strengthens the patient surprisingly.'

23 JANUARY 1786

The *Maidstone Journal* seemed greatly satisfied at the outcome of this affair:

The desperate duel fought on Thursday se'nnight at Chatham lines, having been misrepresented in some of the public prints, we are authorised to give the following particulars from respectable authority. The cause of the quarrel arose from Lieutenant G having shown some symptoms of ill-temper at having lost a bet of five guineas to four guineas, with Lieutenant M, at a gentleman's apartments in Brompton. Some very harsh language and blows passed on both sides, and the next morning the parties met. No compromise could be settled by the seconds, and Lieutenant M fired first, hit his antagonist in the upper part of the back of the thigh. Lieutenant G directly fell, but suddenly starting up, as Mr M advanced towards him, discharged his pistol, and the ball shattered the humerus (or upper bone) of M's arm, a little above the elbow. Here the seconds interfered, and the combatants were taken to their quarters. On Monday last Lieutenant M's arm was amputated, and we are assured both of the gentlemen are in a fair way of recovery, and are, by the mediation of their friends, perfectly reconciled.

24 JANUARY 1791

Even though bare-fist fighting attracted huge crowds and remained popular for many more years, *The Times'* report of a fight at Wrotham is severely censorious. It refers to the contestants as 'boxing blackguards' and while it admits that spectators are increasingly turning their backs on 'so depraved an indulgence,' it asks if there can be any satisfaction in 'displays of such brutal practice.' And what of the two Canterbury magistrates who were present? Even if they have no care for their private reputations, *The Times* sternly reminds them, they ought to preserve the dignity of their public office.

25 JANUARY 1842

Gangs of navvies worked on the railway system of Kent for thirty or more years from 1840. Despite their valuable work, they brought little comfort to the towns and villages they passed through. The *Maidstone Gazette* observes:

> In Staplehurst and Marden scarcely a night passes without a robbery by excavators employed or seeking employment on the railroad. One night last week five farmers lost their poultry and one two pigs. On Friday last a poor woman returning from market was robbed by five men of her week's provisions. Every woman who leaves her house unprotected is liable to be robbed or indecently assaulted.'

Another witness writes:

> Drawn together from all parts by thousands – most of them men of prodigious strength, violent passions, and ignorant to a fearful and almost incredible degree – separated from the kindly influence of family and friends and from the usage of civilised life – having no home but the public house by day, and a barn or shed or temporary hut, in which several are packed together by night – having no other pastime, after their hard toil, than drunkenness and fighting, for which their large earnings furnish them but too abundant stimulus – enjoying little or nothing of a Sabbath either in body or soul; as appears from most with whom I have conversed – and all this carried on for 5, 6 and more years, with a large proportion of the number – they are literally a mass of heathens, in the bosom of a Christian land.

26 JANUARY 1903

Frederic Barter, alias Dowling, a labourer, and his wife Amy were summoned at Bromley Petty Sessions for neglecting their four children aged 15, 13, 10 years and 20 months. The first three were the husband's children by his first wife and the youngest was the child of the defendants. A teacher said that when the 10-year-old came to school in the morning he had to be sent to wash himself. Even when he had washed himself he had to be kept apart from the other children because he was still filthy. He was dressed in rags and his boots had no soles. The stationmaster at Beckenham said the same boy often hung about the station. He had seen him there at half past six in the morning and as late as eleven o'clock at night. On occasion, because he had been out all night, the boy went into the waiting room and stood by the fire to dry his clothing. Sometimes, because he was in such a filthy state, he had to be turned out of the waiting room. The stationmaster had on occasion fed the boy, as had PC Clay, who said he had seen him pick scraps of bread and apple out of the gutter to eat. The court heard about the family home which had practically no furniture in it. What passed for bedding was filthy. The father earned 32s a week while the eldest boy, who slept in the dog kennel with the dog, gave his mother 6s 6d a week. The defendants were each sentenced to two months' hard labour.

27 JANUARY 1860

A huge landslip – more than 100 tons of earth – occurred at a cutting at Bekesbourne on the London and Chatham Railway just minutes after the five o'clock bell had sounded for the men to leave off work. Had it occurred any earlier, many workers would have been submerged. As it was, only three or four unfortunates were buried alive. Rescue work began almost immediately and continued through the night, even though there was the ever-present danger of a second fall of earth. Despite the heroic efforts of the navvies, they were unable to locate their workmates' bodies. With daylight, the work was pursued in a more systematic manner, the sides of the cutting being boarded up. There was of course no hope that the victims would be found alive. When the bodies were recovered there would be an inquest. Questions were already being asked: This was not the first such disaster. What was the company intending to do to ensure that there was no repetition?

28 JANUARY 1927

Twenty-two miners with pneumatic drills were clearing rock and sandstone at the bottom of a 1,900ft deep shaft at Betteshanger Colliery when, at 7.30 a.m., there was a deafening explosion. Even so, there seemed to be nothing remarkable about that for miners constantly used gunpowder charges to release obstacles and to make seams more accessible. But this explosion caused the deaths of four men and injuries to eleven others. At the inquest the following day, after hearing witnesses' accounts, the coroner concluded that the correct safety procedures for firing explosives, laid down in the Mines Act Regulations, had not been followed. But summing up, he said that it was no part of his duty to throw blame on a dead chargeman and recorded a verdict of death by misadventure.

29 JANUARY 1832

At about 2 a.m., a party of twenty or more smugglers landing a cargo of contraband goods were surprised by Lt Ross, a naval officer, and a member of his coastguard patrol. Despite the smugglers being armed with long heavy clubs and in some cases with guns, the lieutenant tried to arrest some of them. There was a desperate resistance in which two of the smugglers were severely wounded, one of them fatally. At one point Lt Ross was struck down and beaten with clubs but he recovered and, undeterred, set off with his patrol in pursuit and overtook the smugglers. They turned and fired on the coastguards, who returned fire, but the cover of darkness and the difficulty of terrain allowed the smugglers to escape.

30 JANUARY 1869

Despite the demands of the law, 25 per cent of children born in the Woolwich Union were not vaccinated. In order to discover the exact situation, Dr Seaton, the Metropolitan Inspector of Vaccination, visited the registrars at Woolwich, Plumstead and Charlton, to discover the names of those who had not returned certificates showing that their children had been successfully vaccinated during the last twelve months. Orders were given that all

MR. GLADSTONE AT Greenwich

VACCINATION.

PEOPLE of GREENWICH,—

Mr. GLADSTONE is going to address you. Now remember, that so long as the **blood-poisoning** produced by Vaccination, continues, other matters are of little importance. By Vaccination the Government is spreading a pestilence throughout the land, which keeps up a sickly and diseased population.

Will you allow such a thing to continue? Surely not. Then we conjure you to ask the following questions of the Prime Minister; and mind you *get an answer*.

Yours &c.,
A MEMBER OF THE ANTI-VACCINATION LEAGUE.

October 13th, 1871.

1. Will you suspend the vaccination laws, which are nothing else than a system of blood-poisoning?
2. If vaccination be **proved to be wrong**, will you not be poisoning **thousands of children before the meeting of Parliament in February next?**
3. Has not the Queen suffered from her re-vaccination in the spring of this year—and do not the symptoms **clearly prove** what she has?
4. Do you think it right that honest citizens should be sent to **prison** because they **refuse** to poison their children by vaccination?
5. Is not vaccination a worse dogma than that of the infallibility of the Pope?
6. Does not **the Report of the Select Committee** of the House of Commons on the vaccination question **prove** that the former legislation had been wrong?
7. Assuming vaccination to be wrong, are you not from day to day producing the most fearful results as regards the population?
8. If you **believe** vaccination to be right, **state your reasons.**
9. Does not the late amount of small-pox, both in England and France clearly prove that the more vaccination there is, the more small-pox we have?
10. Did not **the late Sir Robert Peel,** when in office, **protest against compulsory vaccination,** as being **contrary** to the constitution of the country?
11. Did not Sir William Jenner say before the Select Committee of the House of Commons that **he** was 'no authority' on vaccination? and if not, **who is an authority?**
12. Although you are not a Doctor, do you agree in the evidence given before the Select Committee by Sir Dominic Corrigan, M.D. & M.P., that unvaccinated Children are bags of Petroleum, or barrels of Gunpowder? And further, do you agree with Sir William Jenner, and Dr. Gull, **that it is immaterial** whether we vaccinate from **healthy** or **unhealthy** subjects?

A vehement attack on vaccination and dire warnings of blood poisoning. *(Courtesy of the Greenwich Heritage Centre)*

defaulters were to be served with notices and where these were ignored, offenders were to be summoned to the Woolwich Police Court.

31 JANUARY 1845

Another 'melancholy accident', this time at Dungeness where, at about 9 a.m. during a severe snowstorm, an outward-bound boat was grounded at low water. The stranded boat was spotted by Lt Combe of the coastguard, who ordered his rescue boat to be manned. The lieutenant's crew of four men carried their vessel across the sands before reaching the water and then, after a desperate struggle, for the sea was running high and the wind blowing strongly from the north, they succeeded in getting alongside the grounded boat. But in the violent waters the coastguard boat was upset and the four crewmen were thrown into the sea. Only Lt Combe managed to clamber into the floundered boat in which he had set out to help. Despite unremitting efforts to rescue the stricken men, only two were saved. Shortly afterwards, two Deal boats and another coastguard boat from Dungeness came to their assistance and finally, after three attempts, the stranded boat was floated and Lt Combe and his two surviving colleagues were helped back to land.

FEBRUARY

MURDER

OF

Mr. Bird and his Housekeeper.

Greenwich, Vestry Meeting, Feb. 24th, 1818.

WHEREAS, a Reward of £500. has been offered by the Vicar and Churchwardens, for the Apprehension and Conviction of the Person or Persons concerned in the horrid Atrocity, recently committed in this Parish, a Vestry Meeting was held, on Tuesday, the 24th Inst. for the purpose of taking into consideration the most eligible mode of raising the said Reward.

At this Meeting a communication having been made by Mr. BIRD, the Son, through the medium of the Churchwardens, that he was desirous to contribute £300. towards the said Sum—It was unanimously

RESOLVED,

That the remainder, with such expences as have been already incured, by endeavouring to discover the Person or Persons concerned in the perpetration of this Atrocity, be raised by Subscription.

This Resolution was adopted, in order to afford to every Inhabitant of the Parish, an opportunity of testifying his or her abhorrence of the crime committed, and of voluntarily contributing, how small soever may be the Contribution, towards the the discovery and Conviction of the Guilty.

RESOLVED,

That for this purpose, a Book be left in the Vestry-Room, for receiving the Names of all who may be inclined to Subscribe; the Reward not being payable, and the Subscription Monies, therefore, not required, till after conviction.

RESOLVED,

That if the amount of Subscriptions should not be sufficient to cover the Reward and other expences, the deficiency be made good by a Parish Rate.

RESOLVED,

That the thanks of this Meeting be returned to the Vicar and Churchwardens, for the meritorious zeal and promptitude which marked their conduct on this distressing and melancholy occasion.

EVEREST & BICKNELL, Vestry-Clerk.

N.B. And it is particularly requested that, any Persons who were at or near Mr. BIRD's House, between the Hours of 7 and 10 o'Clock, on the Evening of the 7th of February, and

---

A reward notice offering £500 for the apprehension and conviction of the murderer of Mr Bird and his housekeeper. *(Courtesy of the Greenwich Heritage Centre)*

1 FEBRUARY 1915

Henry Williams was arrested in London and charged with bigamy. After a whirlwind courtship, he had 'married' the genteel Bessie Mundy in August 1910, taking off within weeks with her savings. Over the next two years, using a variety of aliases, Williams pursued the same course with several women. Then, in March 1912, perhaps by chance, he met Bessie again and she forgave him unhesitatingly. The couple set up house at 80 The High Street, Herne Bay. This time they made wills in each other's favour. On 10 July 1912, Williams took his wife to the doctor, concerned that she was having epileptic fits. She had not known that she was suffering fits until her husband had told her. Three days later, Bessie was found drowned in a small zinc bath in front of the fire. The doctor had no doubt that she had had an epileptic fit. The widower arranged the funeral, asking for it to be 'moderately carried out' at the cost of seven guineas. The zinc bath, for which he had paid 37s 6d on approval, he returned to the hardware store. Now affluent with the money from Bessie's will, he purchased several houses in Bath and opened accounts in several names in various banks.

George Joseph Smith and Bessie Mundy. (*Illustrated Police News*)

Two other women suffered a similar fate. First, Alice Burnham married Williams on 3 November 1913 and, heavily insured, died in a bath in Blackpool eight days later. She had the cheapest possible funeral. Moving on and calling himself John Lloyd, the constant widower met Margaret Lofty, a clergyman's daughter with little cash but a good insurance prospect. They married on 17 December 1914 and the following evening, in Holloway, shortly after neighbours heard him singing 'Nearer my God to Thee' with harmonium accompaniment, Margaret was found dead in the bath. It was too good a story for newspapermen to ignore. The headline 'Bride's Tragic Fate' in the *News of the World* led Alice Burnham's suddenly suspicious father to contact the police.

George Joseph Smith, a man of many names, was tried at the Old Bailey for the murder of Bessie Mundy. Found guilty, Smith was executed at Maidstone Gaol on 13 August 1915.

A police photograph of George Joseph Smith. (*Daily Graphic*)

2 February 1790

The *Maidstone Journal* printed the following list of prisoners committed to Maidstone Bridewell: 'Nicholas Smith of Wrotham, butcher, for refusing to maintain his family which has become chargeable to that parish. Elizabeth Bull, for stealing from the premises of Joseph Delves, at Tunbridge Wells, three linen cloths, his property. John Foreman of Frindsbury, labourer, for incurring a penalty of ten pounds, through using a wire for the destruction of game, and having no goods and chattels to levy the same.'

3 February 1909

The *East Kent Times* reported that a women's branch of the Anti-Suffrage League had been formed recently at a meeting in Southwood, Ramsgate. After the election of the committee, Miss Mary Angela Dickens, granddaughter of the novelist, addressed the meeting. She said, 'Women's work lies in being a good wife, mother and friend, and as long as she interests herself thus, what time has she to devote to the study of Imperial politics? There are about one million more women than men in England, so the tone of government would be womanly. It is presumably not denied that women are less virile than men, therefore our government would be less virile than governments of other countries where men predominate, and the results in cases of conflict would be the weaker – and that weaker would be England – go to the wall . . . Women's suffrage would result in a hugely increased irresponsible vote, ultimately petticoat government and a weakening of respect for law and order.'

Lady Rose Weigall, who lived locally, said: 'I do not think that any benefit would result from women entering Parliament as men are so jealous they would resent women's interference if they became mixed up in party politics openly and publicly. It will destroy any good influence that a woman can have.'

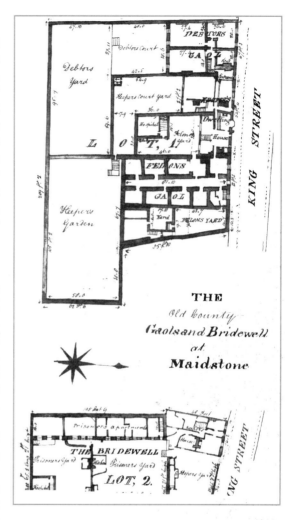

THE
Old County
Gaols and Bridewell
at
Maidstone

4 February 1845

When the jury foreman fell ill, Mr Carttar, the West Kent coroner, decided to postpone the inquest into the death of Joseph Morgan, who had died, it was alleged, after ill-treatment aboard a fishing boat. The jury would convene again, the coroner said, only when the foreman was recovered and witnesses who were now at sea were available. Mr Carttar's postponements had previously annoyed many inquest juries. Thirteen months earlier, he had adjourned an inquest into the death of Maria Monckton who had been poisoned under suspicious circumstances.

Treadmill, House of Correction, Brighton, a smaller version than the one at Maidstone. *(Sussex County Magazine)*

5 February 1824

The treadmill at Maidstone Prison was completed under the superintendence of William Cubitt, the original inventor of this form of prison discipline. Newspaper reports suggested that the machine at Maidstone was 'the most perfect building of its kind in the country.'

The machine cost £3,000. There were eight distinct shafts, all communicating with the great central wheel. There was 18in elbow room for the men as they stood in a row, ceaselessly climbing, step by step. This mill was capable of holding about 100 persons at the same time. It was built to dress corn and ground 12 bushels an hour or 18 quarters of wheat a day.

But it was a bestial invention. Treadmills were dangerous: men fell off them or became entangled in the revolving machinery. There is no evidence that they acted as a deterrent and they were eventually abandoned. Those employed on the 'endless ladder', the frail and unfit as well as the robust and sturdy, are estimated to have walked the equivalent of 12,000ft each day in winter. In summer, with longer hours, they climbed as much as 18,000ft. At St Augustine's House of Correction some years later, figures showed a minimum ascent of 10,692ft in winter and 14,107ft in summer.

6 February 1899

In a letter to a friend, Bertha Peterson wrote: 'God . . . told me to do what I have done. I shot the man JW.'

Bertha, a 45-year-old religious fanatic and frighteningly unbalanced, was arrested for shooting John Whibley in the head immediately after the previous day's morning service at which she had played the harmonium.

Months later, at Maidstone Assizes, the story of Bertha's murderous obsession came out. Whibley had been a teacher in

The ladylike Bertha Peterson. *(Kentish Express)*

the Sunday school when Miss Peterson lived in the village with her father, the rector. There had been a rumour in Biddenden that Whibley, the local shoemaker, had indecently assaulted a little girl though there was no proof of this. But Bertha never had any doubt of his guilt.

In recent years, she had been working in a home for inebriates at Reigate where she had become increasingly delusional. Suddenly she returned to Biddenden for a few days, writing to Whibley and two others who had previously incurred her wrath. She intended, she said, to present the school with a painting. Would Whibley and the others come to the little ceremony in the schoolroom after Sunday morning service?

But only John Whibley turned up. As soon as he went over to see the painting, Bertha pulled out a revolver and shot him in the back of the head. 'I had to do it to protect little children,' she said.

John Whibley.
(Daily Graphic)

The case was abruptly halted by the jury who decided that it should not proceed, returning a verdict of guilty but insane. Bertha Peterson spent the rest of her life in a mental institution.

The body in the schoolroom.
(Kentish Express)

Whibley's home at
Biddenden. *(Kentish Express)*

7 FEBRUARY 1802

In the early hours of the morning a Margate hoy carrying thirty passengers and a crew of five was caught in a violent storm. The hoy was stripped of its rudder by the combined power of wind and sea. Now, the craft, almost unmanageable and constantly pitching and rolling, was shipping water from the tremendous seas. The force of the waves drove her back towards the beach where she eventually halted but then mountainous waves from all directions washed nearly all on deck overboard. Three of the crew and one male passenger managed to struggle to dry land but the master, determined to do all he could for his passengers, refused to quit the wreck. He, along with twenty-five of the passengers, were drowned. In the course of the day the bodies of nine victims were thrown upon the shore and fourteen bodies were found in the cabin. The few who were saved had climbed into the shrouds. A *Maidstone Journal* report tells us: 'Nothing could present a more awful spectacle than the repeated arrival at Margate on Sunday of various carriages with the bodies of the sufferers from the wreck.'

8 FEBRUARY 1786

It was reported that hardened criminal John Shepherd was once more in jail awaiting trial. He and a fellow thief, Sullivan, had been to visit McNeal, a convict (though whether he was still serving a sentence is unclear). On their return, they robbed a man and his wife at Hanging Wood Lane outside Woolwich, violently beating the man about the head with a pistol. Shortly afterwards they were captured.

A public execution.

Several years earlier Shepherd had received a last minute respite at Tyburn: just as the executioner was about to drive away the cart from under him, his pardon arrived. This time he was less fortunate.

9 FEBRUARY 1911

George Richardson, Henry Elliott and Samuel Hunter were charged at Chatham police station with breaking and entering into Gillingham post office on 2 February and stealing £555 in cash and postage stamps. At 2 a.m. the burglars had entered the premises through a window and then, after breaking through the door leading to the sorting room, had found the heavy iron safe. They had manhandled it into a position where they could rip off the back using jemmies and a saw. It took them nearly two hours to complete the work. The police arrested the men only hours after the offence.

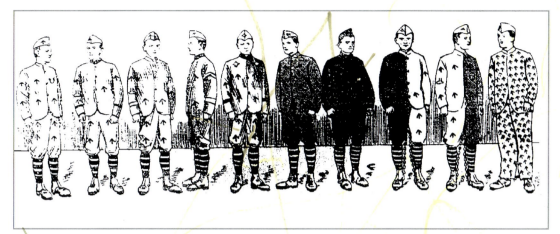

The distinctive dress of various classes of convict. (*Courtesy of the NCCL Galleries of Justice*)

Later in the year the three men appeared at Kent Assizes and all received prison sentences. In court it was said that Elliott and Richardson were two of London's cleverest safe breakers, although from time to time Elliott had given police information against his friends when he himself was perpetrating robberies. The day before the Gillingham robbery he had been to Scotland Yard to offer information on other matters. He and Richardson were given six years and Hunter three years.

10 FEBRUARY 1918

The body of 16-year-old Nellie Trew was found on Eltham Common, opposite Shooters Hill cemetery, a quarter of a mile from her home. She had been savagely beaten, raped and strangled.

Chief Inspector Francis Carlin from Scotland Yard, heading the investigation, was immediately interested in two items picked up near the body. One was a metal badge of the Leicestershire Regiment. The other was a bone button with a piece of wire threaded through its holes. Carlin had photographs and drawings of the badge and button published in newspapers. Within twenty-four hours he learnt that a young man, David Greenwood, had called at Tottenham Court Road police station. He recognised the badge: he had sold it to a stranger on Saturday, the day Nellie Trew was murdered.

Nellie Trew.

Carlin interviewed 21-year-old Greenwood, who had recently been invalided out of the army with shell-shock and heart trouble after being buried alive in an explosion. He worked at Hewsen Manufacturing just off Tottenham Court Road but lived only 100 yards from where the body was found.

A drawing of the badge discovered near the murder scene.

During the interview Carlin became aware that Greenwood's overcoat had no buttons. In every place save one, threads showed where there had been a button. But where the top button had been, there was a small hole as if the button had been torn away. Greenwood's workmates told the policeman that Greenwood had buttons on his coat when he left work on Saturday lunchtime. They also recalled that his top button was held in place with a piece of twisted wire instead of being sewn with thread. And that kind of wire, Carlin discovered, was made only at Hewson Manufacturing.

It was too much of a coincidence that Greenwood had not only sold his badge to a stranger but also that he had used company wire as a temporary measure on his top button.

Charged with murder, Greenwood appeared before Mr Justice Atkins at the Central Criminal Court in April 1918. It was the wire that clinched the case for the prosecution. He was found guilty and sentenced to death, though the jury recommended mercy. He was reprieved on the eve of execution and sentenced to life imprisonment. He served fifteen years in gaol.

Of Greenwood's guilt there was no doubt but had there been no wire attached to the button, would the prosecution's case have then seemed so strong? And would the jury have added their strong recommendation to mercy had they not known of Greenwood's army service?

11 FEBRUARY 1821

At 2.30 a.m., preventive officers, led by Charles Newton, came across members of the notorious Aldington gang, 200 of them carrying casks of spirits, and another hundred, all armed, forming a protective cordon. Undeterred, Newton's numerically inferior force challenged the gang and the so-called 'Battle of Brookland' began. The running fight across five miles of country ended with the deaths of four smugglers and one preventive officer. Only two men were captured and subsequently charged with smuggling at Lydd. At the Old Bailey, Cephas Quested was found guilty. A second man, Richard Wraight, whose pockets contained shot and powder when he was taken, claimed that he had wandered quite by chance into the preventive party and that he had nothing to do with any smuggling. An unlikely story but he had powerful witnesses to vouch for his probity. But then so had Quested, leader of the Aldington gang, but he was hanged.

12 FEBRUARY 1798

An order issued by General Bonaparte clearly indicated his intention to launch an invasion on the south coast:

DUNKIRK 12th February 1798

General Caffarelli will repair at once to Boulogne and take measures for the improvement of the harbour; it must be capable of accommodating 50 gunboats . . . one or two divisions of horse transports; six ships of 100 tons for the Staff; six ships for artillery; six ships for the official management; six ships for hospitals.

He will inspect the batteries defending Boulogne, and increase them if necessary . . . he will send privateers with an engineer officer to reconnoitre the English coast from Folkestone to Rye to ascertain the real conditions of defence on that part of the coast and to take note of the batteries which it would be necessary to carry, or to take by surprise, so as to effect a landing.

BONAPARTE

13 FEBRUARY 1930

The inquest on the deaths of a honeymooning couple, Albert and Edith Hodges, who were killed when a French airliner crashed at Marden, opened at Staplehurst. Four key witnesses, the pilot and his two mechanics and the only other passenger, who all escaped with injuries, were in Maidstone Hospital and unable to attend.

Mrs Hodges' father had identified her body only by a wristwatch and ring. Eyewitnesses who saw the aircraft immediately before the crash were confident that the rear right-hand tail wing was broken. The plane was flying very low as if there was some attempt being made to land but it suddenly went into a nosedive and, on hitting the ground, burst into flames before exploding.

Hugh Curson, the surviving passenger, would later say that the aircraft became unsteady. 'I cannot say how long we remained like that but it seemed ages to me. Suddenly we dived. There was the noise of a crash and I did not remember any more until I found myself in the wreckage.'

The inquest was resumed at the end of March when a verdict of accidental death was returned. The plane was only a year old and was regularly serviced. There was no explanation for the accident. The pilot was unable to account for the broken tail wing.

14 FEBRUARY 1868

A report says that in the previous year, punishment at Maidstone Gaol was inflicted 2,406 times on males and 83 times on females.

	Males	Females
Whipping	11	–
Irons or handcuffs	1	–
Solitary or dark cells	820	83
Stoppage of diet	1,574	–

Male prisoners also performed shot drill. In this form of hard labour, they responded as a group of up to thirty-two men, to warders' orders. They had to stoop down and, without bending the knees, pick up a cannon ball. The ball was raised up to the chest and when the order was given, the men took three steps sideways and then replaced the ball on the ground. They were then ordered to take three steps backwards and the procedure commenced all over again.

Stone breaking, beating rope, picking oakum and pumping water were other mind-numbing tasks to be performed. Work continued throughout daylight hours in winter and in summer from 6.30 a.m. until 6 p.m.

Oakum-picking, a hated task, was given to women as well as men. The task was to separate strands of rope into thin threads. Working at this task day after day made the fingers painful and bloody. The reconstituted threads were sold on to make string or mattress stuffing – hence the saying 'money for old rope'.

Shot drill. (*Courtesy of the Governor of Inverary Gaol*)

15 FEBRUARY 1894

A skinny little Frenchman had lunch in Fitzroy Square. Afterwards, he makes for Westminster Bridge where he caught a tram to Greenwich. According to one witness, he was carrying a bulky package in his pocket. Another to see it, a gardener in Greenwich Park, said the package was about the size of a brick. The Frenchman made his way up the path towards the Royal Observatory. At 4.51 p.m., when he was only 50 yards from the observatory, there was an explosion and the little man lost part of his left hand and received severe injuries to the abdomen and chest. Yet, when anxious bystanders rushed up to him, he asked to be taken home. He was too badly injured for that and they sent for a doctor. He was taken to the Royal Naval Hospital and admitted at 5.15 p.m. They put him to bed. He told them that he is cold and at 5.40 p.m., only twenty-five minutes after admission, he died.

Martial Bourdin, a man devoted to the anarchist cause, was only 27 years old. Where did he get his bomb? Who made it? This is not altogether clear although a recipe for a bomb, copied from a book in the British Museum, was found on his body.

Did the first terrorist on British soil intend to blow up the Royal Observatory? Some say he was simply going to test it on open ground. Others suggest that he intended to pass it on to a fellow anarchist.

16 FEBRUARY 1885

The newspapers carried accounts of the inquest at the Railway Hotel, Beckenham, on five men who were killed by the explosion of a boiler at the Mid-Kent Brickworks on 13 February.

At the time of the explosion the five men were all in the engine house where the bricks were made. They appeared to have been crushed to death. One of the men had his brains blown out and the others received dreadful head injuries. The explosion, heard many miles away, totally destroyed the engine house. Not a brick was left standing and the machinery lay scattered in thousands of pieces. The inner tubes of the boiler, over 2 tons in weight, were blown 100 yards and some parts went even further.

The coroner said that the only man who could have thrown any light on the case was the engine driver and he was dead. He ordered a thorough scientific inquiry to discover the cause of the accident. The enquiry later reported that the boiler was worn out, defective and dangerous. Its maintenance was entirely the responsibility of the engine driver but, the report concluded, 'the generality of drivers know little or nothing as to the strength of boilers and in such cases on no account should the inspection of the boiler be left to them.'

Three of the dead men each left five children.

17 FEBRUARY 1937

At Kent Assizes, Langford Duncan was given five years' penal servitude for robbing an aged widow, Mrs Annie Cleave, at Stanstead. He knew the woman's daughter and had even stayed weekends at her cottage on various occasions. On 27 November Mrs Cleave gave him 3s for his return ticket to London, but he spent this on drink at a public house. He then returned to the cottage and robbed her of 12s after hitting her with a poker.

Duncan came from a respectable family and acknowledged in court that he had made a failure of his life. Recently he had contemplated suicide. He had tried unsuccessfully to buy a revolver and had thought of throwing himself under a train, but he 'hadn't the guts'.

The maximum sentence for this crime was penal servitude for life and a flogging with the cat-o'-nine-tails. There was a medical report which indicated that he was unfit to be flogged. How fortunate. The judge told him that he would have remembered it all the rest of his life.

18 February 1861

Order was at last restored at Chatham Prison. On the previous Monday, 10 September, more than 700 convicts had mutinied but by now they were confined to their cells. Of this number, seventy-six were expecting further and more stringent punishment. Now, only 100 prisoners at a time were permitted to exercise under the close supervision of warders, and soldiers who had been called in. The Director General of Prisons, Captain Gambier, had been brought in to investigate and resolve the situation and the leaders of the mutiny had received severe punishment. Forty-eight of them were given thirty-six lashes, administered with an unprecedented severity, by the strongest army drummers and farriers. The convicts as a whole were chastened by the harshness of the punishment. Later, there were complaints in Parliament about soldiers being required to carry out such punishment on civilians. Only the 150 prisoners who had played no part in the mutiny were allowed to resume work in the dockyard.

It was said that the mutiny had erupted after complaints about the quality of the soup. Certainly on the Friday there had been some minor disorder when a few had complained about their soup, but the general conditions within the prison and the convicts' treatment by prison staff also played a part.

Not that all saw it that way. One correspondent attributed it solely to the food complaint. 'Outrageous,' he said. 'Men in the position of criminals, who get 27oz of excellent white bread, 5 or 6oz of good beef, three-quarters of a pint of by no means indifferent soup and cocoa and gruel in addition, as their ordinary diet, cannot be said to have much grievance on the ground of quantity.' And certainly, as far as diet was concerned, prison diet was better than in most workhouses and in many homes.

19 February 1920

At Kent Assizes, Frederick Cullender (18) alias Frederick Smith, and William Scutt (17), both inmates of Rochester Borstal, pleaded not guilty to the murder of warder Edward Adams. Cullender had escaped from the institution but was recaptured. Almost immediately after his arrest, Cullender made a statement, saying, 'I did not mean to kill him. We only wanted to get away. My mate who was working with me and I had planned this for a week. I don't know if he got out. The last I saw of him was when I was getting over the wall. His hand was on top of the wall. The whistle blew and I ran away.' He said that he and Scutt had intended to knock Adams out and steal his keys. He had, he said, 'just tapped the officer on the head.'

Scutt, however, denied Cullender's version of events. Cullender was no friend of his, he said, and he had had nothing to do with any escape plan. He claimed that he had tried to stop Cullender climbing over the wall. When asked why he had not called for help, he replied that he was afraid of Cullender.

Another inmate, Elias, said that he saw Cullender with the warder's truncheon in his hand and was warned to get out of the way. Because he too was afraid of Cullender, he stepped aside but he saw the two men at the boundary wall. It appeared to him that Scutt was trying to stop Cullender from climbing over. It was at this point that Scutt had been taken by warders and accused of the attack on Adams and of attempted escape.

The jury found Scutt not guilty, but Cullender was sentenced to death, although later he was reprieved on appeal.

20 February 1904

The *Tonbridge and Sevenoaks Standard* reported the following tale of neighbourly discourse. Lizzie Wheatley of Quarry Road was summoned by Walter Giles for assault the previous week. He told the Maidstone Police Court that at about 11.30 p.m. the defendant had come to his house and had started hammering on the door. When he opened the door, she hit him with a poker.

Asked by Mr Ellis for the defence where she had hit him, Giles replied, 'On my arm. I have lived there seven years and have had six years of misery.'

Mr Ellis: Then why on earth haven't you moved? Did you knock her down that night?
Walter Giles: I never got outside the door.
Mr Ellis: Is your arm broken?
Walter Giles: No.

Mrs Harriet Hawkes gave corroborative evidence.

Mr Ellis: It's a pretty noisy district, isn't it?
Harriet Hawkes: Yes, it is.
Mr Ellis: There is plenty of bad language used there?
Harriet Hawkes: Yes, there is.
The Mayor: Was the defendant intoxicated?
Harriet Hawkes: Yes, she was.

Edward Hawkes also gave evidence. Lizzie Wheatley had hit him with the poker too.

The Clerk: Did you hear any quarrelling going on?
Edward Hawkes: We are so used to it that we don't take any notice of it.

Lizzie Wheatley said that Giles had pushed her against the water barrel, tearing her dress and bruising her. She had never had a poker until they all set on her, she said, and she denied hitting Giles with it.

The Clerk: You say you picked up a poker?
Lizzie Wheatley: No, it wasn't a poker. I haven't got a poker in the place.

For the assault, a fine of 5s and 14s costs was imposed and for the obscene language Lizzie was given a fine of 5s and 10s costs. If she was unable to pay, she was told she would go to prison for fourteen days on each charge.

21 February 1935

The settlement of an action against Mr H.G. Tyrwhitt-Drake, the former mayor of Maidstone, was announced at Kent Assizes. A 16-year-old had been mauled by a bear at Mr Tyrwhitt-Drake's private zoo, as a result of which he had an arm amputated. Then septicaemia set in and the boy had died.

No one had seen how the bear caught hold of the boy but when the alarm was raised, Mr Tyrwhitt-Drake and his keeper ran to the boy's assistance.

The parents alleged negligence, a charge which the owner denied, although he did accept liability. He paid £70 into the court with an additional £25 costs.

22 February 1937

Two airmen were killed and two others were injured when an RAF aircraft crashed during a snowstorm at Ewell Minnis between Dover and Folkestone. After hitting the ground, the plane had bounced several hundred yards along a field before crashing through two hedges, crossing a road and finally turning over completely. Wreckage was scattered over nearly a quarter of a mile and the two engines were hurled more than 50 yards. The machine was returning to Manston Airport when it was caught in the storm. One of the dead men was found at the controls and the body of the other lay 50 yards away. The two injured men were both found lying outside the plane.

23 FEBRUARY 1934

The marriage of Maximilian Habsburg, Prince of the Realm of Austria, to Cathleen Manning took place at Dartford. At the Kent Assizes four months later, not only did he face a charge of bigamy but it was also revealed that rather than being a Continental blue-blood, he was a chef, the son of an army private. Frank Vernon Carruthers had told his bride that his first marriage was illegal and that he was therefore free to marry her. His army career was as chequered as his civilian life. After marrying his first wife at Woolwich ten years earlier when he was a gunner in the Royal Artillery, he had transferred to the Royal Marines from whose service he had deserted while stationed in Bombay. Carruthers was sentenced to nine months' hard labour.

24 FEBRUARY 1930

Frank Smith, a 27-year-old farm labourer from Headcorn, was sentenced to seven years' imprisonment and Edward Philpott, a pensioner from Sittingbourne, to twelve months' imprisonment with hard labour.

A man referred to as Mr X had been stopped in the street by Frank Smith. Smith told the man that he was out of work and down on his luck. Mr X had taken him home and given him a meal after which Smith asked if there was anyone else in the house. When he was certain that the house was empty, Smith had said, 'If you don't give me some money I shall make out a serious case against you.' He told Mr X that he was a police constable and said that he would tell the police that he had been assaulted. Mr X was frightened and over a period of about five weeks, handed over £510 of which Philpott received £60 for supporting Smith in his accusations. It was only when Mr X attempted to gas himself that the story came out.

Mr Justice Rowlatt, in passing sentence, said that Smith had committed an abominable crime. Had the offence been committed by a professional blackmailer, the judge said that he would have sentenced him to penal servitude for life. But Smith was a humble man, poorly educated, and there was no suggestion that he was a professional blackmailer. 'This crime must be stamped out,' said the judge, 'and it will be stamped out mercilessly in any court in which I preside.'

25 FEBRUARY 1791

The *Maidstone Journal* related the following:

The last store-ship going to Botany Bay with convicts sailed from Deptford to Gravesend to join the other vessels. The whole of this fleet are to rendezvous at Portsmouth the 10th of March, and from thence sail under convoy to the place of destination in the Southern ocean.

The *Mary Ann*, bound for Botany Bay, sailed from Gravesend on Friday last with near 200 women convicts on board. The *Matilda* also sailed at the same time to receive convicts at Portsmouth. Two other ships have sailed within these nine days, the *William and Anne* and the *Britannia*, both with men convicts, supposed to have had on board about 208 each. The other ships still lying at Gravesend to receive the men convicts from Newgate are the *Armagh*, the *Barrington* and the *Active*.

26 FEBRUARY 1798

The *Maidstone Journal* related the following 'melancholy accident' at Dover Castle where soldiers were billeted: 'The soldiers who have families have built huts for them under the bank. The late severe frosts, having penetrated the ground above them, a quantity fell on one of them and buried a man, his wife and two children; a third, two months old, was providentially saved by the unfortunate mother throwing her arm over it. The man's name was Hans White and he was a gunner in Major Lewis's company of the Royal Artillery.'

27 FEBRUARY 1925

The River Medway inundated huge tracts of land in and around Tonbridge and many acres of hop fields were under water. The two cricket fields were submerged and in the High Street neighbourhood the water rose over River Walk and flooded the side streets. At Hildenborough the London road was impassable.

The flood at Maidstone was one of the worst in years. The waters rose so rapidly in the early hours that by 7 a.m. houses and business premises in the low-lying part of town were under water and their occupants stranded in the upper floors. Floodwater poured into the cellars of the general post office and the electricity works.

At Deal hundreds of acres of grazing land were under water. At Cottington on one farm alone, 60 acres of pastureland were flooded to a depth of 3ft. Pigs, cattle, horses and sheep were drowned.

28 FEBRUARY 1815

Late on a Saturday night, going on for midnight, passengers enjoying a trip below deck on the Gravesend ferry had already had enough to drink but seemed cheerful enough, laughing, joking and singing. A jolly little chap, a hump-backed fellow who knew popular comic songs and could even dance, entertained them. They quite forgot his deformities, his smallness. It didn't matter – he was a great entertainer. At least, it didn't matter to most people. But one man, Charles Rose, was not enjoying the five-minute celebrity. Perhaps he thought that Robert Clarton was showing off. He began heckling, making coarse remarks and personal comments. 'You're a Birmingham man!' Rose called out at one point. 'You're just made up of odds and ends of men!'

Hurtful? Clarton did not seem to think so. Plenty of good things came in little packets, he told Rose.

It is not clear how his fellow passengers took the interruption and possibly some thought it was just good-natured chaff. Clarton went on with his performance, encouraged by the others in the cabin. And at one point the two men shared a bottle of beer.

Then came the threat that no one at the time believed. 'You'll never reach Woolwich!' Rose called out. 'I'll throw you overboard before you get there!' Perhaps his listeners laughed or exchanged glances, shaking their heads at Rose's crass behaviour.

As the passengers left their seats to disembark, Rose gripped hold of the little man up on deck. Then what happened? An accident? Did Clarton trip on a rope and lose his balance? Did he fall overboard, or was he pushed?

At the Assizes, Rose, a journeyman breeches-maker, was charged with the wilful murder of Clarton who had drowned in Galleon's Reach. The jury tussled with questions of intent and accident and concluded, perhaps with some misgivings, that Rose was guilty of manslaughter for which a sentence of nine months' imprisonment was passed.

29 FEBRUARY 1820

From the *Maidstone Journal*: 'Numerous depredations have been lately committed in the neighbourhood of Harrietsham and Lenham which has occasioned a patrol to be established in those places. Although William Baldwin, Esquire, of Steed Hill, a few days since, generously distributed to the poor four hundredweight of pork and a large quantity of bread, yet the villains attacked the mansion of that worthy gentleman and stole from the larder a considerable quantity of pork and other articles, and on the same night they broke into the Court Lodge at Harrietsham and stole several things from thence.'

MARCH

Black Maria, used from about 1860 to convey prisoners between court and prison.
Inside were separate locked cubicles. *(Courtesy of Kent Police Museum)*

1 MARCH 1905

A party of sixty beaters succeeded in flushing out from woodland the animal which had in recent months savaged flocks of sheep between Sevenoaks and Tonbridge. And now the predator was dead, shot by a gamekeeper. It had been thought that perhaps a wolf was on the loose. Its mode of attack, the biting of the victim's shoulder, the disembowelling, led to that conclusion. The culprit was in fact found to be a jackal. Earlier in the year a predator at Gravesend had slaughtered thirty sheep in the same fashion. Was it the same beast? Had it changed its hunting ground? Or was there another animal on the loose?

2 MARCH 1773

The *Sussex Weekly Advertiser* related this horrific accident: 'A man who was brewing at the Bull Head Inn, at Cranbrook in Kent, unfortunately fell into a cooler of hot wort [malt] whereby he was so terribly scalded that he expired the next day in great agonies.'

3 MARCH 1924

The adjourned inquest on the Erith explosion reconvened and reached a verdict of 'death by misadventure from shock and burns due to accidental explosion while breaking down Verey lights.'

The appalling accident at the Slades Green Filling Factory near Erith had occurred on the morning of 18 February. One man and twelve women, one 16 years old and the rest in their early twenties, lost their lives. One of the females had started work at the factory only an hour before the explosion.

One eyewitness was Mr Pepler, the assistant manager, who had been outside the shed at the time. He had seen smoke issuing from the roof of the hut in which there were twenty-six workers. He was preparing to investigate when the shed exploded and he ran towards it. He could hear cries from inside and when he reached the door, he saw a girl standing, her arms extended and evidently blind.

'Keeping my coat in front of me,' Pepler said, 'I gripped her on the arm and pulled her towards me, partly dragging and partly carrying her to safety. The impression I had then was that the whole interior was one red flame. This poor girl was standing in the flames and was on fire from head to foot.' The girl was taken to hospital but later died. None of the corpses was recognisable.

At the inquest it transpired that Slades Green was a government factory, run under government regulations but under the management of Messrs Gilbert and Co. The manager ensured that all workers – they were mainly young women – were aware of safety regulations. Their task was to empty Verey light cartridges of their explosive. The powder was poured into a small tray on the workbench before its almost instant removal.

Highly qualified safety experts considered the evidence and concluded that most girls died at their workbenches of asphyxiation. Possible causes of the explosion were either that an unstable rogue cartridge had found its way into those requiring disposal or that a cartridge had been dropped on the floor with the inevitable consequence or that two cartridge rims had struck together and caused a spark.

4 MARCH 1926

At Canterbury Police Court, Sid Ballard, a motor mechanic, and John Hills, a waiter, faced four charges of forging and uttering £1 notes. The two men had arrived a fortnight earlier at Whitstable and soon came under police surveillance. A warrant was obtained and their lodgings in Station Road were searched. Here the police found tools and equipment for forging notes. Both men admitted their guilt and confessed to having passed notes in

Canterbury, Faversham, Herne Bay and Southend. Ballard said that he had been making notes for the past year and had been associated with Hills since December.

Eva Beasley said that months earlier she had lived with Ballard and he had forced her to change £1 and 10s notes that he had made. She had left him but met him again in January when she had moved in with the two men and another woman. They had been obliged to leave a house in Eltham because detectives were after them. Beasley said she saw the notes being made but that she was not allowed out of the house alone and was not permitted to send letters in case the postmark gave their address away.

At the Assizes the men were both sentenced to five years' imprisonment.

5 MARCH 1798

The *Maidstone Journal* reported the following distressing story, which took place in St Dunstan's, Canterbury.

In the morning Mr T. Chaplin, a shopkeeper, his wife and three children, each took what was supposed to be cream of tartar and brimstone as physic. The effect, however, soon proved deleterious as the whole family were affected with such alarming symptoms that the most skilful medical assistance proved ineffectual. One of the children died in the afternoon, in the evening another and at night their mother. The father and the third child were alive on Thursday but in so bad a situation that very little hope remained of their recovery. The infant, having taken but a very small quantity of the mixture, is the only one expected to survive. The cause is supposed to have been a fatal mistake in mixing sugar of lead with the brimstone instead of cream of tartar, the sugar of lead having been kept in the house among other articles as the man frequently acted as a doctor to his own horses which he worked in a cart for hire.

On Wednesday last, a coroner's inquest was taken on the bodies of the woman and the two children who died in St Dunstan's when a jury returned their verdict that 'they died through excessive vomiting by taking some medicines which could not be ascertained.' We are sorry to add that the man also died on Thursday evening.

6 MARCH 1841

The *Kent Herald* reports another dramatic sea rescue. One night in the previous week, the brig *Amelia*, with a cargo of wheat, was driven in stormy weather onto the Herne Sand off Reculver and began to sink straight away. The captain, his wife and seven crewmen had barely time to jump out of their berths before the inrush of water overwhelmed them. They all managed to climb up the rigging but had no means of making any distress signal. They lashed themselves to the shrouds and were there next morning when they were spotted by Lt Lake of the Reculver Station Preventive Service. He set off in a boat through heavy seas to their rescue. One of Lake's crew, a Whitstable man, Robert Wood, sprang into the shrouds of the stricken ship and made his way to the captain's wife who, to his astonishment, refused his help, directing him to her husband, who was lashed to the shrouds next to her. Wood released the captain who, exhausted as he was, was scarcely able to comprehend what was happening. But his wife was still alert. 'How many would Wood's boat take?' she asked. 'Four', he told her. 'Then, take two of the crew next,' she said, 'and when they are in the boat unleash me and I will make the fourth.' All of this activity was conducted in a towering sea, with a shrieking wind; the *Amelia* swaying violently from side to side. The first of those saved were taken to Reculver and afterwards Lake returned for the rest of the survivors.

7 MARCH 1829

When Mrs Jane Gardner fell ill shortly after breakfast she spoke to Fuller, her gardener, who worked at her Kennington home. It must have been the tea she had that morning, she told him. It had a funny taste, she said, really rather disagreeable and she had not drunk it all. Even so, she had been very sick. Just as well she had not finished it or she might have been seriously ill, she thought.

Fuller looked in the teapot, the tea caddy and the milk jug, but found nothing to arouse suspicion. It was when he looked in the sugar basin that he saw a whitish substance which was certainly not sugar. To test it he put it in a cup of water and later found traces of white powder in the bottom of the cup. He was concerned and went to Mrs Gardner, suggesting to her that she had been poisoned and that she was lucky to have escaped.

Mrs Gardner sent for Martha Epps, her 16-year-old live-in servant, with whom she had always been on the best of terms. What passed between them is not recorded but presumably Martha denied any knowledge of how the white substance had found its way into the morning tea. In any event, it seems that the girl was not reprimanded. The following morning, however, Martha sought out Fuller, asking him why he had told Mrs Gardner that she had tried to poison her. But he had not accused her, Fuller insisted. Yes, he had spoken to the mistress, he said, but he had made no accusation about Martha. But he must have had serious doubts, for two days later he called on the constable, who arrested her. Presumably Fuller had shown him a paper packet purchased from Mr Cochrane, an Ashford chemist, marked 'Poison'.

Martha appeared later in the month at the Assizes, charged with administering poison with intent to kill. But was it likely that Martha would try to murder her mistress? They had always been on such good terms and Mrs Gardner had only once previously reprimanded the girl. She had gone home for the day and instead of arriving back at Kennington at nine o'clock, was an hour late. 'How could you think of staying out till this late hour?' her mistress had asked her. Martha had replied that her brother had misled her about the time – it is likely that no one in her labouring family's house had a watch – and she apologised for her mistake. By the next morning, it had all passed over. Mrs Gardner, having thought matters over, felt that perhaps she had been unduly harsh on the young girl.

But what about the purchase of the poison? Yes, on 6 March, when she had a free day, Martha had gone to Ashford. She had been asked to do some errands when she was in town though she could not quite recall the exact names of two of the items she had been asked to purchase. She told one witness, Mrs Birch, that she had had to go to the chemist to buy something which started with 'cam'. 'Cam?' Well, Mrs Birch told her, that must be camomile. Martha had agreed that it must. And then there was something she was to buy for her uncle's ulcerated leg. 'Sugar of lead?' Mrs Birch had suggested. Ah yes, that sounded right, Martha had said.

So deliberate poisoning or sheer forgetfulness and confusion? Had Martha put her uncle's ulcer remedy in her mistress's tea? In the absence of motive and bearing in mind that it was Mrs Birch who had put the idea of the sugar of lead in Martha's mind, the judge had no doubt that it was no more than pure ignorance and advised the jury to lean on the side of mercy and find the girl not guilty, which is precisely what they did. Whether Mrs Gardner continued employing Martha is not known. But if she did, did she feel easy in her mind as she sipped her morning tea?

8 MARCH 1796

Sailors aboard HMS *Defiance* mutinied in October 1795. As usual – and it would be repeated in the more serious Nore and Spithead mutinies of 1797 – the complaints were related to appalling conditions; dreadful food; irregular pay and the brutality of some punishments. The *Maidstone Journal* described how matters finally turned out:

Sheerness: At nine o'clock this morning the signal for execution was made on board the *Defiance* man-of-war, by firing a gun, and hoisting a yellow flag at the fore top-gallant masthead. A lieutenant in a boat manned and armed was immediately sent from each ship to witness the awful scene. The crews of the respective ships were called on deck and the Articles of War read to them by their captains who afterwards warned them to take example from the fate of the unhappy men who were about to suffer. The Reverend Dr Hatherall, Chaplain of the *Sandwich*, administered the sacraments to all of them except Michael Cox and Martin Ealey who were Roman Catholics. After praying with them until eleven o'clock, they were brought on deck and the ropes fixed around their neck when John Hunt, George Wythick, John Lawson and William Handy were made acquainted that his Majesty had been pleased to pardon them. At quarter past eleven the signal for the execution of the remainder was made by firing a gun when Michael Cox, Robert McLaurin, John Sullivan, Martin Ealey and William Morrison were launched into eternity.

9 MARCH 1891

The night and following morning saw one of the most violent hurricanes ever experienced in the channel. The wind blew with fearful force and then a blizzard set in. Within hours the streets of Dover were 2–3ft deep in snow. Everywhere was enveloped in a thick veil of sharp frozen particles of ice and snowdrifts. Outside, in the country, roads were quite impassable and at one village near Dover, drifts 12ft high were reported. At Shepherd's Well, the railway cuttings had even deeper drifts.

The Elham Valley railway line was blocked with snow, and rail traffic between Dover and Canterbury was suspended. Three engines on the South Eastern Railway ran off the line during the night. Earth and iron railings were washed away from the quay near Folkestone lighthouse.

10 MARCH 1936

The haunting of Dene Manor had been talked of for years. As well as a suicide, a servant girl had been murdered and countless other awful events had occurred over the centuries at the old house. Harry Price, the country's pre-eminent investigator into the paranormal, arranged to broadcast via BBC Radio a scientific investigation of the strange goings-on at the house. He rigged up all manner of equipment around the building – microphones, cameras, heat sensors and special lighting. Starch and graphite were sprinkled on floors and window ledges and lead seals were placed on windows to ensure that there was no cheating. And from 8 p.m. until midnight the nation waited, listening to the broadcast. But the nation was to be disappointed. No ghost put in an appearance. There

The haunted door at Dene Manor. (*The Listener*)

A thermograph installed in the cellar at Dene Manor. *(The Listener)*

was not so much as the slightest footfall or tiniest creak of an opening door. The experiment failed. But was there – is there – any substance in the old stories?

11 MARCH 1877
A fire at Ashford resulted in the death of five members of the Cook family; the father, his wife and three girls aged 5, 3 and 1. They lived in the centre of five very old wood-built cottages on the mill bridge over the Stour. The two houses immediately adjoining also caught fire and the inmates fled for their lives. A witness climbed up to the bedroom window and hung on as long as he could, calling out to the occupants. He could see Cook inside the blazing room, unable to save either himself or his family. Later the charred and limbless trunks were found. The origin of the fire was unknown.

12 MARCH 1853
William Collins (45) was charged at Kent Assizes with setting fire to a wheat stack at Henry Everist's farm at Strood.

Mr Everist explained to the court that at about midnight on the night the fire broke out he and his family were roused by shouts of 'Fire!' He went outside and found the stack blazing and it was eventually totally consumed. He had seen Collins, a total stranger, earlier in the evening lying under a nearby hedge.

PC William Lorshoo said that at midnight he saw the prisoner, who crossed the road to ask him whether there was any place where he might find a night's lodging. The constable recognised Collins, who two or three years earlier had been before the court charged with setting fire to a haystack. When he challenged Collins with that fact, he replied that he had just been doing the same thing. He was immediately taken into custody. He was found to be carrying matches, a pair of spectacles and two pipes, one of them full of partially smoked tobacco. PC Lorshoo's superintendent also remembered the original case against Collins, but recalled that Collins was acquitted on the grounds that there was no proof that he had set fire to the stack deliberately. Had what had happened to Everist's wheat stack also been the result of an accident? Could a man cause such an accident twice?

In court Collins challenged his accusers in a manner described as 'very impudent and insulting' saying that they were telling lies and that they had no proof of his guilt. On the day in question, Collins said that he had walked from Wrotham to Strood. At times he had lain under hedges and at night, when it began to rain, he had gone to Everist's stack and had covered himself with sheaves for protection. He had lit his pipe and had set the stack alight.

The jury retired for a very short time. They found him guilty and he was sentenced to transportation for ten years.

13 MARCH 1761

From the *Sussex Weekly Advertiser*: 'At Chatham three men and several women were committed to trial at Maidstone. These, and several others who were being sought, had obtained letters of administration and with them had impersonated the heirs of dead seamen and received their outstanding pay. The gang had swindled the government of huge sums of money from several naval offices.'

14 MARCH 1867

At the Spring Assizes Thomas Smith was charged with the manslaughter at Dover of a man named Cramp.

There had been a dispute between the two men over a plank laid from Smith's boat onto a neighbouring boat. For some unspecified reason, Smith forbade Cramp from using the plank which belonged to him. If Cramp dared put so much as a foot on the plank, Smith swore he would throw him in the water. Cramp defied Smith and was using the plank when he fell into the water and drowned.

In court two witnesses said that they saw Smith move the plank as Cramp was crossing. The defence was that as the plank belonged to Smith, he was entitled to move it because Cramp was trespassing. Musing, the judge asked the prisoner's counsel whether, if anyone put his head to the mouth of a loaded gun, the owner had a right to pull the trigger and kill him.

Summing-up, the judge said that if the prisoner had deliberately moved the plank, he would be guilty of manslaughter. In fact, it might even lead to a charge of murder. A man who acted wilfully and unlawfully, knowing that what he did might lead to another's death, was guilty of murder. It was absurd to think that because a man was trespassing, he could be thrown into the water and drowned. In substance, the question was this: did the prisoner move the plank while the man was on it or did Cramp slip accidentally? If they were not satisfied that Smith moved it on purpose, the judge told the jury, they ought to give him the benefit of the doubt.

A verdict of not guilty was returned.

15 MARCH 1805

The *Kentish Gazette* reported: 'Last week, the wife of one of the men employed in cutting the canal at Shorncliffe, was conducted by her husband to the market place, at Hythe, with a halter round her neck and tied to a post; from whence she was purchased for sixpence by a mulatto, a drummer belonging to the band of the 4th regiment, lately in barracks at that place. She was a young woman, apparently not more than 20 years of age, tall, and of a likely form and figure; her face, however, exhibited evident marks of incompatibility of temper; vulgarly, she had a pair of black eyes; notwithstanding this, the new partner led her away, with much apparent satisfaction from his bargain.'

At a time when divorce was too costly for the poor and when desertion could have led to demands for maintenance, this exchange with its curious ritual of the halter, recorded in other such cases, was seen as an effective way, quasi-legal as it was, of handing on responsibility to a new 'owner'!

Stagecoach. *(Luton Museum and Art Gallery)*

16 MARCH 1751

A letter from Canterbury, printed in the *Sussex Weekly Advertiser*, reads:

> About nine Years ago the Canterbury Coaches were robbed several Times by two Highwaymen, and then the Masters of the said Coaches hired a Man to go and guard them, and soon after they were both taken, one hang'd, and the other, by Friends, got off for Transportation for fourteen Years. The Coaches have not been robbed since, till this Winter, which has been three Times, by a single Highwayman, once at Shooter's Hill, once at Bexley Heath, and once, on this side of Dartford; then the Masters of the said Coaches not only hired a Man armed to guard them, but gave great encouragement to any who would endeavour to pursue and apprehend such a Villain, which has had the desired Effect, for on the 6th instant three Men who were at Work, seeing one Peter Forlonger, who liv'd at the Three Sugar Loaves, in Duke Street, in the Park, Southwark, rob Capt Montague in a Post-Chaise, a little beyond Welton, they left off and pursued him, and on Sunday took him at an Alehouse just by his own House. He owns robbing all the above Coaches, and that he returned a Family Watch the last Time he robbed them. He says he took a thousand Pounds within a Month at Christmas but it all went as it came. He has three Horses where he says shall never be known of.

Peter Furlonger, a noted highwayman, was hanged at Maidstone on 12 April 1751.

17 MARCH 1833

Fifty-two-year-old Mary Hogg died from unspecified causes in the newly-built Kent County Lunatic Asylum at Barming. She had been the first patient, having been admitted on 4 January. On arrival, Mary, the mother of fourteen still-surviving children, was covered in bruises. Her daughter attributed this to her father's ill-treatment. Mary suffered from giddiness and more alarmingly, from the delusion that people were trying to poison her. At times she would tear off her clothes and try to shred them.

18 MARCH 1872

The inquest into the death of Thomas Callis took place at Dartford Workhouse. On the previous Friday, both bare-fist fighters Callis, a cabman, and 20-year-old John Connor had been engaged in a prizefight. When John Varley, a police inspector, stepped into the ring to interrupt the fight, Callis fell to the ground unconscious. He was carried away first of all to the nearby Long Reach tavern where the inspector saw him lying on a table dreadfully injured. Later he was taken to Dartford Workhouse, where he died the following day. At the inquest it transpired that a fight between the two men had been stopped by police at Horley earlier in the week. Witnesses were to say that before the Dartford fight his face was already bruised and swollen.

At Kent Assizes in July four men faced a charge of manslaughter. Found guilty, Connor was sentenced to one month in prison and heavy costs were imposed on him.

19 MARCH 1806

At Maidstone Assizes, Sarah Pearce, servant to the Revd James Andrews at Marden, said that on the night of 26 December, at about 11 p.m., just before going to bed, she was letting the cat out. As she opened the back door five men immediately rushed into the house. Two of them wore masks; two had black silk handkerchiefs over the lower part of their faces and the fifth – the accused, James Danes – had his face covered with catgut 'such as is used for the lining of bonnets.' Sarah was dragged upstairs and at the top she saw her master with two men holding pistols to his head. They told him that they did not want to murder him: they only wanted his money. Mr Andrews then gave them money but this was not enough. Unless he showed them the secret drawer which held his cash and notes, they would most certainly kill him. Mr Andrews handed over his keys and the robbers helped themselves. After this the men broke open chests, drawers and cupboards. They stayed for about four hours, helping themselves to food and drink.

During this time Sarah Pearce saw James Danes, for his catgut mask sometimes slipped. She particularly remembered his nose, which was large and aquiline. She had no doubt that he was one of the men who had robbed the house.

Danes was found guilty of stealing 40s, was condemned to death and was hanged on 3 April.

20 MARCH 1836

At the Assizes, John Billing, found guilty of burglary in Wick Street, Maidstone, was sentenced to death. At the conclusion of the case, Mr Justice Vaughan said that it was a disgrace to the county of Kent that the police were not under more strict surveillance. He had tried a great number of burglaries at the Assizes, nearly all of them committed in and about Maidstone. In the last two days there had been four burglaries in the town, which suggested that criminals were not deterred by any fear of the Assizes. The judge recommended that magistrates and gentlemen of the county keep a sharp look-out over the police because it seemed to him that either they were conniving at the offences or were failing in their duty.

21 MARCH 1806

When 'Mendoza the Jew', as he always insisted on being billed, met Harry Lee at Grimstead Green near Bromley, those in the know – 'the fancy' – might have been a shade uncertain how it might end, for the great man was now 41 years old and past his prime. It was lack of money that had taken him back to the ring that he had graced as the Champion of England, bringing science to the brutal bare-fist game which at the time allowed biting, eye-gouging and hitting below the belt. But Daniel Mendoza, slightly built and no more than 5ft 7in tall, had defeated powerful opponents with his measured approach. Could he repeat this now at Grimstead Green? Lee had had little experience but he was young and strong.

Illustration from *Boxiana* by Pierce Egan, the earliest sporting journalist.

Pierce Egan, acknowledged as the first sports journalist, gives a detailed account of how Mendoza, a 'star of the first brilliance,' felled his challenger time and again. Poor Lee was knocked down or thrown down more than forty occasions in the bout which lasted one hour and ten minutes.

As early as the second round, Lee was bleeding copiously but continued throughout to fight courageously. But at various times he was 'punished out of the ring;' he was 'hit in the throat,' his weakness 'palpably visible.' On and on, the two men exchanged massive blows, both were cut, both were breathless, the blood ran down their faces. And the crowd urged them on, wanting more, placing their bets in the hope of some miracle. Time after time Lee rose, unable to damage the great man seriously but in yielding after 53 rounds, he had not disgraced himself. He has, says Egan, acquitted himself 'rather in a superior manner.'

22 MARCH 1911

A postman calling at Pluckley Grange, a lonely country house about two miles from Bethersden, straight away saw signs that the animals and poultry had not been fed. It was very unlike the Berndts to neglect their livestock. Then the postman saw a note pinned on the back door. 'Send for the police', it read.

When a policeman arrived at the house he found all doors locked and had to climb in through an upstairs window. He found Mrs Berndt on the bed, dead from a gunshot from a double-barrelled gun lying in the room. In the kitchen, Louis Berndt lay with a shot to his chest. A revolver lay at his side.

The Berndts, a German couple, had lived in the house for only two or three years. Theirs was a secluded life and no one appeared to know them at all well. It transpired that there had been a visitor to the house on the day before the bodies were found. He had been accompanied by a railway porter and was thought to be a relative of one of the Berndts but as there was no answer when he called, he had presumably left the district. He no doubt saw the note on the door but, knowing no English, simply imagined that his relatives had gone away. The porter had apparently not seen the note.

Documents addressed to the coroner described the way in which Berndt had intended to kill his wife and himself but there was no indication of any motive. In one place in the document he referred to his wife as 'my darling'.

23 MARCH 1827

Two Dutch cavalry officers were driving in a gig down a hill into Broadstairs when the wheel of the vehicle nudged the porch of a door. Both men were immediately thrown out of the gig. The local surgeon went to help one of the officers and he recovered enough to return to his post the following day. The second man, a 21-year-old, the more gravely injured, was less fortunate. For three days he was in the hands of the local apothecary whose skills apparently fell short, for his commandant asked that he be transferred to the care of the surgeon. But it was too late. His somewhat florid obituary, typical of the period, says: 'The early fate of this interesting young man, has left a melancholy impression on the minds of all who witnessed his sufferings. He was elegant in person and manners, highly accomplished, most amiable and sincerely beloved and deeply lamented by both officers and privates.'

24 MARCH 1827

Henry Matthews, en route from Lewisham, arrived in Deptford where he picked up a prostitute, Sarah Emery. She took him to 'a low public house' where they drank so much that Matthews 'fell off his seat in a state of insensibility.' At this point Sarah pleaded with a young man to help her take her 'husband' home to what turned out to be a common brothel. Many hours later, when he came to in the streets of Deptford, Matthews realised that he had been robbed. He immediately put an advertisement in the paper which led to Sarah Emery's arrest. Before Deptford magistrates she faced a charge of stealing a £50 pound note, a £20 note and some coins. In court, Emery claimed that Matthews had paid her the money for her services. As he had no recollection of the circumstances, the jury found her not guilty.

25 MARCH 1801

Richard Sheppard, Robert Morley, James Seamans and Patrick Summers hanged at Maidstone for highway robbery. A peak year for executions; there were 219 in England and Wales, as opposed to the usual average of eighty.

The footpads had stopped a post-chaise on the road between Shooter's Hill and Blackheath, robbing the passengers of nearly £100. When a horseman, Mr Taylor of Crayford, came upon the victims they asked him to keep an eye open for the robbers. Further along the road, Taylor saw them entering a wood between Charlton and Woolwich. He rode off and informed the local garrison what had occurred. While some soldiers surrounded the wood, others went inside in search of the gang who were soon caught. The money they had taken was found hidden in a ditch. The men were in possession of eleven loaded pistols and were suspected of having recently shot the guard on a Dover coach.

26 MARCH 1796

Tax on hair powder for wigs was introduced by the Pitt government and designed to help pay for the war. But then all sorts of odd taxes have been paid over the years – on servants, dice, hats and gloves. This tax, around £75 at today's value, was resented and it outstayed its welcome until 1869. This advertisement appeared in the *Maidstone Journal*:

HAIR POWDER TAX
West Kent Stamp Office
Rochester, March 22, 1796

Notice is hereby given that the last year's Certificates for wearing Hair Powder will expire 5th of April, 1796; from and after which time they are to be renewed for the succeeding year.

Certificates are now ready to be delivered by ARTHUR HANCLARK, Stamp Officer, Rochester, and (for the convenience of the Public) by his several Agents in the following towns in West Kent, where the proper printed forms of entry required by the Act to be filled up in writing, and delivered in previously to the issuing of any certificates, will be furnished gratis to the persons applying for such certificates.

There follow the names of the agents at Bromley, Chatham, Cranbrook, Dartford, Eltham, Goudhurst, Gravesend, Greenwich, Lenham, Maidstone, Malling, St Mary Cray, Sevenoaks, Tenterden, Tonbridge, Tunbridge Wells, Westerham, Woolwich and Wrotham.

The Distributor for West Kent thinks it right to apprise the public, that the old certificates all expire on the 5th of April, although many were obtained long after the commencement of the tax; and as the Act has given no limited time after the 6th April for their renewal, he recommends them to make as early application as possible for Certificates to prevent any vexatious informations which they may be liable to from delay.

It all sounds rather stern, and 'vexatious informations' has a hint of menace about it!

27 MARCH 1905

A vicious crime carried out by two low-level criminals would have been long forgotten had it not led to the first murder trial to feature fingerprint evidence. The Stratton brothers,

Alfred (22) and Albert (20), take their place in crime's long corridor of infamy solely because of this single fact. Their trial was a landmark in the history of forensic evidence.

Scotland Yard officers had been finger-printing criminals for several years but prints were only reluctantly accepted as evidence. Then came the double murder in Deptford High Street. Thomas Farrow, manager of a chandlery for more than fifty years, lived above the shop with his wife, Ann. Every Monday morning, the shop's owner used to call for the previous week's takings of about £12. This routine was known to the

The Stratton brothers. *(Daily Sketch)*   Strattons.

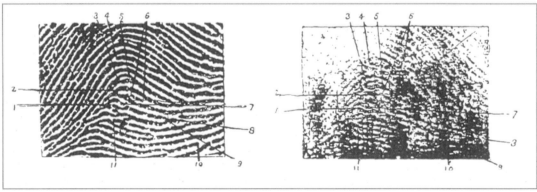

The right thumbprint (left) of Alfred Stratton and thumbprint (right) found on the cashbox.
(Daily Sketch)

The chandlery where the murders were committed.

When the young assistant came to work on that Monday morning in March he found the old man downstairs with his head battered in. Upstairs, his wife was unconscious and she survived only four days.

An empty cashbox with a smudged thumbprint was found in the bedroom. Enquiries led to the arrest of the brothers and Alfred's right thumbprint matched the one on the cashbox. At the Old Bailey trial the judge was dubious about the fingerprint evidence but the jury returned a guilty verdict. The Stratton brothers, unwilling makers of forensic history, hanged together.

28 MARCH 1839

An inquest took place at St Mary's Cray on the body of a pauper called Burgess who had died at Cudham Workhouse. Burgess had applied to the relieving officer, Mr Palmer, for admission to one of the Lewisham workhouses. But his upkeep would inevitably fall on the Lewisham district ratepayers and as Burgess originated from Cudham near Bromley, Palmer insisted that he go there for support. Burgess, Palmer maintained, was not the responsibility of Lewisham ratepayers. So the pauper was given a letter to hand over to the Cudham Workhouse master and sent off in an open horse-drawn cart. Shortly after his arrival at

Cudham Workhouse at Leaves Green. *(Photograph by David Orchard)*

The inscription reads:

Cudham workhouse was Built ate the Charge of the said Parish Anno Dom —1731—

(Photograph by David Orchard)

Cudham, Burgess, who was obviously seriously ill, died. The workhouse doctor was of the view that his journey had contributed to his demise.

At the inquest held at St Mary Cray, the coroner asked the jury to consider if Burgess's death was the responsibility of the receiving officer. Had he been neglectful in sending a sick man off in the way he had? Palmer denied being aware that Burgess was 'in a dangerous state at the time of his removal.' But if that was the case, why was the man sent in a cart? Was it because he was ill, because he was unfit to walk? And did Palmer not know that?

The jury was out for an hour and a half and on their return the foreman declared that they found Palmer guilty of neglect of duty, not knowing the state Burgess was in at the time.

This was not good enough for the coroner, who wanted a more precise response.

Coroner: But what is your verdict in reference to the deceased?
Foreman: We find there has been great neglect of duty. We can't soften it.
Coroner: Do you intend a verdict of manslaughter or not?
Foreman: We leave that to you, sir.

Dissatisfied, the coroner sent the jury out again and this time they were away for two hours after which they returned a verdict of manslaughter.

A public execution at Maidstone Gaol.

29 MARCH 1849

Seventeen-year-old farm labourer George Millen, convicted for the murder at Bethersden of William Law, an 82-year-old man, was hanged at Maidstone.

Millen and 16-year-old Henry Sheepwash had broken into Law's cottage late on a February evening. They found nothing downstairs so then, with a chisel, they took the staircase door off the hinges and went up to where the deaf old man was sleeping. His bed-curtains were pulled apart and straight away, according to one version of what occurred, Sheepwash hit Law with an iron bar, calling out, '**** you, take that!' The terrified old man called out for mercy and tried to catch hold of the weapon. 'Hit him!' Sheepwash shouted. More blows were struck, though by whom is not clear.

Law was now barely conscious and the boys began to search the cottage. But there was no money there. They looked at the old man, bleeding freely. 'I think we've killed the old ****,' Sheepwash said. They came away with their booty: a pair of breeches and three sausages, which they eventually threw in a pond.

Within days both boys were under arrest. Earlier they had talked openly of what they planned and witnesses were quick to come forward. Sheepwash quickly gave his version of events and then in prison Millen told the man's son his version. It was after this that the old man died.

At the Assizes, Millen accused Sheepwash of striking the old man. Both boys were condemned to death but Sheepwash was reprieved on grounds of mental incapacity and sent to a lunatic asylum.

30 MARCH 1861

In his annual report, the Inspector of Prisons mentioned that in Dover Gaol many inmates were soldiers who had committed offences in the hope of being dismissed from army service. Some of them had said that they would commit another offence in order to prolong their time in gaol. In his view, the inspector said, prison was unsuitable for such men. He feared that they might attack officers who came to see them. The report also observed that there was still too little useful work for prisoners, even for those sentenced to hard labour. At Maidstone Gaol, there had been eight cases of corporal punishment for offences committed inside the prison. Two of the prisoners were boys aged 14 and 16, one of them receiving corporal punishment for the second time. The inspector said: 'I feel called upon to observe upon the infliction of the punishment upon them with the cat-o'-nine tails instead of the usual instrument, the birch rod, not only because it is contrary to the usual custom, but also because the enduring scars which are occasioned by the cat operate injuriously upon the individuals in after life, rendering them inadmissible into the army.' At Sandwich Gaol the inspector had found two sailors, summarily convicted for refusing to sail in a merchant ship on the ground that she was not seaworthy. After the men's imprisonment, the vessel was inspected at Woolwich, was found to be unseaworthy and was condemned. But the men were still confined. The Inspector had made the case of the men known to the ship's owners, leaving, it seems, the resolution of the matter to them.

31 MARCH 1769

The *Sussex Weekly Advertiser* reported the following:

> Bowland, the highwayman, who robbed the mail on the 19th of last month, was, after several hours' examination on Thursday last, committed to Maidstone Gaol to which place he was conveyed by Messrs Wright and Ellis (who apprehended him) and under a strong guard.
>
> Being charged with tearing and destroying several letters and material law pleadings going to the Assizes on the Northern Circuit, and leaving them scattered upon an open common near where he committed the robbery, he answered that when he opened the mail, he took out of the letters such enclosures as he thought would be of service to him, then returned all the letters into the bag and tied it up and left it on the roadside where he was sure it would be found the next morning. It is therefore imagined that some person who found the mail in the morning where Bowland left it, mutilated the letters in the manner they were afterwards found about the country, for he, tho' several times asked by the gentlemen of the Post Office, positively denied the doing of thereof, so there is great reason to believe there was a second robbery of the mail committed by another person.
>
> The highwayman had put his boxes with all his clothes and papers on board a Holland trader and was to have sailed in half an hour after he was so apprehended. He is said to have committed the robbery near to the place where he was born and though he was well known in Greenwich, where he had been a letter-carrier, he was so infatuated as to dance all night at a public ball in that town after his name and person was described in the papers.

APRIL

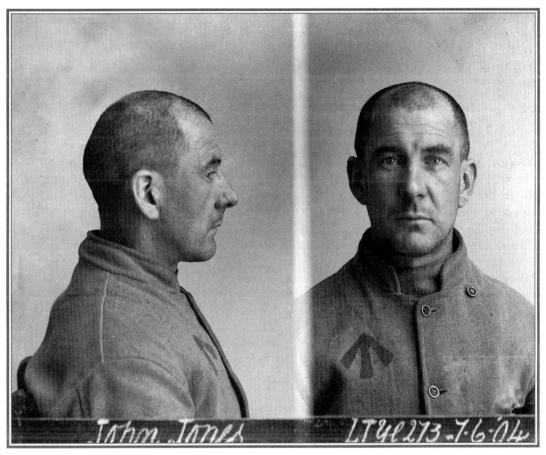

Convict John Jones, 1904. *(Author's Collection)*

1 April, 1819

James Morgan (39), guilty of the theft of 101 sheep from a farm at Bowhill and William Bowra, a highway robber from Tunbridge Wells, were conveyed on a wagon from Maidstone Gaol to Penenden Heath. Despite making the usual preparations, the hangman appears to have bungled the affair. While the 19-year-old Bowra's departure went off without a hitch, the heavily-built Morgan fell down so far that his toes were touching the platform and he appeared to be standing up straight with the rope around his neck. The very full report in the *Maidstone Journal* said that 'the persons surrounding the scaffold with great celerity and presence of mind almost instantaneously got away the platform from under his feet.'

Dead Man's Hand. Women would press the hand of the newly-executed felon to their throats hoping that this would cure them of goitre. *(From a print by Isaac Cruikshank, courtesy of the Neil R. Storey Archive)*

If this episode was not horrifying enough the *Journal* offers more detail. 'After the criminals had hung some time, the usual disgusting scene took place of persons afflicted with wens applying to the executioner for the purpose of having the swellings rubbed with a hand of the deceased which the credulity and ignorance of the afflicted or their relatives led them to suppose it would be an effectual cure. On this occasion, many persons of both sexes, and of various ages underwent the operation. One decent, pretty-looking girl about 17 years of age presented herself at the moment when the body of Morgan was about to be cut down and she actually got upon his coffin to stand sufficiently high for the hand of the corpse to be drawn several times over her neck.'

2 April, 1801

After the execution of twelve men on Penenden Heath their bodies were taken down. Nine of these were buried under the gallows. Three others were handed over to their families for burial. The *Maidstone Journal* took the opportunity to regret what it referred to as 'the depravity of the present time.' William Neale, one of those executed, especially aroused the newspaper's disapproval:

A number of spectators from all parts was greater than ever remembered and notwithstanding the terrible example they had just witnessed, we are sorry to say the behaviour of many that same evening, but too much evinced the depravity of the present time.

'The terror of approaching death does not always bring hardened sinners to a just sense of their actions during the short limits of their existence. A criminal's denying the fact for which he is going to suffer, while a halter is about his neck, is presumed to proceed from a delusive hope that the sheriff may have a respite in his pocket to save a man persisting in his innocence to the last moment of life. But a man under sentence of death endeavouring to implicate in his guilt, in the minds of the people, the evidence which brought him to his deserved punishment is a new species of villainy. Neale, the horse stealer, informed his acquaintance, and those that called on him out of curiosity after his condemnation, that Pretty who apprehended him had been concerned with him in stealing a horse and the day before his execution, told several that his last words at the gallows should be to the same purport. His not repeating those words he engaged to do, exculpates Pretty, and it is hoped the malefactor made his peace with God for endeavouring to injure the peace of mind of a man that did but his duty.

3 April, 1786

In the evening Mr Hurd, described as a contractor from Dartford, was returning from the corn market when he was held up by three footpads on the road between Crayford and Bexley Heath. One of the men had a pistol which he pointed threateningly, unaware that Mr Hurd, wise to the dangers of the road, had pistols ready primed which he fired. The robber fell to the ground and Mr Hurd spurred his horse, riding off to Crayford where he collected a posse. They went in search of the wounded man whom they found on the heath, lying hidden among furze bushes. They took him to Crayford where a surgeon removed the bullet, which had hit him in the chest. Aware that he faced a capital charge, the robber confessed all. One of his companions, he said, was a calico printer and a few nights earlier they had robbed another man in the same neighbourhood. A newspaper report concluded: 'There are but few hopes of his recovery.'

4 April, 1861

Three privates of the 4th King's Own Regiment, stationed at Chatham, appeared before Rochester magistrates charged with having entered the shop and home of Nicholas Lean, a Chatham grocer.

On the night of the robbery, at a time when they ought to have been back in barracks, the three men had been seen lurking outside. Between 9 p.m. and 10 p.m. they broke into the shop and were confronted by Mrs Lean. Two of the men who were carrying sticks beat her severely while the third emptied the till and stole some tobacco. But Mrs Lean's cries for help roused the neighbours and the robbers ran off. One of them was almost immediately captured and the other two were taken in what one newspaper described as 'one of the low neighbourhoods at Chatham.'

In a report of the court proceedings the soldiers were described as 'men of the most depraved character.' The oldest, William Gater, had been tried at the last Assizes on a charge of setting fire to a wheat stack on a farm at Chatham Hill but had been acquitted for lack of evidence.

The men were committed to trial at the next Assizes.

5 April, 1859

The *Maidstone and Kentish Journal* relates this horrific tale: 'A frightful accident occurred in Chatham dockyard to one of the workmen, named John Gallavan, who was literally torn to pieces. The unfortunate deceased was employed in attending to some portion of the ponderous machinery used in the dockyard when, from some unexplained cause, his clothes came in contact with a portion of the machinery, and he was immediately drawn in and almost instantly deprived of life, the machinery, before it could be stopped, tearing him limb from limb. The unfortunate deceased, who was a very steady man, has left a widow and numerous family.'

6 April, 1786

From the *Maidstone Journal*: 'INSANITY – Gentlemen and ladies unfortunately so affected continue to be accommodated with those Attentions which 14 years past have ensured so decided a preference to the Practice and Situation of Dr PERFECT of West Malling, whose Advice and Attendance as a Physician, both in this and every Branch of his Profession, may be commanded upon the usual terms.'

7 April, 1826

The *Maidstone Journal* carried what it describes as 'a very melancholy circumstance [which] occurred at Hythe, early in the morning of Wednesday.' A naval officer, Lieutenant George Dyer, on the coast blockade service, was on the lookout for an armed gang of smugglers reported to be in the area.

At the inquest, George Lewis, a petty officer, stated that when he heard a gunshot in the direction of Shorncliffe, he called out to the lieutenant who was further along the beach. A seaman, James Lemon, accompanying Lewis, almost immediately fired a shot. 'You fool,' Lewis snapped at him, 'what are you firing for?'

Lemon answered that he did not know who was coming and that he had shouted out but had had no reply. But Lewis was annoyed. Firing like this was completely against orders. There was to be no firing at anyone until they had been fired at or at least had been threatened with some form of violence. And then came the shout from Michael Divine, the lieutenant's orderly. 'My God! Mr Dyer is shot.' Lewis found him stretched out on the beach. The lieutenant was dead. Lewis made arrangements for the body to be transferred to Sunderland Fort.

Despite his protests, no-one had heard Lemon's challenge. The court was told by Petty Officer Walker that both he and the lieutenant had repeatedly directed the men generally, and on one or more occasion Lemon individually, that if a suspicious party came on the beach, no-one was to open fire unless violence was first used towards them.

The jury returned a verdict of manslaughter recorded against Lemon who was to stand trial at the next Assizes.

8 April, 1761

This item of news from Chatham appeared in the *Sussex Weekly Advertiser*: 'This Town is full of Pensioners and Cripples, who are come to attend the Chest at this place, for Relief for their Loss of Limbs and Wounds on board His Majesty's Ships of War.'

The Chatham Chest was established in 1588 by Sir Francis Drake and Sir John Hawkins after the defeat of the Armada. The aim was to ensure that old sailors and soldiers, incapacitated in the country's service, should not starve. The chest may be seen at Chatham Historic Dockyard.

Two Old Sweats — 'Descriptions of Battles by Sea & Land'. *(Courtesy of Greenwich Heritage Centre)*

9 APRIL, 1802

The *Maidstone Journal* reported 'The following affair happened at Rochester on Monday se'nnight. A young gentleman, son of a Mr S— of Woolwich, decamped from his father a day or two before with a considerable sum of money, in company with a female, and slept at the King's Head Inn in Rochester, on Sunday night; his father, with a friend, arrived early in the morning, and finding his son in bed, sent his friend upstairs to the room for admittance; during which the son, hearing his father's voice on the stairs, immediately took a pistol from his trunk, and discharged its contents below his temple. A surgeon immediately extracted the ball and he lingered from six o'clock in the morning till two in the afternoon, when he expired. The jury returned a verdict – Lunacy.'

10 APRIL, 1808

The following is a correct statement, taken from the Parish Register, of the number of soldiers buried at Ashford, from 1 March to 6 April 1808, out of about 1,600 men, of which the garrison then consisted.

In the course of 37 days, 47 men in the seriously overcrowded barracks had been buried. The symptoms were fever and the appearance of a slight cold. Death occurred after two or three days.

The report continues:

The disorder, we are sorry to add, is not in the least abated, though, happily for the inhabitants, it is by no means infectious, not a soldier or a person living in the town, having died of the same complaint – a positive proof that the malady is entirely owing to the unhealthy situation and construction of the barracks. But what shall we say of the criminality of those who, knowing the cause of this mortality, and possessing the power to terminate it, by removing the men, still permit the evil to continue! No satisfactory excuse can be offered for continuing the men in these barracks for a single day longer. If a remedy be not instantly applied, we shall not be deterred, by any consideration whatever, from holding up to merited execration and contempt those who can be so criminally callous as to turn a deaf ear, for a single hour longer, to the imperious call of duty and humanity.

The above appeared in two unnamed Kent newspapers and is quoted in *The Times*.

11 APRIL, 1913

In the early hours of the morning, the pavilion at the Nevill cricket ground at Tunbridge Wells was burnt down. Damage was calculated at £1,500. Inside the pavilion there had been a collection of valuable sporting prints, which included a particularly fine example illustrating the first cricket week at Canterbury. There was no doubt about the culprits. Copies of the magazine *Votes for Women* were found nearby. On top of one of these was a photograph of Mrs Emmeline Pankhurst, the suffragette leader, and the woman who contributed most in the fight for the enfranchisement of women in the early years of the twentieth century.

12 APRIL, 1877

Late in the evening Harriet Staunton (37), emaciated, filthy, her head alive with lice, was brought by four people to lodgings in Penge. She died the following morning weighing 5st 4oz.

Two years earlier, Harriet, with a personal fortune worth about £200,000 at today's value, had married Lewis Staunton, an auctioneer's clerk, ten years her junior. From this point, her money was gradually transferred to Lewis's account.

Harriet gave birth to a boy, Thomas, and as she was increasingly unable to look after the child, she moved to Woodlands, a remote cottage at Cudham, near Bromley, where Lewis's brother, Patrick, an artist, lived with his wife, Elizabeth. Back in London, Lewis conducted an affair with Alice Rhodes, the sister of Elizabeth. He visited his wife at weekends. Harriet was never to know that in October 1876 Lewis and Alice moved into Little Greys Farm, only a mile away from Woodlands.

On 8 October, Thomas, now aged 1, was taken to a London hospital by Lewis, Patrick and Elizabeth. The child died three days later. He had been starved to death. Only twenty-four hours later Harriet was taken to die at Penge.

The Stauntons and Alice Rhodes were tried, and, found guilty, were sentenced to death. They were later reprieved and although Alice Rhodes was released, the others served life sentences.

Harriet Staunton.

13 APRIL, 1928

At a meeting of the Royal Sanitary Institute, Dr Alfred Greenwood, County Medical Officer of Health for Kent, spoke about the sanitation of hop-pickers' camps. He argued that the by-laws relating to sanitation were being ignored. Conditions in some of the camps constituted a danger both to the occupants and to local residents.

Dr Greenwood referred to a serious typhoid epidemic in Maidstone in 1897. This had been due to the pollution of water from a hop-pickers' encampment. In the summer of 1927 there were many similar sources of pollution which, had they happened to be typhoid-infected, would have caused a grave epidemic.

Turning to accommodation, Dr Greenwood went on to make suggestions for lighting, ventilation and the prevention of overcrowding. He asked that fires in front of huts should be discouraged as these had led to considerable numbers of burns and scalds, especially among children. There ought to be an adequate water supply within reach of the pickers and the use of streams for drinking water should be forbidden. All camps, Dr Greenwood said, needed adequate numbers of latrines. In some hop gardens there was only one latrine for 200 hop-pickers. As a result of this woeful provision, many camps were in a disgraceful condition and great suffering was inflicted, especially upon women and children. While there had been some improvement over the years, some of the hop gardens were a disgrace.

14 APRIL, 1832

A letter to *The Times* from F.M. refers to three men – Cornelius Fitzgerald, described as 'an Irishman of respectable appearance'; Robert Self, a one-legged 35-year-old ex-soldier; and George Betts, a 'shabbily dressed man' – who appeared before the magistrates at Greenwich.

All three men had been arrested early the previous morning. At Deptford, two policemen, James Jefferies and Luke Kenney, had noticed a cart being driven very slowly and two men walking on each side of the horse. The constables recognised the men as notorious resurrectionists (body-snatchers). The policemen sent for help and then took the cart and the men to Greenwich police station.

When the cart was examined it was found to contain the bodies of two old men. Almost at once word was out that the two dead men had been 'burked' (murdered preparatory to sale to a medical school). A crowd of thousands assembled at the police station, demanding that the three 'Burkites' be let out so that they could attend to them. Eventually, late at night the three prisoners were escorted by forty police and taken before the magistrates at Deptford. As they passed, the mob hurled stones and bricks and missiles of every kind at them. It was only with difficulty that the prisoners were brought into the room with the magistrates. The magistrates then remanded the prisoners until the corpses could be identified.

The next day (Saturday 14 April), the bosun of the *Justitia*, a convict ship lying off Woolwich, identified the deceased. They were both convicts, one aged 84, the other 65. They had died on board on the Thursday night. They had, he said, been speedily interred at Plumstead and just as speedily dug up by the three men who, later that morning, had been arrested. Now the magistrates ordered the bodies to be interred once more and the prisoners were again remanded.

On Monday morning (16 April), Jefferies and Kenney were again patrolling the area where they had been on the previous Thursday. Yet again a cart came past and once again they stopped the driver. Looking inside, the policemen saw the same two corpses, which had been disinterred a second time. This time a man named Hollis was charged.

The prisoners were removed to Maidstone Gaol and appeared at the next Assizes.

15 APRIL, 1878

Mr Charles Nye, a Chatham watchmaker, was sentenced to one month in Maidstone Gaol for refusing to have his children vaccinated and refusing to pay the fine imposed. He had already undergone six or seven terms of imprisonment for the same offence. He was secretary of the local Anti-Vaccination Society.

16 APRIL, 1915

Police Constable Simmons was on the East Cliff at Ramsgate after 10 p.m. at night. There were sentries on guard there and he stopped to chat to them. Suddenly they noticed a very bright light coming from the direction of Albion House. A sentry commented on this as at night there was a restriction on cars on the seafront and regulations which required headlights to be kept as low as possible.

When the car reached the corner the sentry called out 'Halt!' and, when it did not immediately stop, he shouted out the order three more times. Even then, the car did not slow down and so the sentry fired. Within yards, the car came to a halt. Inside, Lt Ronald Winch, a passenger, lay dead.

At the inquest, the driver said that he had not heard any challenge but the car was rather noisy and the hood was up. Witnesses said that they had certainly heard the sentry's challenge. The sentry told the court that he had fired at the wheel.

Returning a verdict of death from misadventure, the jury said that no blame was attached to the sentry. They recommended, however, that sentries should carry lights. Had the sentry in this case carried a lamp, perhaps a dreadful error would have been avoided.

17 April, 1798

After sitting for three weeks, the Special Commission published the indictment against five Irishmen, charging them with High Treason.

The men were accused of conspiring to levy war and asking the King's enemies – the French government – to support them with ships and soldiers. All of the accused men were members of the United Irishmen movement which sought civil, political and religious liberty in Ireland.

At the trial held in Maidstone on 21 and 22 May, four of the five accused were acquitted but the Revd James O'Coigley was found guilty of carrying a coded letter inviting the French government to assist the Irish rising. The letter was allegedly found in his overcoat pocket some days earlier at a hotel in Maidstone.

There will always remain some doubt about O'Coigley's guilt. He would always deny having had such a letter. Was it planted on him? Did the British, hard pressed in a war against the French and anxious to nip in the bud a rebellion in Ireland, concoct false evidence against the most influential Irish leaders? Were the witnesses corrupt? More than one had had a reputation for swearing away the lives of the King's enemies in Ireland. And what about the Bow Street Runner, described as 'a most unreliable class of fellow – a creature who was a cross between a low bailiff and a lower process-server'? Could such a man be believed when he said that he had taken the letter out of O'Coigley's topcoat in that hotel in Maidstone? And what about the handwriting in the letter? Was it the accused's?

At home, O'Coigley had been a victim of Orange Order violence: at Maidstone, was he the victim of a government desperate to hang onto Ireland and fearful of the French and the Irish becoming allies?

O'Coigley's execution on 7 June did not prevent the Irish outbreaks throughout the summer nor the French invasion of Ireland in the autumn. Despite most of their leaders being already rounded up, the rebellion in Ireland was widespread and violent. The British repressed the rebels and repulsed the French invasion but in the process, thousands were slaughtered.

18 April, 1851

At the Ashford Magistrates Court William Cotton (65) was charged with fraudulently obtaining 12s from Jemima Maxted, an old lady living at Belting, near Godmersham. Cotton lived at Rolvenden where, according to the *Sussex Express*, he was known 'by the ignorant' as Dr Cotton, 'a cunning man' (a witch), capable of curing diseases, foretelling events, explaining dreams, telling fortunes and finding lost property. 'Hosts of silly girls,' opined the *Maidstone Journal*, 'have contributed to his fee for undertaking to show them in their dreams the men whom they were certain to marry and the period when this happy event was to take place. Many letters were found on him when apprehended from different persons, requiring his magical aid, some of which betrayed a degree of superstitious credulity which could scarcely have been expected to exist in any part of England in the present day.'

Mrs Maxted who, so the *Journal* said, 'is considered a little deranged', believed that she was suffering from a spell put on her by a neighbour, Mrs Tollest of Lenham Heath, who also enjoyed the reputation of being a witch. Widow Fenn of Ashford and a Mrs Hines of Hothfield persuaded the sick woman to consult Dr Cotton. They told her that he would be the only person able to drive the evil spirit out of her.

Mrs Maxted consulted Cotton twice for which she paid him 25s. But while after each visit she felt there was some slight improvement in her health, this was not sustained. She began to think that Cotton only drove the devil out of her temporarily and then let him in again. She thought that it was his way of getting her to visit him continuously. She therefore went to the police station at Ashford where she asked Superintendent Gifford either to rid her of the devil or to compel Cotton to do so by law. The policeman told her to write to Cotton – she was illiterate but Mrs Hines obliged – and invite him to her house. The Superintendent prepared her with marked coins. When Cotton arrived at Belting he refused to move until the old lady had handed over 12s. She gave him 2s, promising to give him the outstanding 10s if he would meet her at the New Inn at Ashford and would promise to remove the spell forever. Cotton agreed to this. At the New Inn she handed over the 10s and in return he gave her a receipt on which he wrote, 'The spell will be removed for ever and ever and never trouble you any more.' At this point Superintendent Gifford arrested Cotton who was sentenced at court to two months' imprisonment as a rogue and vagabond, to be served at St Augustine's House of Correction.

19 April, 1867

The Court of General Session heard reports from the governors and surgeons of Maidstone and Canterbury Gaols on the effects of the Government dietary, which had been in force for nine months.

Mr Joy, the Maidstone surgeon, said that the new diet was insufficient to keep prisoners healthy enough to be able to work the scheduled nine hours on the treadmill. In recent weeks, he said, there had been an unusual amount of sickness and diarrhoea and in consequence, he had had to increase the diet of many prisoners. The governor, Major Bannister, claimed that weakness and hunger were visible on the faces of the convicts within a week of their arrival. He had difficulty in preventing them from picking up raw potatoes and potato peelings.

While the Canterbury surgeon, Mr Reed, had observed no serious deterioration in the health of prisoners, he, like Mr Joy, felt that the diet was not compatible with continuous hard labour at the treadmill. He was also of the opinion that released prisoners could not go out into the world and straight away earn a living after three months on the treadmill.

The meeting decided that hours of labour should be temporarily reduced in accordance with the reduced diet.

Canterbury Gaol.
(*Kent Messenger*)

20 APRIL, 1747

Armed to the teeth, the Hawkhurst Gang, which for years had terrorised great tracts of Kent and Sussex, attacked the village of Goudhurst. The smugglers were outraged that the villagers had decided that they had had enough of being subjected to the tyranny and cruelty of this ruthless gang. That the villagers had now had the effrontery to establish their own defence force, the Goudhurst Militia, and publish their determination to resist the smugglers was an insult too far. Thomas Kingsmill, leader of the gang, gave fair warning of what was to happen. He and his men would descend on Goudhurst, sack the village and slaughter its inhabitants. Doubtless he was confident that when the assault began any resistance would crumble, but the villagers had prepared in recent months for this day. They had advice from a former military man, George Sturt, recently returned from the wars. Under Sturt's command they gathered what weapons they could, cast bullets from the lead of the church roof, dug trenches, dispersed themselves into strategic places and awaited the arrival of their enemies. Accounts vary as to the duration of the 'Battle of Goudhurst' but at its conclusion, three of the gang lay dead and the rest had taken to their heels. This encounter did not defeat the Hawkhurst Gang. They continued to be a powerful force but their days were nearly ended. Their arrogant raid on the Poole Customs House six months later and the subsequent brutal murder of two old men led to trials at Chichester and the Old Bailey in 1749. The verdicts smashed the power of the Hawkhurst Gang and their close allies in Sussex. Thomas Kingsmill was among those hanged at Tyburn in April 1749.

21 APRIL, 1826

The *Maidstone Journal* carries a sad but not totally unfamiliar tale: 'A child named Turmaine, whose parents reside in St Dunstan's, Canterbury, about sixteen weeks ago was bitten by a dog, supposed at the time to be in a rabid state, from the circumstance of the animal having seized one or two other persons; little notice, however, was taken, further than dressing the wounded parts; but we are sorry to say symptoms of hydrophobia made their appearance a few days since, in the case of the child; and that the little sufferer, after exhibiting all the symptoms attendant upon the disease, died on Sunday in excruciating agony.'

22 APRIL, 1814

Should there be evidence required of the ruthlessness of smuggling gangs, it is here inscribed at Minster on the headstone of this unknown man, thought to be an informant:

> O EARTH COVER NOT MY BLOOD SACRED TO THE MEMORY OF A MAN UNKNOWN, who was found MURDERED, on the morning of the 22nd April, 1814, near SCRAP'S-GATE in this PARISH, by his Head being nearly Severed from his Body. A SUBSCRIPTION was immediately entered into, and ONE HUNDRED GUINEAS REWARD offered on the conviction of the PERPETRATORS of the HORRIBLE ACT, but they remain at present undiscovered.

But who would risk his life for a reward of £5,000 in today's terms? People knew what happened to informers. It has been suggested that it was the culprits themselves who cynically offered the reward.

23 APRIL, 1868

The Report on the Prisons of Great Britain indicates that on the day of the Inspectors' visit to Canterbury the male prisoners were employed as follows:

Treadmill	50	Shoemaking	1
Beating rope and oakum	2	Cleaning	2
Oakum picking (3lb daily)	17	In punishment	1

24 APRIL, 1916

Hundreds of visitors were out on the seafronts at Dover, Deal, Ramsgate and Broadstairs. It was not the usual chilly Easter Monday: this time it was a bright morning, which had encouraged visitors and locals to take leisurely walks along piers and promenades. Then, at about 11.45 a.m., a German aeroplane was spotted over Dover, circling the town at about 6,000ft. The warning siren sounded, calling out the special constables, and the crowds scurried for shelter. Then the anti-aircraft guns, heard at Deal, started up and the aircraft turned back.

Sirens also sounded warning of the approach of hostile aircraft at Ramsgate and Broadstairs. This was the first time the siren was sounded before the actual arrival of hostile aircraft.

On this occasion, the day was not ruined. No bombs fell. But there would be other occasions when the consequences were less happy.

25 APRIL, 1786

The Chairman, the Revd P. Cromp, opened the Quarter Sessions for the Western Division. In his remarks to the Grand Jury, he was reported by the *Sussex Weekly Advertiser* to have said:

> The number of capital convicts, gentlemen, at the last Lent Assizes throughout England, amounted to 286; Kent stands foremost in the list; nearly one tenth of all the capital convicts in England were condemned at this bar: this fully evinces the necessity of attempting to stem this torrent of vice and licentiousness, which seems ready to overflow its banks and to carry away all government and order before it.
>
> The principles of licentiousness (falsely called Liberty) which have been so widely disseminated, and the love of luxury and dissipation have jointly contributed to abolish almost all that is valuable among us. By the first, men are taught to disregard all laws and to abhor all government; by the other, they are reduced to commit any crime which will enable them to gratify their inordinate demands.

26 APRIL, 1871

At 4 a.m. a police constable on patrol in Kidbrooke Lane, always popular with lovers, found a girl with horrific injuries to her face. Her jaw was fractured, one eye was almost torn out of the socket and brain matter protruded from the right temple.

Doctors at Guy's Hospital, where she died four days later, said the girl had been bludgeoned, possibly with a hammer. But it had not been a sex attack nor was it a robbery. She was two months pregnant although the child she carried had been dead for at least a week. Her calloused hands and knees suggested she was in service.

At the murder site, which attracted 20,000 onlookers on the following Sunday, police found footprints and blood on stones by the nearby brook where the attacker had washed himself. In the grounds of Morden College, a mile away, they found a bloodstained hammer. An ironmonger in Deptford High Street recalled a short, black-bearded man in his late twenties who had purchased one recently.

Edmund Walter Pook. *(Illustrated Police News)*

Jane M. Clousen.

Mr and Mrs Trott had read of the murder and went to the police station wondering if she was their niece. Only with difficulty did they recognise her as Jane Maria Clousen. She was 17 years old.

Only days earlier, Jane had told her uncle and aunt that she had been dismissed from her employment because she was pregnant. She also told them of her secret lover, Edmund Pook, the son of the house. Edmund, she had said, was going to take her away with him to the country and on Tuesday, 25 April, at 7 p.m., they were to meet at the top of Crooms Hill in Greenwich to make final arrangements.

When police interviewed handsome 20-year-old Edmund Pook, he denied having seen Jane since her dismissal three weeks earlier. He described her as 'a dirty young woman'. Edmund's father said that she had been an unsatisfactory employee though other witnesses were to say that she was clean, respectable and hard working. Edmund said that on the Tuesday night he had gone to Lewisham but a girlfriend he had hoped to meet had not arrived. He had returned about quarter past nine. On 1 May Edmund Pook was charged with murder.

At the trial, witnesses from the ironmongery said that Edmund was not the man who had purchased the hammer. Blood on his clothing was explained away as the consequence of frequent epileptic fits during which he bit his tongue. And how could he have murdered the girl and made his way back to Greenwich in forty-five minutes?

Illustration of the murder.
(Illustrated Police News)

Murder in
Kidbrooke
Lane, 1871.

After a four-day trial the jury took twenty minutes to find Edmund Pook not guilty. But then who did kill Jane Clousen? The mystery remains.

27 APRIL, 1917

The following announcement was made by the Secretary of the Admiralty after 100 shells were fired from German ships: 'On the night of 26–27 April several enemy destroyers opened fire from seaward in the direction of Ramsgate. The fire was immediately returned and the enemy were driven off after they had fired a large number of rounds.'

The following communique was issued by the Field Marshal Commanding in Chief, Home Forces:

The damage and casualties occasioned by the enemy during this bombardment of the East Kentish coast are as follows:
Killed: one man; one woman
Injured: one man; two women
Damage: 21 dwelling-houses; two stables (one horse killed).
The larger number of the projectiles fell in the open country.

At the inquest the jury added to their verdict a rider asking whether 'in view of the recurrence of bombardment additional protection could be afforded to this part of the Kentish coast.'

28 APRIL, 1820

CUSTOM-HOUSE, LONDON
28th April, 1820
Whereas it has been represented to the Commissioners of his Majesty's Customs that in the night of Monday the 17th instant, JOHN COOK, HENRY LAWS, and WILLIAM RIDDEN, who had been committed to the Gaol of Folkestone, in the County of Kent, for having on the 11th instant, within the liberties of the said town, feloniously assembled with divers other persons to the number of three or more, armed with firearms, in order to be aiding and assisting in the illegal landing, running, and carrying away certain goods liable to pay duties, which had not been paid or secured, made their escape from the said Gaol by forcing the doors with iron crows, in which they were assisted by forty or fifty persons dressed in round frocks, as countrymen; and that two large sledge hammers, together with two ladders which had been used for the purpose of effecting their escape had been found in the said Gaol.

The said commissioners, in order to bring to justice the three persons who escaped, and also those who assisted them therein, are hereby pleased to offer a Reward of
ONE HUNDRED POUNDS
to any person or persons who shall cause the said JOHN COOK, HENRY LAWS, and WILLIAM RIDDEN, or either of them to be taken and safely lodged in the said Gaol of Folkestone, or some other of his Majesty's Gaols in Great Britain, and the like Reward to any person or persons who shall discover, or cause to be discovered, any one or more of the persons who aided the escape of the said three persons, so that such person or persons may be apprehended and dealt with according to law, to be paid by the Collector of his Majesty's Customs at the port of Dover.

The said JOHN COOK is about 30 years of age, is of a dark complexion, has dark hair, rather crooked legs and is about 5 feet 8 inches high, and had on when he broke Gaol a light grey frock coat, was a journeyman butcher and lived in the Town of Folkestone.

The said HENRY LAWS is about 27 years of age, is a dark complexion, has brown hair, is stout made and about 5 feet 7 inches high, had on when he broke Gaol a short brown gaberdine, was a waggoner, and lived in the town of Folkestone.

The said WILLIAM RIDDEN is about 25 years of age, is of a dark complexion, has brown hair, is of an athletic make, and is about 5 feet 11 inches high, had on when he broke Gaol a long dark gaberdine.
By Order of the Commissioners,
G. Delavaud, Secretary.

29 APRIL, 1882

It was a complex, disturbing case but finally the jury returned a verdict at variance with the direction of the judge.

A woman and a little girl had left the train at Paddock Wood, arriving there from Charing Cross at 4.10 p.m. It was a grey, drizzling afternoon, only five days before Christmas. They went towards Yalding, taking the long way round.

They were spotted passing the Kent Arms, walking on into country bounded by orchards, studded with the occasional silent cottage. There was a fog now; the air was raw; the road was empty; there were neither stars nor moon.

Stephen Moore and Esther Pay. *(Illustrated Police News)*

At the Queen's Head, Brenchley, a heavily veiled woman called in briefly for a glass of gin. Later that evening she took the child into the New Inn at Laddingford where she bought three penn'orth of whisky and the tired little girl had some cake.

During the evening a man in Yalding heard a cry in the night but dismissed it as a rabbit screaming its life away.

Earlier that day, in Pimlico, 7-year-old Georgina Moore had gone to afternoon school but did not come home. No one could find her but a little boy said he had seen her on the way to school with a tall lady wearing an Ulster coat.

That sounded like Esther Pay, a woman Georgina loved and who had often taken her out. But Esther later denied having seen Georgina that day.

There was some history between the Moores and the Pays. Esther Pay and Stephen Moore, the child's father, had been lovers. But, in July 1881, when William Pay, a brutal drunkard, discovered that he was being cuckolded, he gave his wife a severe beating. The relationship was then severed by Moore, a relentless womaniser. Was Esther Pay now showing her resentment at how matters had turned out?

But now, with little Georgina missing, Esther's association with Stephen Moore started up once more. Nevertheless, Moore had doubts about Esther, asking her if she was responsible for his daughter's disappearance and reminding her that she had once said that if they ended their affair, she would steal Georgina and bring her up herself.

And then Georgina's body was found in the river at Yalding. She had been strangled and round the body was tied some wire attached to a brick, evidently used to sink the corpse.

When arrested, Esther tried to put the blame on Moore but the police were sure that she was the culprit. After all, Esther Pay came from Yalding and her parents still lived there.

At the trial, held at Lewes in the hope of an unbiased jury, it was the prosecution's case that Esther Pay had murdered Georgina to avenge herself upon Moore.

It was a lengthy and complicated case but it was impossible for the prosecution to prove that Esther Pay was the woman who had left the train at Paddock Wood with the little girl. And anyway, was that child Georgina? Despite the judge's direction, the jury returned a verdict of not guilty.

30 APRIL, 1892

A fresh outbreak of foot and mouth disease was reported in the Sittingbourne district. There had already been outbreaks in the county but it had been hoped that the thorough precautions that had already been taken by the local authority had produced the desired effect. But then the disease appeared among a flock of sheep at Bapchild. Police were immediately drafted into the area. A force of 130 police constables – about one third of the full strength of the Kent County Constabulary – was stationed around the whole of the infected area, which was several miles in extent. A complete restriction on movement in and out of the area was imposed. The report says that 'not even birds or animals are allowed to cross the boundary.' This outbreak lingered on and in June, at Parsonage Farm on Great Belmarshes, 200 sheep that had been in contact with infected cattle were reported. Cattle and sheep were destroyed in huge numbers.

MAY

Tenterden Police, c. 1890. The man standing fulfilled the dual role of chief constable and local butcher. *(Courtesy of Kent Police Museum)*

1 MAY 1835

An extract from a Select Committee report into the 'State of Gaols and Houses of Correction' describes one day on board the *Euryalus* hulk at Chatham. This was used exclusively for about 250 boys. Eight and nine-year-olds were confined there until they were fifteen, at which age they could be transported.

At Five o'clock in the Morning 'All Hands' are called, Ports opened, Hammocks lowered and lashed up, the Boys washed and examined. At Half past Five a Signal is given to prepare for Chapel, when the boys stand round in their respective Wards, after which they go in, headed by the older boys of the Ward, who place them in their respective Seats with profound Silence: the Morning Hymn is sung, and Prayers read by the Schoolmaster; the Officers and a Portion of the Guards being present. After Prayers they return to their respective Wards and still in Ranks till the Breakfast is served down at Six o'clock, equally divided and examined by the Steward and others; he then desires the boys on One Side of the Deck at a Time to go to their Table, hold up their Bread, give Thanks, and sit down. At Half past Six the Boys commence coming on Deck, each elder Boy heading his Division, and his Deputy bringing up the Rear. Hammocks stowed, Boys filed up into their respective Divisions by the elder Boy of their Ward, after which the Officer orders all elder Boys on the Quarter-deck for the Purpose of making known anything that might have occurred since their last Report, when each of the Complaints are noted down in order that they may be inquired into. The Boys return below, in a single File, to clean their respective Wards, with the exception of those who are appointed to wash the Main and Quarter-deck. At Eight o'clock the boys are set to their respective Work, when Silence is observed. At Nine the elder Boys, accompanied by those of whom they complain, state their complaints to the Commander, when each correction is awarded as the Nature of their Offence i.e. by stopping their Dinners or correcting them moderately with the Cane, or by Solitary Confinement on Bread and Water, not exceeding Seven Days; but should anything of consequence occur during the Day it is immediately inquired into. At Twelve the dinners are served down, under the inspection of the Steward; all Quarter-masters and Guard are in Attendance, for the Purpose of seeing that each Boy eats his proper Allowance. At Half past Twelve Boys sent on Deck for Air and Exercise, but not permitted to make the least Noise. At Half past One Boys filed up as in the Morning and sent below to their respective Work. At Two a Division consisting of One Third of the Boys sent into the Chapel for the Afternoon, when they are taught reading and writing. At Five the Boys leave off work, clean their Wards, and wash themselves. At Half past Five supper is served down, after which the Boys come on Deck for Air and Exercise. At Half past Six the Boys file up as usual, and take their Hammocks down. At Seven the Signal is given to prepare for Chapel, when they proceed in, as in the Morning; after which a Portion of the Boys are catechised, the Evening Hymn sung, and Prayers read by the Schoolmaster. The Boys return to their respective Wards. At Eight the signal is given to prepare for Muster, when each Boy stands with his Hammock placed before him, till the whole of them are mustered; the Signal is then given for them to hang up their Hammocks. At Nine profound Silence throughout the Ship . . . The Watch consisting of two Guards, one of which is placed below, and the other on Deck, relieved every Three Hours and a Half, the Bell struck, and 'All's Well' called every Half Hour through the night. On Saturday the Boys are washed all over in tepid water and soap.
(Courtesy of Jill's Black Sheep Search)

2 MAY 1786

From the *Maidstone Journal*:

STOLEN
Out of the stable of Mr HARRIS at the ROE BUCK,
at Harrietsham, on Sunday Morning last,
A BLACK GELDING, Full-Aged, Fourteen Hands and a half high, with a long Broom tale, a Star in the Forehead, writing on the Withers on the off side under the Saddle. Whoever will give information to G. GREEN whose property the said Horse is, or to Mr HARRIS, of Harrietsham so that he made be had again, shall receive TWO GUINEAS reward, and all reasonable charges.

3 MAY 1938

Bromley magistrates heard an odd case. William Reed, a 19-year-old Royal Navy torpedoman and accountant Guy Bell (29) had recently become very friendly. Reed told Bell that he wanted to get out of the Navy. If he committed an offence which would earn him three months' imprisonment, the sailor said, he would be dismissed from service. The two men concocted a plan.

They drove to Hayes Common in Bell's car and there, Reed hit Bell over the head with a jackknife wrapped in a handkerchief. He then drove off in Bell's car.

Bell reported to the police that he been violently assaulted by a sailor to whom he had given a lift. The same man had stolen his car. Shortly afterwards, Reed surrendered to the police admitting to assault and to the theft of the car.

The case came up at Bromley Petty Sessions and after Bell gave evidence against him, Reed was sentenced to three months' hard labour. But Wandsworth Prison was even worse than the Navy and Reed gave notice of appeal, admitted all, and his sentence was reduced to one day. And he was now out of the Navy. On being questioned by police, Bell admitted precisely what had happened.

The magistrates sent the case to the Assizes and Reed was sentenced to four months' imprisonment and Bell was bound over for two years.

4 MAY 1835

Lack of work and living on handouts were causes of much rural distress in the early nineteenth century. The poor feared that they faced a lifetime of poverty. In consequence, there were frequent disorders and demonstrations. On this occasion food vouchers were being offered to distressed families but a mob of 200 labourers, armed with bludgeons, met at Throwley and after that, they went on to Rodmersham, Linstead and Doddington to harass the Parish Relieving Officers who, in the view of the angry crowd, were selling them short. There were threats of violence; shouts of 'See if you can find a pond to give the bugger a ducking.' The conduct of the mob, according to one witness, was 'very tumultuous.' William Butler (22), prominent that day, wore a notice in his hatband which declared, 'We want no tickets – we will have money or blood.' What they really wanted was work and a decent living wage. Several of the officers and guardians of the Milton and Faversham Workhouse Unions were assaulted.

At the East Kent Quarter Sessions held at Canterbury in October, Butler and Richard Cox were found guilty of riotous assembly and assault. Cox was sentenced to two years' imprisonment with hard labour at Maidstone and Butler was given nine months at St Augustine's Gaol.

5 MAY 1891

Matthew A. Adams, Medical Officer of Health for Maidstone visited the slum houses in Paradise Row and was concerned at what he found.

Two years earlier, Adams had inspected the well supplying nos 14 and 15. A child had died of diphtheria in one of the houses and in Adams's view, this was directly attributable to the water being polluted. The well was situated close to the closets and the soil round about was saturated with the filth of past generations. Samples of water had been taken and the conclusion was that it was unsafe for drinking and a serious danger to health. As a consequence of this inspection the Sanitary Committee ordered that the pump handle be locked and a chain and padlock was purchased for that purpose.

Returning two years later in May 1891, Adams found that there was no lock on the pump handle and that occupants were still using the well. One of the residents complained to him that there was no source of drinking water nearer than the hydrant in Stone Street and that on some occasions she had had to walk all the way to the Town Hall to collect water in her pail.

In his Special Report to the Sanitary Committee, Adams wrote: 'In a town like Maidstone . . . there is an abundance of good water, in a situation like Paradise Row, accessible to all, and common to many people; people, too, of a class, ignorant, thoughtless, indeed in many cases reckless, it is absurd to suppose that an order to keep a handle of a pump locked, will always be faithfully obeyed; or to trust to a label to warn such people that a given water is not to be used for drinking purposes. As practical men, we know that in dealing with people of this class, the only way to command obedience in matters of this kind is to put disobedience beyond their reach.'

Adams's view was that the well should be made completely inaccessible.

Sanitary Inspector

WELL WATERS.

Special Report upon

WELL,

Supplying 14 and 15, PARADISE ROW,

MAIDSTONE,

BY THE

Medical Officer of Health.

Front cover of the special report on the well supplying Paradise Row.

6 MAY 1821

The robbery at the Revd Dr Piggott's house at Mereworth began with a reconnaissance. Late at night, when the household had settled down to sleep, Emanuel Willis and John Cable along with Nathaniel Ford, armed with the tools of their trade – crowbar, screwdriver and centre-bit – went into the farmyard and waited there, just checking doors and windows so that at some future time they might return with major decisions about entry already having been resolved.

On 14 May, confident that they could manage the job, they came back with an extra man, Bell. Once the house was settled, they broke through one of the shutters with the centre-bit. Later in the year, Nathaniel Ford, by then a prosecution witness, was to tell the court how he put his arm through the hole, broke a pane to open a window and climbed into the house. From there, he went through the house and opened the area door to let in his masked companions. Then began the thefts – greatcoats, silver spoons, coins, watches, handkerchiefs and rings. They took three umbrellas and two pairs of pistols, finally making bundles of what they had stolen. During a pause in their activity they had a meal with what they had taken from the larder. Then, after each of them put on half a dozen or so fine shirts, they made their way out into the night. It had been a fine night's work. Dr Piggott estimated that he had lost property worth £250.

At Wrotham they hid the greatcoats and shirts in a wood. Willis went straight off to sell the gold and silver articles in London. Next, they made arrangements to retrieve the greatcoats and shirts from Wrotham and for this enlisted yet another man, John Friend. When this was successfully completed, they shared the booty but shortly afterwards were arrested at Meopham.

At the trial Nicholas Ford proved an excellent witness. After five minutes' deliberation the jury found Cable, Willis and Friend guilty. Willis and Cable hanged at Penenden Heath. Friend was sentenced to fourteen years' transportation.

7 MAY 1838

Three boys, all of them workhouse inmates, were brought before the magistrates at Tunbridge Wells and each sentenced to three weeks' imprisonment with hard labour for the following offence against the New Poor Law: 'The prisoners had got up early in the morning, putting their bolsters in the places in bed, and letting themselves out of the window they scampered for some hours over the country, returning at breakfast time.'

8 MAY 1786

At an inquest the jury heard of a man walking his dog by a pond at Halden the previous day. He saw something of a whitish colour in the water and thought it was a dead sheep. Thinking that he might take the carcass home to cut up for the dog, he tried to bring it out with a stick. But it simply would not budge. Only after a considerable time did he make any headway. The corpse began to move and then 'a human hand was raised to his view.'

When, with the assistance of another man, the body was ultimately brought out of the pond, they saw that 'the deceased had no other clothing when discovered, than a shirt, breeches and stockings; around his neck was tied a grindstone and to his legs was fastened a very heavy stone.'

The coroner's court heard that the man's skull was fractured and that he had been dead for five or six weeks.

The jury returned a verdict of 'wilful murder by person or persons unknown.' But there was no suspect. No one had been reported missing and the case was never resolved.

9 MAY 1862

An accident at Ospringe on the London, Chatham & Dover Railway resulted in the death of two passengers. Three others were severely injured. The train which left Victoria at 7.10 a.m. was due at Dover at 9.20 a.m.

At the inquest, Edward Packer, a Faversham miller who had been working in the field by the side of the track, gave a graphic account of what he had seen. He had heard a tremendous noise and as he looked up, saw four out of the five carriages running off the line and rolling down the embankment. As they went, they broke down a wall in the process of which two of the carriages were completely shattered. Then as the coupling broke, the engine came adrift from the carriages. The rails, he said, were torn up.

Packer ran for help and on his return he found one of the passengers sprawled on the embankment at the point of death. Part of a carriage was on his back. Another passenger was at the bottom of the embankment, lying under the fragments of the broken carriage.

The jury returned a verdict of accidental death and added, 'We believe that the engine left the rails in consequence of the defective state of the [rail] road.'

10 MAY 1927

The girl who knocked at Mrs Harland's door at 4.30 a.m. was clearly distressed. She was also naked, wearing nothing but shoes and stockings. And her body was completely black – not that this was her natural colour. She had been 'boot-blacked'.

The police were called and, following the 22-year-old's hysterical story, went to the nearby woods and found a tin of polish, a pair of blackened leather gloves, a length of cord and pieces of cotton wool.

At his trial at Maidstone on 29 June, Sir Gerard Arthur Maxwell Willshire was charged with having 'unlawfully and indecently assaulted and ill-treated Jean Olds at Thurnham'.

Willshire had taken Miss Olds, a city worker, for a drive from London. In the early hours of the morning, they had called at the Star Hotel in Maidstone where one of Willshire's friends was staying. They both had a whisky and soda before continuing the drive. At Thurnham, Willshire stopped the car, telling Miss Olds that he would show her where he used to live. They walked into some woodland and here Willshire attacked her for the first time. She struggled free and they both went back to the car. She thought he was going to take her straight back to London. Instead, once in the car, he ordered her to take off her clothes. Terrified, she did as she was told. Willshire tied her hands behind her back and then proceeded to black her body. Somehow she managed to escape and ran for help.

In court, Willshire, a married man, pleaded guilty although he said that he could not remember anything of what had happened. The court was told that he suffered the results of trench fever and that sometimes he acted abnormally. Drink, he said, sometimes had a serious effect upon him and at the time of the offence he had been 'tight all week'. He was sentenced to six months' imprisonment.

11 MAY 1795

'RUN AWAY – on the 11th May, and left his wife and family chargeable to the parish of Meopham, William Hunt, aged 25 years, about 5ft 7 or 8 inches high, full faced, dark hair rather inclined to curl, had on when he went away a smock frock, flannel waistcoat, high shoes, and a bound hat; supposed to be in the Hundred of Hoo as he was seen in Rochester going that way. Whoever will give information to any of the officers of Meopham aforesaid, by letter or any other means, so that he may be brought to justice, shall receive a reward of One Guinea when taken; if brought home and delivered to the officers, two Guineas.

George Smith Esquire
Joseph Parker   } Churchwardens
W Mungram
Thomas Salmon   } Overseers

12 MAY 1818

James Dyson, 80 years of age and very infirm, was walking near the edge of the lower pier at Margate when he suddenly fell down. 'Shocking to relate,' said the *Maidstone Journal*'s report the following day, 'his head came in contact with the pier crane with such force as to precipitate him over the side of the pier into the harbour, a distance of more than 40 feet!' The tide was out and the old man had fallen into mud but although help came quickly and although no bones were broken, the shock he received was so great that 'the unfortunate gentleman remains totally devoid of sense. We regret to add that it is a hopeless case.'

13 MAY 1904

George Jones (22) of no fixed abode, was summoned by the NSPCA for cruelty to a gelding. Inspector Easedown of the Society told the court that at about 4 p.m. on 12 May he was at a cattle sale in the Lock Meadows. He noticed the defendant trotting the gelding about the field, trying to sell it. The animal was very old, extremely lame, in a distressingly poor condition and totally unfit to be moved. The inspector cautioned Jones but about half an hour later he saw him again trying to coax the horse to gallop. Inspector Easedown then asked the defendant whether the animal belonged to him. 'No, it doesn't belong to me,' Jones said. 'It belongs to another bloke and I am trying to sell it for him.' He had brought the animal by rail from Ticehurst that morning. The owner claimed that the horse was all right when he left Ticehurst but that he was perfectly willing to have it destroyed.

The bench imposed a fine of 40s with 8s costs or one month's hard labour in default. The fine was paid by the owner.

14 MAY 1872

Foot and mouth disease had broken out in West Kent and inspectors were bringing cattle owners before the magistrates when they failed to give notice that their animals were infected. There was some concern that in the magistrates courts, differing levels of fine were being imposed. Thomas Wallis, a cattle dealer from Eltham, appeared before the Bench at Woolwich, charged with failing to inform the authorities that he had twenty cows in the Plumstead Marshes suffering from the disease. He was fined £2 10s per head plus costs, a total charge of £51 5s. On the other hand, Bromley magistrates were more lenient with Richard Sawtell, a Southborough farmer, who had ignored the fact that eight of his cows were affected. He was fined only 5s a head.

15 MAY 1855

The Great Bullion Robbery puzzled police in both England and France. How could £12,000 worth of bullion disappear from a train travelling from London Bridge to Paris? What a challenge it was. Bullion consignments were placed in iron-bound boxes. These were placed in an iron safe, secured by Chubb locks, then sealed, weighed and locked before leaving London Bridge. The safe was never opened until it reached Folkestone when the boxes were transferred to a safe on the ferry. There were two locks to the train safe and keys to these were kept in London, in Folkestone and also by the ferry captain, an employee of the South Eastern Railway Company.

Edward Agar, alias Jenkins alias Adams, a top-class safe-cracker, masterminded the robbery. William Tester (26) a former stationmaster at Margate and now a senior railway clerk, James Burgess (35) a railway guard, and William Pierce, a professional gambler, were his accomplices. The great exploit was a story of duplicate keys; of lead shot replacing the gold in the boxes as the train travelled from London to Folkestone; of the gold then being transferred to travelling bags and these being nonchalantly carried out of Folkestone station by innocent looking travellers. On their return to London a furnace was set up in the grate of a private house to smelt the gold into ingots.

The Great Bullion robbers — William Tester, Edward Agar and James Burgess. *(Illustrated Police News)*

The robbers got away with the silkiest of robberies until there was a falling-out among thieves. Then, three of the men were transported, only the cunning Pierce escaping with a sentence of two years' hard labour.

16 MAY 1860
Joseph Radley, Superintendent of the Rochester police, was at a loss. He had been asked to be on the lookout for 29-year-old Ann Dent who had left her mistress's employment in April, taking with her £305 as well as a gold watch. Dent was said to be in Kent, spending lavishly, but where she might be he was unable to discover as she kept moving from place to place, never staying anywhere for very long. But how could a policeman be expected to track down such an elusive woman in an extensive county like Kent? Although there was the telegraph, there were no telephones, no motorcars and no e-fits. All Radley knew of Ann Dent was that she had been lodging in Troytown, Rochester, before moving on to Faversham, and thence to Canterbury, her trunks labelled 'Griffin'. But where was she now?

Then came the breakthrough. Despite the ponderous and uncertain communication, Radley discovered that she was in Dover, staying at four different addresses. Off he went by train to Dover. At last he tracked her to Charlton Green and because he was aware that she was cautious, he called on her, introducing himself as a foreman rope-maker at the dockyard, and telling her that he had a message for her from an acquaintance who was working with him. At this, she admitted that she was Ann Dent and straight away Radley arrested her, charging her with theft.

At the Assizes, the judge felt he ought to be lenient as it was her first offence and he sentenced her to two years' hard labour. Considering current attitudes to crime and punishment, perhaps this was extremely light. As for the indefatigable Superintendent Radley, he was commended for his zeal and given a gratuity of £5.

17 MAY 1834
Magistrates sitting at Maidstone Town Hall threw out cases against several beershop keepers who, according to two professional informers, Stowell and Swinton, had sold beer illegally after 10 p.m. at night. Not only were the charges dismissed but evidence was given also that the informers, who claimed to have forty-two charges ready to bring to the court, had asked

beershop keepers for £30 to ensure their silence. While dismissing the case the magistrates did not – or perhaps could not – bring charges of bearing false witness and the threat of blackmail against the two men. Nevertheless, an angry crowd outside the Town Hall became increasingly threatening and the mayor ordered that until matters had quietened down, the informers should for their safety be locked inside the jury room. The mob, however, forced their way in through the door and a window via a ladder placed against the wall. Only hastily sworn-in special constables saved the two men from serious injury. They were hidden first in a downstairs cupboard and later smuggled into a chaise in which they escaped from the town.

18 May 1797

From the *Maidstone Journal* came information of treasonable behaviour: 'Some vile and desperate wretches dispersed and distributed among the soldiers quartered in this town a quantity of Hand-bills tending to stir them up to mutiny and sedition, which so far from having the desired effect, was considered by the soldiers as a gross insult to their character; and in order to detect and convict the infamous incendiaries, they have, highly to their credit, among themselves, actually subscribed the sum of Ten Guineas and offered to deposit it in the hands of the Mayor for that purpose.'

Two days later, Henry Fellowes was charged with printing and publishing a handbill containing certain words and sentences 'tending to incite or stir up the people to hatred or contempt of the person of his Majesty, or the Government and Constitution of the realm.'

19 May 1911

The guardians of the Tonbridge Workhouse considered a letter sent to them by the Local Government Board. The letter contained complaints about 'brutal treatment' meted out to an aged inmate by officers of the workhouse. According to the letter, on 21 April, the invalid inmate had refused to have a bath. He had objected to his bathing being supervised by another inmate instead of the officer who was paid for this duty. As a consequence of this, the man had been roughly handled. It was alleged he had had 'his head knocked on the bricks as hard as they could until the breath was nearly knocked out of him. He was then dragged across the bathroom.' It was alleged that one particular officer involved in the incident then stripped off his jacket ready to fight the old man. The letter-writer reported that 'the officer jabbed his knees into the inmate's stomach.' The letter concluded by asserting that a large number of witnesses could substantiate the charge.

A sub-committee had been set up to investigate the matter. Their conclusion was that there was no cause for the complaints. No inmates were willing to corroborate the charges. It seemed that the man in question had refused to have a bath, saying he would 'die first.' The officer involved had made him have a bath and subsequently the inmate had apologised to him.

It was said, furthermore, that the inmate had previously complained about the treatment of his wife and that upon investigation, none of his complaints were found to have any foundation.

20 May 1794

NOTICE

WHEREAS JOHN WHIBLY alias BADGER of the parish of Brenchley, has left two bastard children chargeable to the parish of Benenden –

The said John Whibly alias Badger is about 5ft 7 or 8 inches high, has a dark complexion with light brown hair and disposed to be in the smuggling line. Whoever will apprehend and bring the said John Whibly alias Badger to the parish officers of Benenden shall receive FIVE GUINEAS reward of

| JOSEPH HALL | } Churchwardens | T. THIRKEL | } Overseers |
| J. BUCKLAND | | R MILLS | |

21 MAY 1912

At Brooklands aerodrome, where there had previously been only one flying tragedy, Edward Fisher, described in the press as 'the young and daring pilot', and his passenger Victor Mason, an American millionaire, were killed when their Flanders monoplane crashed. Fisher had not totally recovered from a motorcycle accident several weeks earlier and was piloting the aircraft with the upper part of one arm strapped to his body. This inconvenience did not prevent the inquest jury from returning a verdict of 'accidental death' in both cases. The jury added that they did not consider that Mr Fisher, who had qualified as a pilot only twelve months earlier, was in any way to blame.

22 MAY 1858

William Roberts, a convict working at Chatham dockyard, managed to escape in daylight. He slipped into the Medway and swam out to the HMS *Cleopatra*, managing to climb aboard unseen. Once there he hid himself until the next morning when, dressed in a stolen naval uniform, he took one of the ship's boats and rowed ashore. After three days, and now in a wretched condition, he was captured at Chalk and taken back to Chatham Prison. Roberts had previously been transported though whether he had made the actual journey to Australia is unlikely. He probably served his time aboard a hulk and worked in the dockyard. Then, in 1857, he had been sentenced at Liverpool Assizes to six years.

23 MAY 1786

The following advertisement, which appeared in the *Maidstone Journal*, is typical of many that appeared in newspapers in Kent over the years:

For the Good of the Public, that the Afflicted may know where to apply -

My wife being afflicted for many years with the Gravel [kidney stone], together with a gathering in her womb, which almost deprived her of life, it being attended with such excruciating pains that it is almost impossible for any human being to imagine, without they saw her lay in such misery, for it kept continually gathering and breaking for upwards of a twelve month, in which time I can declare she did not know what it was to have one night's rest, nor even two hours together, but always laid screaming and crying, hoping every hour to be her last. I had all the advice of the most eminent of the faculty, both in town and country, but to no effect, for they could not find out her disorder. In this scene of misery, she might have remained till it had pleased God to call her, had not divine providence directed me to Dr Lamert, who as soon as he saw her, pronounced her complaint to be a gathering in her womb, which with the blessing of God, broke in thirteen days after she took his medicine, and kept continually discharging both by stool and urine; at length she found her pains decrease daily, and her appetite come again, and could rest well at night; in short, she gained her strength so fast that it overjoyed all her friends and neighbours who in her extremity constantly prayed to the Lord, as well as myself, to take her out of her misery; so that she now enjoys a better state of health than she has done since she was twelve years old; therefore I return you my sincere thanks, and consider it a duty incumbent upon me to publish this, in hopes it may be the means of relieving others labouring under the same calamity.
I am, sir, your most humble servant,
Thomas Bratten
At Bexley in Kent.

Witness . . . John Merralls, son of Mrs Merralls of Tenterden, afflicted with Convulsion Fits, was cured in two months. April 5, 1786

John Beak of Ham Green, Withersham, after judging his Complaint a Dropsy, agreeable to Opinion of the Faculty, applied to me, whom I immediately convinced was Worms, and administered such Medicines as caused him to void a Number, many a Yard long. He received a perfect cure in three weeks. April 15, 1786

The Doctor or his Assistant is to be spoke with at Mr Goldsmith's, East Lane, Maidstone and Mr Swift's, Bell Lane, Tenterden.

24 MAY 1774

Greenwich and Deptford suffered what was described as 'one of the most daring riots . . . as perhaps was ever committed in a civilised country'. Sailors from the *Cumberland* man-of-war, bound for Portsmouth but delayed by winds, had come ashore at Greenwich the previous day. Totally undisciplined – admittedly badly fed and probably unpaid – they had descended on Greenwich in huge mobs, stealing from gardens and shops and even farmyards from where they carried pigs, ducks and fowl back aboard.

Local constables were told by magistrates to be very vigilant and they succeeded in arresting five men who were put in the watch houses in Deptford and Greenwich. The result was that in the evening 300 sailors came ashore, armed with crowbars, pikes, hatchets, iron bolts, staves and cutlasses and immediately broke down the watch house at Deptford and released three of their comrades. They then moved on to Greenwich where their other two messmates were confined. They swore that they would hang in the market place every magistrate and constable they could find. By seven in the evening, their number swollen to 2,000, they totally demolished the watch house with cleavers and hammers stolen from shops. The inhabitants, terrified, shut their shops and barricaded their houses. Finally the mob dispersed, leaving the inhabitants of Deptford and Greenwich, accustomed to a degree of disorder, shaken by scenes such as they had never before experienced.

25 MAY 1827

The *Maidstone Journal* tells of a Rolvenden farmer who was on his way home from Tenterden fair. He decided to break his journey and called in at a public house. He was drinking his ale – and it may be that he had had several earlier in the day – when a stranger offered to bet 5s that he could produce more money there and then than anyone else in the room. The farmer had had some successful sales that day and accepted the challenge and took £25 from his pockets. The stranger was aghast. He could not match that sum, he said, and he did not in the least doubt the farmer's honesty but might he, he asked, just check the notes to ensure that he was not being deceived. And he was not. There it was, £25 in good English money. The stranger ruefully handed over the 5s and the farmer went on his way, happy that the day had turned out even better than he had expected.

It was only when he reached home, now sobered up perhaps, that he took the parcel of notes out of his pocket and found blank sheets of paper. He had lost £25.

26 MAY 1940

In the evening, Operation Dynamo was underway, its task to rescue the 400,000 British and French troops stranded on the beaches of Dunkirk. The British Expeditionary Force, in retreat from Europe, was under threat from the fast-moving German Panzer divisions, which had in recent weeks forced the surrender of Belgium, Holland and France.

The beleaguered army of the only nation still at war with the Germans waited helplessly while day in and day out enemy aircraft strafed and dive-bombed them relentlessly and the artillery of land forces bombarded them ceaselessly.

And now the remarkable rescue mission, planned in the space of a single week at Dover Castle by Admiral Ramsay, swung into action. Fifteen passenger ferries set off from Dover as well as another twenty from Southampton aiming to pull off the most remarkable evacuation of an army ever recorded. But even with air cover and the accompaniment of destroyers and minesweepers, the first attempt to evacuate the soldiers was unsuccessful as the ferries were unable to get alongside the piers. The plan then changed. Now the ships got as close to the beaches as possible and remarkably, supported by hundreds of smaller craft, manned by civilian volunteers, 338,000 men were returned to Britain. But it was the story of 'little ships,' sailing from Kent and other parts of the coast, that most of all added a proud chapter to a nation's history.

27 MAY 1858

Two well-known bare-fist fighters, Johnnie Walker and Bob Travers 'the Black', arranged to fight for a purse of £100. The newspapers described how 'a considerable portion of the

Second contest between the great champion Thomas Cribb and the former slave Tom Molineaux. *(Courtesy of Greenwich Heritage Centre)*

low blackguardism of London' made their way to the fight venue at Greenhithe. Remarkably, there was no riot when Walker decided that he did not wish to fight and Bob Travers claimed the purse. Perhaps it was because two other bruisers, Haley and Sullivan, stepped in and fought a bloody, brutal fight. Then two friends, James Morris, 'The Brighton Pet', and Phillip Redwood, faced up to each other, their bout lasting an hour. It concluded when Redwood fell to the ground, unconscious and severely bruised about the face and neck. There was obviously an emergency but to reach the Gravesend infirmary, the stricken fighter had to be taken there by boat and then by cab. He died within an hour of his arrival. In the opinion of the surgeon, Redwood, a rather slim-built man, had not been physically fit enough to take part in a boxing match.

None of these men was the equal of those giants of the past, Tom Cribb and his opponent Tom Molineaux. Of their second fight in 1811, Pierce Egan wrote: 'To distinguish the combatants by the features would have been utterly impossible so dreadfully were their faces beaten.' Cribb won this fight, held in Leicestershire, in the thirty-fourth round.

Title page of Pierce Egan's *Boxiana*, printed in 1812. *(Author's collection)*

28 MAY 1833
Mr Budd, a surgeon at Tunbridge Wells, was riding at a gentle pace when a sudden gust of wind blew off his hat. A friend accompanying him immediately jumped off and found the hat but Mr Budd's own attempt to catch his hat had startled his horse which raced off. The surgeon was unable to control the animal and eventually, outside Ephraim House, he was thrown. 'The force of the fall,' the *Maidstone Gazette* tells us, 'split the petrous portion of the temporal bone, taking a straight direction from ear to ear.' Mr Budd died within thirty minutes.

29 MAY 1931
As a senior member of the Erith Education Office with thirty years' loyal service, Charles Lewis had a reputation for reliability. And he was thought of equally highly in the local bowling club and in the Conservative Association. With his pince-nez and his business suit, he was the image of dependability. Charles Lewis was certainly not murderer material. He did not look the part. But then, Assistant Education Officers rarely do.

Lewis made two phone calls early on the Wednesday morning when work was to resume after the two-day Whitsuntide break. One call, brief and totally lacking in detail, was to the office: his wife, Maude, and daughter, Freda, were dead, he said.

The second was to his daughter's teacher training college. She would not be in college for a day or so, Lewis said. He would write an explanatory letter. Then, the following day, his brother-in-law in Wales received a letter from Lewis. Maude and Freda were dead, it said, without further elaboration.

Maude Lewis. (*True Crime magazine*)

Freda Lewis. (*True Crime magazine*)

Alarmed, the brother-in-law contacted another relative. Both men went to 37 Erith Road, Belvedere, to find the house empty. They called the police whose initial search of the house failed to explain the absence of the occupants. And then they turned their attention to the garden and the unfinished fishpond. It was here, under the concrete, that they found the bodies, both in nightclothes, woollen jackets, and covered with sheets and a carpet.

On the Friday, more or less about the same time as the bodies were discovered, 60-year-old Charles Lewis threw himself into the sea from a passenger boat bound for Leith. The ultra-respectable man, acting totally out character, was found to have embezzled the local authority of £600.

30 May 1789
Goodman, said to be one of a gang of highwaymen who had committed many robberies in Kent, appeared before magistrates at the Bow Street office. A witness, a man named Griffiths, said that on 18 May, when he was returning to London in a post-chaise from

Highwaymen at work.

Dartford, he was stopped near Blackheath windmill by four men, all armed with pistols and cutlasses. They had taken his silver watch and about £3 in money. He was certain that Goodman was one of the men who robbed him. Mr Griffiths was bound over to prosecute Goodman at the next Maidstone Assizes. So, this is how prosecutions were carried out. It was incumbent on the injured party to lay the case. Perhaps for this reason, as well as the expense and time, many found it all just too much bother to proceed. There is no record of the outcome of the trial.

31 MAY 1811

The hulk *Sampson* at Gillingham was used exclusively for French PoWs and particularly for those who had been recaptured after escaping. Others who had proved themselves troublesome on other hulks were also imprisoned on the *Sampson*. The discipline maintained on this hulk was rigid. In May, the captain, as a reprisal for damage done on board, reduced rations savagely.

Angered at the reduction, the prisoners went on a forty-eight hour hunger strike, refusing to eat what they had been given. After two days of starvation they went up on deck and asked the captain to increase their food allowance. This he refused to do, saying that they would have no more than that already given to them. He ordered the prisoners back below decks. But the prisoners refused to move. Now it was stalemate. One of those present, Sergeant Major Beaudouin, left an account of what occurred next:

> Hardly had they made this declaration than the captain gave the word to the guard, which was at once done, the crowd being fired upon. The poor wretches, seeing that they were being fired upon without any means of defence, crowded hastily down, leaving behind only the killed and wounded.

Reinforcements arrived from other ships to help the captain restore order. There is some dispute about the numbers but it seems that six men were killed and many more were wounded.

Another French prisoner, Dr Fontana, who was on one of the neighbouring hulks, claimed that the English had shot 'poor half-starved wretches who had been deprived of all food for twenty-four hours and who only demanded their rations, offering to pay forthwith for the damage of which they had been accused.'

JUNE

Senior officers and sergeants from Dover Borough Police,
seen here at the beginning of the twentieth century. *(Courtesy of Kent Police Museum)*

1 June 1799

Travelling in his chaise from Lewisham, Lt-Col Peter Shadwell and his servant stopped at the Bull at Wrotham to refresh themselves and their two horses. Two men from the 17th Light Dragoons came by and Shadwell spoke to them. They told him that they were on their way from Maidstone to London but Shadwell was suspicious of them and asked to see their passes. At this point they walked away and Shadwell, suspecting them of being deserters, tried to catch hold of one of them. He was shot in the heart and died almost instantly.

The men, John Keggan and Philip Keating, each carrying a pistol, ran off but were followed and as their pursuers caught up with them, Keggan threatened to shoot them but soon threw down his weapon. Keating was more stubborn and only yielded after being shot.

Philip Keating, who had fired the shot which killed Lt-Col Shadwell, was hanged. Keggan was extremely fortunate and was found not guilty.

Some accounts say that Lt-Col Shadwell was the leader of a smuggling gang which used the Bull as one of its staging points for contraband. One incorrect version of the incident says that the deserters were pursued by gang members, caught and beaten to death.

The Bull at Wrotham.
(David Orchard)

The plaque at the Bull at Wrotham. *(David Orchard)*

2 JUNE 1927

Sonia Ramsay's mother, Mrs Heilgers, noticed that her daughter had not returned home to the house they shared in Lindenthorpe Road. The following morning, uneasy, she took herself off to the Chinese Lantern Café which Sonia had opened in Harbour Street in Broadstairs the previous year.

The café always had some elegance. So had Sonia, flitting around the tables in silk Oriental gowns, her hair immaculately styled. She was a striking woman, whose husband, an RAF pilot, had been permanently crippled in a flying accident. But he always trusted his faithful wife enough to encourage her to go dancing in the ballrooms of Margate, Ramsgate and Broadstairs.

And now, upstairs, Mrs Heilgers found her daughter dead in one of the rooms, her back hard against the door. She was fully dressed, wearing a brilliant scarlet Chinese robe, gold dragons embroidered on the back. A white sheet had been draped over her and this concealed the severe blow to her head and the towel round her neck. There was a considerable amount of blood on the floor and on the lower part of the walls.

The Chinese Lantern Café. (Isle of Thanet Gazette, *courtesy of Margate Library Local Studies Collection*)

A trail of bloody footsteps led from the room to a bedroom on the opposite side of the stairway where the police found a bloodstained hammer and a pair of men's shoes, their soles caked with dried blood, and a man's suit stained with blood.

And on the dressing table was an eight-page letter confessing to the murder. It was written by Charles Robinson who lived above the café, of which he was part-owner.

Since the Ramsays had arrived in Broadstairs two or three years earlier, Robinson, separated from his wife, had lived at the café. He was a first-class nurse and a highly trained masseur who also looked after Mr Ramsay.

Police now searched for Robinson, described as a fascinating man, 'a most able and entertaining conversationalist.' He was found after a week lying among some shrubs near the cliff edge. He was unconscious, his face blue, his tongue swollen and a yellow froth oozed from his mouth. On his left temple was a bruise; there were abrasions on his knuckles and one eye was discoloured. On the grass beside him was a large medicine bottle containing a yellow liquid, a small aspirin bottle, and a bottle of whisky. Robinson was rushed to Ramsgate Hospital but within two hours he died.

The two inquests – Sonia's at Broadstairs police station and Robinson's at Ramsgate Town Hall – combine to reveal a tale of obsessive love. Robinson, infatuated with Sonia, had even begun dancing lessons but when he asked if he might accompany her to dances, he was rebuffed. Sometimes he threatened to turn up at dancehalls where she was; at other times he objected to her dancehall visits.

Inquest witnesses spoke of Robinson's nervous breakdown; a doctor said that he seemed at times to be on the borderline of insanity. The letter he left was described as 'a letter of an insane man smarting under an insane delusion that he had been grievously wronged by the deceased woman.'

Though perhaps it may not seem so, both were eminently decent, respectable people.

3 JUNE 1940

At the beginning of the war up to 8,000 children from London had been evacuated to parts of rural Kent. Now, in view of the possibility of an invasion by German forces, the government decided to remove all of these evacuated children from such vulnerable areas. Children who had been evacuated to certain Kent towns had already been moved out of the county, principally to the Midlands and South Wales.

Some parents expressed anxieties that the government intended to send their children to Canada or Australia and it was made clear that no children would be sent abroad except at the wish of their parents.

4 JUNE 1842

Perhaps when Ensign George Bradin of the 26th Regiment of Foot arrived at Chatham, he was unaware of the ill-feeling, brewing for weeks, between officers of the garrison and seamen belonging to the various colliers berthed on the Medway. If that was so, then he must have been in for a rare surprise when, along with a friend he was going to the Sun Hotel with late on the Saturday night, he heard shouting, swearing and saw a mob gathering in the High Street. A remark by a passer-by alerted him to trouble: some officers, she had heard, were going to be murdered.

That was enough for Bradin who at once made for the crowd to find out what was happening and found several officers being brutally beaten. Bradin intervened, pushing his way through the ring of onlookers hoping to effect a rescue. As he made his way through the jostling, jeering crowd, a man aimed a blow at him. Bradin shouted at the man, telling him that there was no reason to try to hit him. He was a stranger to Chatham, he said. But his assailant swore that Bradin had fought with him a few nights earlier. As it was clearly impossible to calm matters down, Bradin decided that retreat was the better part of valour. But he had not made much headway before he was knocked down and set upon by a dozen or more colliers who kicked him about the head and face, shouting out that they would 'kill the bloody marine.'

Finally, an onlooker, equally outraged at what was happening, managed to extricate Bradin and take him back to the hotel. The officer's bloodied face was dreadfully cut and both of his eyes were closed. The following day his face was swollen as if it had been blown up.

Two days later, two men, brothers George and Thomas Langford, appeared in front of the magistrates at Rochester. They heard that in view of the violence which they faced whenever they went into Chatham, officers would go there only if they were carrying their swords. Some of the officers were laid up and would be for several days after this outbreak. George Langford had been in the thick of things, saying that he 'would make their chops rattle.'

The magistrates declared that this was an assault case of a most atrocious character. Although Thomas Langford was acquitted, his brother George was fined 40s with 16s and 6d costs. Unable to pay, he was committed to the House of Correction for six weeks.

5 JUNE 1934

Eighteen-year-old Frederick Johnson had the responsibility for delivering the wages to a gang of workmen. He was cycling down Berengrave Hill at Rainham and carrying an attaché case containing £103 when three men suddenly rushed at him from behind a stationary car. Johnson was pushed off his cycle and into the gutter. When he rose, the case had gone and the car was making off with a fourth man at the wheel.

Later in the year four men were tried at Kent Assizes. Three of them, all from London, received sentences of between three months and a year. The fourth man, George Brown from Chatham, the ringleader, was given three years. Brown had been aware of the way in which the wages were delivered and had invited his London friends to assist him.

6 JUNE 1806

At about 9 p.m. in the evening Mr Ambrose from Bearsted was held up by three men just outside Maidstone. They drew their bayonets and threatened to run him through if he resisted. They stole from him his jacket and waistcoat, two handkerchiefs, his hat and smock along with 8s. They left behind a jacket of the kind worn by soldiers of the 52nd (Oxfordshire Regiment). Later that night, in the same neighbourhood, a farm labourer was assaulted by three soldiers who stole his hat and his smock. It was presumably the same three men who shortly afterwards stole a £10 banknote, a half-guinea in gold and sixpence in silver from the landlord of the White Horse at Bearsted. It was thought that the men were deserters aiming to pass themselves off as civilians. There is no record of the men having been caught.

7 JUNE 1824

After a day drinking with his wife at Wincheap Fair, Benjamin Barrett called in for a drink at the George and Dragon. It seems that he was already drunk, for the landlord, spotting potential trouble, refused to serve him. But that did not stop Barrett who, ready for a fight, began to argue with some 'broomdashers' (rabbit catchers, probably gypsies). He insisted on fighting one of the group, James Baker, and the two men left the pub and went down the street to find a suitable place for what they seem to have regarded as more than just a brawl. It was to be a formal fight and they both engaged friends to act as seconds. It was a raucous enough affair with several spectators encouraging their favoured man.

The men clearly followed the crude rules which applied in professional pugilistic encounters. When there was a knockdown or when one of the two went down on one knee, there was an agreed pause for a minute or two. After seven 'rounds' in which the men gouged eyes, felled their opponent with blows to the throat, kicked him in the groin, bit whatever presented itself, Baker gave Barrett a punishing blow in the ribs. Barrett staggered and fell flat on his face. Within three minutes, he died. His wife, who until then, with her infant child in her arms, had been enthusiastically cheering on her husband, was now, so says the report, in despair and 'gave away to the most extravagant grief'. The body was carried to the nearby Cock public house. A coroner's jury returned a verdict of manslaughter against James Baker.

8 JUNE 1826

The *Maidstone Journal* relates details of a case which went to the Assizes. The extremely wealthy George Gregory who had recently come to live at Willesborough, received the following letter, demanding 20 sovereigns:

> I have wrote a few lines to you and I am in great distress all throu you, for you have a time back engered me of all my property: and now, if not by good will, I must by bad, have 20 sufferens [sovereigns] of you, and you must put them at a private place for me, for if you dont, I will be the death of you in some way or other: if I can't do it slyly, I will do it in the middle of the day, or in the night, or at the first uperunety [opportunity] & if you say anney thing about this, I will murder you the same as if you don't put it there: look down aside your frunt wall and door post, and move the durt, you will find a small purse; put the sufferens in it, secure it again at the same place; if you wish to live, do it; for if you dont, prepare for death; for your time will be short; for hear is four of us, and if you put it there and say nothing about it, fear not. As soon as you receive the letter, put it there, and dont let me hear of it again for if I do, I will not go back of my word; so do it, and then I will never interfear with you; but if you dont, you may depend upon it I will be the death of you now. Dont you disappoint me.

Gregory did nothing about this letter but when a second one, written in the same vein, arrived, he set a trap. He placed the money where he had been told to do so and when the letter-writer came, he was seized by Gregory's servant.

Joseph Finn was found guilty at the Assizes of feloniously sending a threatening letter, an offence which carried the death sentence. He was later reprieved.

9 JUNE 1865

The 'Tidal Express' was an apt name for the train from Folkestone to London, for its departures depended on the tide. It waited at Folkestone for the arrival of the cross-channel ferry and its times were therefore variable. But the railway authorities were well aware of this and always prepared specific timetables for this service. Tragic then that Henry Benge, foreman of a gang of platelayers working on rails over a bridge near Staplehurst, consulted the wrong day on the timetable. He had checked the Saturday times instead of Friday's. The result was that when the 2.20 p.m. train from Folkestone came unexpectedly up his stretch of line, one of the plates holding the rail had been loosened. All too late did a flagman up the line try to warn the train driver; all too late for any action save for Benge and his gangers to jump out of the way before the train keeled over the bridge, seven of its carriages plunging into the stream, a fall of several feet. They were so crushed and shattered that together they did not occupy the space of two whole carriages. It was impossible to know if the travellers inside had been killed outright by the shock or had suffocated as they lay in the water and mud. There were ten deaths and many more injuries. Charles Dickens, a passenger, was commended for his rescue work.

Company rules required that detonating signals should be placed on the line for up to 1,000 yards when track was being taken up. Again Benge had been neglectful. At the Assizes later in the year he was sentenced to nine months' hard labour.

The 'Tidal Express' crash between Tonbridge and Staplehurst, June 1865. *(Photograph reproduced with the author's permission from Frank Chapman's Book of Tonbridge)*

10 JUNE 1797

A correspondent from Queenborough writing to the *Maidstone Journal* records an incident during the naval mutiny at the Nore when some captains defied the mutineers and broke their blockade of the Thames:

Whilst we were drinking our wine after dinner, a most dreadful firing took place amongst the ships at the Nore, caused by the *Leopard* cutting her cable and running up the River Thames; the *Repulse*, in following her example, made for Sheerness harbour, but unfortunately got aground within gunshot of the mutinous ships. Never was a scene so distressing, it is impossible for me to describe to you the manner in which she was fired at by all the ships that could reach her, particularly by the *Monmouth*, the nearest to her which, by the assistance of a spring-cable, was able to attack her in every direction. She fired to such a degree for an hour and twenty minutes whilst the *Repulse* was on shore that it was feared everyone on board would be killed and the ship not able to get off. But how great was the joy of the numerous spectators who covered the ramparts and batteries when she started! I have the pleasure to say that no one on board the ship was injured but a lieutenant who lost his leg.

PS It is now 2 o'clock and since writing the above the *Sandwich* and other ships at the Nore have hoisted St George's Ensign on the main mast but six ships out of the number have got the Flag of Defiance on the fore.

11 JUNE 1798

The *Maidstone Journal* reported this sad story:

A party consisting of two gentlemen, two ladies and their servant arrived at Gravesend from Southend in a little boat, navigated by two men belonging to the latter place. During their stay some of the experienced Gravesend watermen saw that the boat was improperly conducted and strongly advised the shortening of the sail, a caution which was fatally disregarded. Within a few minutes after the party had quitted the town, on the return, the wind increased as they were passing the Cole-house point, and the men, improperly leaving the boat in stays, her head was greatly lifted up, when the gentlemen and ladies taking shelter under the tilt, she instantly went down stern foremost and every soul perished.

The boat was dragged up when the body of a beautiful young woman, apparently about 17, was alone discovered, having her arms closely entwined in part of the furniture. A note was found in her pocket book in her pocket, directed to Miss Lascelles at a clergyman's near Prittlewell [Southend] and from some other memorandums in a pocket book, it seemed that the party were on a visit there . . . The gentlemen, by the initials on their buttons, are supposed to have been members of a Volunteer Corps.

12 JUNE 1889

At Tonbridge Petty Sessions, Rhoda Martin from Pembury laid her domestic troubles before the magistrates. Her labourer husband, Charles Martin, was summoned for persistent cruelty to his wife who was applying for a separation order against him. Martin also faced a second charge of attempting suicide.

The couple had been married for twenty years and Mrs Martin had had seven children of whom four were alive. Her husband was frequently drunk and had on different occasions threatened her with guns, knives and razors. When recently Mrs Martin told her husband that his father who lived with them ought to make some financial contribution, he had flown into a temper telling her, 'If you are the cause of my father going into the workhouse, and you can put up with the irritation and provocation I'm going to give you without going into Barming [the County Asylum] you'll be made of good stuff.'

The argument continued and Martin had tried to hit her but one of their sons intervened. Then Martin threw a knife and fork at her and threatened to murder her. Eventually Mrs Martin called for the police and the following day she left him.

Having heard the evidence, the chairman concluded that the trouble occurred only when Martin was drunk. Could he not give up drinking, Martin was asked?

Chairman: Look how much happier and better off you would be if you gave it up.
Defendant: I will give it up, sir.

That charge dealt with, Martin was then charged with the suicide attempt. He had been drinking at the George and Dragon at Capel. He was very distressed about what had happened and, pulling out a penknife, said he could endure it no longer. He stuck the blade into the palm of his hand and ran off into woodland, shouting as he went that he intended to end it all. In fact, he was found by a pond, his hand bleeding but with no other injuries.

Again the chairman summed up sympathetically, though perhaps rather optimistically. It was a great pity, he said, that the defendant had given way to drink because it had caused both domestic and personal unhappiness. He urged Martin to sign the pledge, which would no doubt resolve their problems.

13 June 1797

The mutiny of sailors on twenty-eight British warships stationed at the anchorage in the Thames Estuary came to an end after a month. The leader of the mutineers, Richard Parker, chosen by his shipmates because of his education and intelligence, was a former naval officer, a man concerned that sailors should have better conditions, better pay and better food. On behalf of all of the crews he put these proposals, along with requests for the end of the press gang and the removal of unpopular officers, to representatives of an alarmed government. But the mutineers lost public sympathy when they damaged trade by blockading the Thames, and when fears grew that the French, with whom the country was at war, might take advantage of the situation. Sensing the swing away from the mutineers, the government refused to accede to any of the demands. The Nore mutiny collapsed. But Parker, the so-called President of 'The Floating Republic', and the principal mutineers were arrested and charged with mutiny and piracy. Parker, a man of undoubted decency, was tried, found guilty and was hanged from the yard-arm of HMS *Sandwich*, the ship on which he had served. In all, twenty-nine mutineers were executed. Others were flogged, imprisoned or transported.

14 June 1796

From the *Maidstone Journal* on this and other dates:

ITCH
The most inveterate cured in forty-eight Hours, in two Dressings only, by an Ointment under the Sanction of his Majesty's Letters Patent, perfectly agreeable in Smell, does not contain a Particle of Mercury or any pernicious Ingredient, but is so innocent that it may be used with the greatest Safety on a Child of a Month old.

Sold by the Proprietor, J. TYCE, No. 96 Fleet-market, London; also by W. Browne, Druggist, and J. Blake, Maidstone; and Mr King, Druggist, Rochester.

One Box, price one shilling nine pence is a Cure for one Person, and divided for two Children. Nothing, perhaps, will more strongly elucidate the superior Efficacy of this Ointment than the frequent puffing Attempt of envious, unprincipled Impostors, to prejudice it in the public esteem, and to substitute, under various Names and Presences, their own pernicious Truth in its stead.

Cured by this Ointment in the course of the last and present year, upwards of Two Thousand Persons.

15 June 1797

From the *Maidstone Journal*: 'TEN POUNDS Reward — Broke out of the County Gaol, early on Tuesday morning last, the following Convicts, viz.

BARNABAS EGANS, born at Woodchurch, in Kent, labourer, 29 years of age, 5 feet 11 inches high, light complexion, with a fresh colour, long straight hair, had on a mixed colour cloth coat and trowsers.

Also JAMES SAVAGE, labourer, a native of Yalding, in Kent, 5 feet seven and a half inches high, 30 years of age, dark complexion, and marked with the smallpox.'

16 June 1928

'The Atlantic Flyer', installed only weeks earlier at Dreamland Amusement Park in Margate in readiness for the new season, consisted of eight gondolas slung from a central pillar. The passengers whirled round and round at up to 30ft in the air in this thrilling aerial experience. Even the name suggested something exotic and daring.

But on this Saturday afternoon, in mid-flight, a bolt securing the rear of one of the gondolas snapped and its eight passengers were hurled to the ground at high speed.

One passenger was flung through the canvas cover of a nearby children's roundabout; another was thrown into the steel framework of 'The Flyer'; yet another crashed into the fence of the scenic railway.

Three men were killed instantly; another died some hours later. Four people received injuries, among them a woman who remained unconscious for several hours; there were shattered knees, broken thighs, facial injuries and deep shock among the four survivors.

At the inquest the next day the jury returned a verdict of 'death by misadventure' and called for stricter supervision of machines of this kind. One of the survivors later received damages for £750 as a consequence of the owner's negligence. Although the machine had been inspected that morning, it was alarming to learn that the man who had tested its worthiness was not a qualified engineer but a former bricklayer.

17 June 1820

After a game of cricket at Chatham, the players spent the evening together at the Artichoke and it was not until midnight that they decided to go home. But they were now in high spirits and decided to have some fun with Joshua Ruck who was sitting in the bar. 'Come-on, Squire Ruck,' they called out to him. 'Your coach is waiting outside.' And with that the gang bundled Ruck out of the pub and into a cart. They drove off towards Ruck's house but as they were passing the river they decided that their joke could be even better and they threw their victim into the water. Off they went, leaving poor Ruck drenched to the skin.

Shortly after this, a furious Ruck met another man on the road. 'You're one of the three Cook brothers,' he said. 'I'll do for you all one of these days.' Ruck claimed that the man's brother, John Cook, had been one of those who had played their rotten tricks on him.

Half-an-hour later John Cook, who had been one of the party at the Artichoke was making his way home. And there, waiting for him in the dark, was Joshua Ruck, who accused him of pushing him into the cart. 'If I was sure you were there, I'd run you through,' Ruck told him. At this point Cook saw the cutlass in the other man's hand, saw Ruck raise the weapon and bring it down and felt the weapon cut him. Frightened and anxious to defend himself, Cook picked up a hedge-stake but it was no use against Ruck's cutlass and he tried to run away. Again he saw Ruck lift the sword and aim another blow at him and he raised his arm to defend himself. Down came the cutlass, severing Cook's hand at the wrist. Even that did not immediately stop the onslaught but Cook eventually managed to get away.

At the Assizes in July, Ruck told the court that he regretted what had happened, saying that he wished he could restore the hand. Witnesses spoke up for him saying that he was a good-natured man if somewhat hasty tempered.

Mr Baron Ward told the jury that they must be satisfied that Ruck acted maliciously before finding him guilty. They were satisfied enough, finding the rather put-upon man guilty of attempted murder. In August, Joshua Ruck was hanged on Penenden Heath.

Convicts
working at
Woolwich
Dockyard.
*(Courtesy of
Greenwich
Heritage Centre)*

18 June 1832

For the past week the outbreak of cholera, which had first appeared in Scotland and the north of England, had become frighteningly serious in the convict hulks off Chatham. Since the outbreak began ten days earlier, there had been more than eighty cases, of whom sixteen people had died. There were now fifty convicts in the hospital ship but others were still working in the dockyard, despite the fact that some of them were infected. Among the dead were a nurse and Dr Conway, who had attended to the sick convicts. At 3 a.m. in the morning he had been taken ill; by 5 p.m. in the evening he was dead.

19 June 1769

From the *Sussex Weekly Advertiser*: 'In the evening at about 9 o'clock, in the lane between Shooters Hill and Eltham in Kent, a post-chaise, with a lady and gentleman therein, and some gentlemen and ladies on foot within fifty yards thereof, who had been regaling on the hill with tea, and viewing the prospect, in returning home from thence, were robbed of their watches and money, by a middle-aged and slim-sized genteel man, and mounted on a slight dark bay horse, with a nag tail, about fifteen hands high. He presented an uncommon large bright horse-pistol, with brass ornaments, and represented himself to be a gentleman in distress, behaved with as much decency as such an attempt would permit, and rode off towards Shooters Hill.'

20 JUNE 1821

Cephas Quested, leader of the Aldington Gang, had been in custody since his capture after the 'Battle of Brookland' in February. His trial was delayed in order to give him time to turn King's evidence in order to incriminate others of his gang. But this he steadfastly refused to do. The *Maidstone Journal* printed his farewell letter to his wife:

Newgate Cell

Dear Loving Wife
I am sorry to inform you that the report came down on Saturday night, and I was ordered for execution on Wednesday. I sent for Mr Hughes on Sunday and he and the Sheriff came in the afternoon, and Dear Wife, they told me that it was best for you not to come up [to the execution]. Dear Loving Wife, I am sorry that I cannot make you amends for the kindness you have done for me, and I hope that God will be a Father and a Husband to you and your children for ever; and Dear Wife, I hope that we shall be happy in the next world, and there we shall be happy. And, Dear Loving Wife, I hope that you will not fret, or as little as you can help. And Father and Mother, I send my kind love to you, and to all my kind Brothers and Sisters; and dear Brothers, I hope this will be a warning to you, and to all others about there. Dear Father and Mother, and Brothers and Sisters, I hope that you will not frown on my dear loving children. Dear Wife, I am happy in mind; thank God for it, and I hope you will keep up your spirits as well as you can. So no more, from your unfortunate husband.
Cephas Quested

Quested was hanged on Penenden Heath on 4 August. His body was to have been hanged in chains but a local magistrate intervened, and persuaded the authorities to allow him to be buried at Aldington.

21 JUNE 1928

John Seaman, a mechanic, who pleaded guilty to robbery with violence, was sentenced at Kent Assizes to eighteen months' hard labour. He had attacked a young woman, the daughter of a Maidstone jeweller, while she was walking through Vintners Park at Boxley. In the judge's opinion there was only one appropriate punishment for offences of this description and he ordered eighteen lashes of the cat-o'-nine-tails. He said that it would teach the prisoner not to use violence on unprotected women.

22 JUNE 1836

George Sanders, a grocer and linen draper of West Peckham, was the victim of professional burglars. After ensuring that his doors and windows were shut, he had gone to bed at about 10.30 p.m. When he rose at 5 a.m. he found that he had been burgled and that the thieves had stolen stockings, silk handkerchiefs, ribbons, waistcoats, dresses and two violins. A pane of glass had been broken and a shutter had a hole in it, cut out with a centre-bit, and large enough to admit a man's hand.

At the time there was no police force as we would recognise it today. Nevertheless, whatever policing existed in Maidstone was in the charge of Thomas Fawcett, the police superintendent. There appear to have been no other paid constables and Fawcett therefore made use of informants, including John Glover, currently on bail for poaching. Ten months earlier Glover had been on the treadmill while serving twelve months for stealing pigeons. Fearful of a repeat dose, he was willing to help Fawcett in the hope that such public-spiritedness would not go unrecognised when he appeared in court.

On the evening before the robbery, Glover had seen three men in the Plough at Maidstone, one of whom had told him that they were going 'to do a concern' that night. But Glover had no further details and although he immediately told Fawcett of what he had heard, the robbery went ahead.

But at least they had suspects and Fawcett, with Glover's aid, was able to bring Michael Rooney and William 'Round Hat' Finn to trial. The third man was not charged. Finn was acquitted but Rooney was sentenced to transportation for life.

That this was a highly professional gang is certain. The stolen articles were being sold in London by 5 a.m., the time that George Sanders was getting out of bed.

23 June 1916

At Kent Assizes, Edgar Middleton, a 21-year-old journalist, was indicted under the Defence of the Realm Act. He was charged with trying to elicit information which might be useful to the enemy.

Until December 1915, Middleton had held a commission in the Royal Naval Air Service but had been invalided out. He then become a journalist. At Dover he told two naval officers that a member of parliament had sent him to ask specific questions about the RNAS.

Although in wartime this was a potential capital offence, the judge was of the view that Middleton had had no evil intention. He was quite certain of the young man's loyalty and had put down his behaviour to immaturity. His questions were, in the judge's opinion, no more than indiscreet. Middleton had already been in custody for six days and he was released with a warning as to his future behaviour.

24 June 1915

When the early morning parcels were being sorted at Woolwich sorting office, Augustus Curtis from Plumstead spotted the nose cone of a small shell sticking out of one of the packages. As he placed the parcel on the rack above his bench, it exploded. Curtis was hit on one side of the face by fragments. Two others were less fortunate. Stephen Roberts took the full force of the explosion and forty small fragments hit him. Charles Baker (18) was also severely injured.

Curtis had had a lucky escape and after a visit to the hospital was allowed to return home almost immediately. Baker was detained in hospital but Roberts died of his injuries within hours.

Fragments of a letter suggested that the shell had been sent from the Western Front and that it was intended as a souvenir. The sender had apparently been unaware that it was live.

25 June 1943

At Maidstone Assizes, Regimental Sergeant-Major James Culliney and Quartermaster-Sergeant Leslie Salter were found guilty of the manslaughter at Gillingham detention camp of Private William Clayton. Culliney was sentenced to eighteen months' and Salter to twelve months' imprisonment.

Discipline in military detention camps was always rigid, controlled by NCOs whose attitudes were much stricter than those of prison warders. In the 'glasshouse,' life was conducted at the double; every item of equipment was polished and re-polished and every minute of the day was spent in earnest activity. Perhaps such rigid regimes were understandable but there were times when rigidity lapsed into brutality. So it was in the case of Private Clayton, who had arrived at Gillingham seven months earlier. The reason for his sentence was not stated but it is most likely that this timid, profoundly deaf 40-year-old was not up to the physical demands of army life.

At Gillingham Clayton was regarded as a malingerer, a man who reported sick whenever he could. They had no time for men like this. On 17 March Clayton was unable to continue marching and was obliged to fall out. QMS Salter was unsympathetic, forcing him to carry a rifle and pack even though he was scarcely able to walk. Then the RSM was called and both men hit Clayton, who collapsed. Shortly afterwards he died.

The post-mortem showed that Clayton had a deep wound at the back of his head, that his lips and nose were swollen and bloody and that the hyoid bone in the throat had been fractured from a powerful blow. He was also suffering from previously undiagnosed tuberculosis.

At the Assizes, the conclusion was that Clayton died of tuberculosis accelerated by the injuries he had received.

26 JUNE 1911

When George Cooper of Edenbridge arrived home at about 10 p.m., his mother told him that labourer John Boakes, a neighbour, was attempting to hang himself in his garden. She was either too squeamish to investigate or she was afraid that Boakes, a mild-mannered man when not in drink, might be aggressive if she attempted to cut him down from the apple tree.

Cooper went down the garden and found Boakes with a handkerchief tied round his neck. This was attached to a strap, which was buckled round a branch. Boakes's toes were just touching the ground, his knees bent to take the weight. He was black in the face and gasping for breath. Cooper cut the handkerchief, laid Boakes on the ground and, applying artificial respiration, restored him to life and took him back into the cottage. When Boakes came round, he implored Cooper to let him go so that he might now drown himself. By turns, Cooper used persuasion and strength to keep the desperate man from doing away with himself. He was in financial trouble, Boakes said, and wanted to end his life.

When the constable arrived at about midnight, Boakes made a dash for the door. The constable finally succeeded in handcuffing him but only with Cooper's assistance. All the while Boakes pleaded with the two men to release him so that he could commit suicide.

At the Petty Sessions held on the following day at Tonbridge, Julia Boakes told the court that when her husband arrived home at about 10 p.m. he was in a difficult mood. He had been drinking but she was at pains to say that he had little capacity for drink. The slightest amount could affect him. Holding out his muffler, he had said to her, 'Do you see this?' She had guessed what he meant but when he went into the garden, she had been frightened to follow him. Several years earlier, she said, he had tried to strangle himself.

Mary Boakes said that when he was in the garden, her father had called out to her three times, but, like her mother, she had been reluctant to go to him because he had previously attempted to hit her after he had been drinking.

After hearing the evidence, the Bench committed Boakes to trial at the next Quarter Sessions. Suicide was against the law.

27 JUNE 1821

Members of the notoriously violent North Kent Gang, fully armed, attacked Faversham Gaol and forced an entry. No one could prevent their releasing two of the gang who had been captured by preventive officers at Whitstable some days earlier. Although a reward of £100 was offered, the two men were never recaptured. Personal safety was obviously more important than a bag of gold. The seemingly invincible North Kent Gang, which had operated successfully for at least fifty years, all along the coast from the Medway to Ramsgate, was broken the following year. Attempts to halt their progress were heightened, following the murder of Midshipman Snow in another fracas between preventive men and the gang. After a trial at Maidstone, four of the gang were hanged at Penenden Heath and fourteen transported.

28 JUNE 1918

At Kent Assizes Tom Wilkinson, alias Tom Williams, a 38-year-old sapper in the Royal Engineers, was convicted of bigamy and sentenced to seven years' imprisonment. He had already received seven years' penal servitude at Derby Assizes on a separate bigamy charge. The court heard that he had 'married' five women. At the time of his arrest he was making arrangements to marry three other women. He had deserted from three different regiments.

29 JUNE 1795

From the *Maidstone Journal*:

> Deserted, from a party recruiting at Maidstone, of the Royal Louth Volunteers, commanded by John Henry Loft, Esq, PHILLIP THORP, aged 23 years, five feet five inches and a half high, pale complexion, dark brown hair, grey eyes, and by trade, a back-maker [cooper] born in the parish of St John's in Norwich, slight made, had on when he deserted a drab coloured great coat, round hat, striped waistcoat, corduroy breeches, and brown coloured stockings; wore his hair curled up in rollers, and said he had worked a long time in Rupert-street, London.

> Also WILLIAM CHAPMAN, a labourer, 26 years of age, five feet three inches high, born at Camberwell in Surrey, fresh complexion, round visage, light brown hair, hazel eyes, worked some time at brick-making near Maidstone, and known by the name of LITTLE WILL the brickmaker; he had on when he deserted a regimental red jacket, flannel waistcoat, white cloth trowsers, round hat, frill'd shirt; remarkably stout made, and his hair long on the top of his head. Whoever will apprehend them, either of them in any of his Majesty's jails, shall receive Three Guineas for each, over and above the 20 shillings allowed by Act of Parliament, by applying to Sergeant Myers at the Ball, Maidstone.

If they will return it is the colonel's desire they shall be forgiven.

30 JUNE 1786

The dreadful hulks, squalid, disease-ridden nests of vice and despair, were frequently the scenes of appalling violence. On this occasion there was a rumour that the transportees were to be shipped to Africa and in consequence the convicts planned to take over the vessel and sail it away, though hulks were in the main no longer seaworthy.

At about 5 a.m., convicts quartered on a prison ship near Woolwich and awaiting transportation, barricaded themselves below. They refused to come on deck and threatened any who dared to try to prise them out. Captain Erskine, the officer responsible, immediately came aboard and ordered the men to their usual work in the dockyard. One man, seemingly disposed

to obey the captain's orders, was set upon by his fellows who hanged him on the spot. Captain Erskine then ordered his soldiers to fire upon the insurgents through the grating. Nine men were wounded, three of them fatally. The mutiny came to a swift conclusion. The first convict ship to Australia sailed the following year.

Prison ship at Deptford.
(Engraving by George Cooke, 1826)

JULY

Two police officers from the Kent police cycle section, 1900.
(Courtesy of Kent Police Museum)

1 JULY 1829

After a body was found in Shooters Hill Wood, a coroner's jury was hastily convened at the Chequers Inn at Eltham.

A witness, Joseph Dell, described as 'a labouring man', had been seeking work in the neighbourhood that morning and at about 8 a.m., after he had eaten his breakfast by the roadside, he went into the wood. He saw what appeared to him to be a man standing upright with his back against one of the young oak trees. 'His face was very black,' Dell said, 'and at first I thought he was a chimney sweep and I called to him but when I got no answer I approached him.' To his horror, Dell found that there was a rope tied very tightly round the man's neck and the slender tree trunk. He had run as fast as he could to Eltham where he reported what he had found to the constable. Dell said that he had never seen the man before but admitted that he could not make out his features.

The dead man was dressed in a snuff-coloured coat, corduroy breeches and shoes. His pockets were searched by the constable but there was little in them save for a woman's glove, a piece of twine, some pieces of old newspapers and a ha'penny. There was nothing there to indicate his identity nor was there anything to show how he came to be found as he was. The jury returned a verdict of 'Found dead in Shooters Hill Wood but the jury have no evidence to lead them as to the manner in which the deceased came to his death.'

The unknown man – a suicide or a murder victim – was buried in Eltham churchyard.

2 JULY 1921

At Maidstone Assizes, four men were tried on charges of attempted grievous bodily harm and of being in illegal possession of firearms, but were found not guilty on charges of shooting to kill. One of the accused, William Robinson, leader of the gang, was sentenced to twelve years' imprisonment and the other prisoners received ten years.

On the night of 16 June there was a serious outbreak of attacks committed by armed bands of masked men in cars. These raids were reported right around the outskirts of the metropolitan area and were directed specifically at the railway service. Railway signalmen were shot at and their cabins set on fire; telegraph and signal wires were cut and the schedules of many trains, in and out of London, were seriously affected.

At Bromley in the early hours the occupants of a taxi began shooting at police. Some of the men escaped but the leader, William Robinson, was wounded and captured.

In court the prosecution said that the affray was part of the 'Sinn Fein campaign which these wild Irishman are endeavouring to carry on in this country.'

In the witness box Robinson admitted being in the cab with three others but he refused to identify them. 'I decline to say anything to incriminate any person who is not here,' he said. He admitted firing one shot. He was out that night, he said, to cut telegraph wires but declined to give the name of the man who gave him his orders. Two other accused denied on oath and the fourth, William Affection, when called into the witness box refused to 'answer any questions about the brothers.'

On their way down to the cells after sentence had been passed on them, the prisoners shouted out, 'God save Ireland.'

3 JULY 1877

Three magazines containing several tons of gunpowder, rockets and fuses, and belonging to Mr Wood of Gravesend, were placed quite near the Ship and Lobster tavern, awaiting transfer to a ship bound for Bombay. In the afternoon one of the magazines exploded and Wood's son and two of his workers were killed. The explosion violently shook the houses round about and the tremor was felt for miles around. The acrid stench was apparent two miles away. How the explosion occurred was a mystery but an investigation was under way. The body of one of the men, shockingly mutilated, was recovered the following day.

4 JULY 1786

From the *Maidstone Journal*:

A most cruel murder was perpetrated on the body of Mary Slavin, a poor travelling woman, in a road leading down to the marshes that joins the churchyard at Minster in the Isle of Thanet. The husband and the unfortunate Mary Slavin, his wife, had drunk pretty freely in the evening of the said night, and were very much in liquor when they went down the said road in order to sleep in a lodge; the woman laid herself down in the lodge, and her husband in a dry ditch adjoining. The husband relates that after they had been there an hour or two, four men came and dragged his wife out from under the lodge into the road and ravished her, each of them by turns, one of them keeping the old man, her husband, confined to the ground, while the others satisfied their brutal lust. The woman's cries of murder were heard several times but before any assistance could get to the spot they had strangled her, it is supposed, by pinching her throat as the marks of fingers were plainly seen on each side of it, and then they made off. Suspicion at first fell on the husband but a person that lives near the spot where the murder was committed swore that when he heard the cry of murder, he looked out of his chamber window, and heard one of them say, 'Damn the old man, keep him down', and he likewise heard the voices of two or three more. The old man has described one of them and says that he had a bridle in his hand, had on a brown waistcoat, and long trowsers, and had lost the forefinger of his left hand.

A suspicion then arose on one John Williams, and who soon after the murder was discovered, absconded, and has not since been heard of, only that he crossed the river in the ferry boat at a place called the Red House. The ferryman says that he seemed to be in great confusion when he came down to the ferry. This said Williams was born in Wingham in East Kent, and is supposed to have gone that way. On Friday, a coroner's inquest sat on the body and brought in their verdict Wilful Murder against a person or persons unknown.

5 JULY 1819

It was either an act of commercial rivalry or pure malice that led John Cruttenden to go by night into Samuel Sander's hop garden and cut the hop binds growing on poles. Cruttenden had in fact offered another man a shilling to do the job but when his offer was refused he cut them himself. At the Assizes in August Cruttenden was charged with maliciously cutting the binds, was found guilty and sentenced to death. He was later reprieved. Cruttenden was indicted under The Black Act, which made certain acts of trespass aimed at stealing or damaging another person's property a capital offence. The Act, introduced in 1723, had originally been intended to combat deer-poaching gangs who went out at night with their faces blacked.

6 JULY 1773

From the *Sussex Weekly Advertiser*: 'A Captain came on shore at Margate in Kent, from the Good Intent, bound from Rotterdam to Cork, which had been drove on the Goodwin Sands, and declared his men had mutinied and that he had been obliged to quit the ship. He took a lodging at Mr Robert Lad's, at the Ship, and the next morning threw himself out of the two-pair-of-stairs window, and was killed on the spot. The jury sat on his body and on examination it appeared that the account of a mutiny was entirely false.'

7 JULY 1931

Twenty-three-year-old Arthur Salvage was arrested for the murder of 11-year-old Ivy Godden. Three days earlier, she had been reported missing and, after a thirty-six-hour search, her body was found in a newly turned-over patch of ground. She was covered with sacking and tied with a rope looped around her ankles and neck. Her dress was drawn up under her armpits and her cotton knickers were round her knees. She had been savagely beaten.

The grave was only 100 yards or so from Sunningdale, the bungalow where Salvage lived with his mother. And in the lean-to shed at the side of the bungalow was found rope similar to that around the child's body, while the sacking in which the body was wrapped was similar to that nailed to the side of the goat house. A bloodhound was called for and twice led his handler from Ivy's grave to Salvage's bungalow.

The forensic evidence – the rope and the sacking – seemed strong enough for police to arrest Arthur Salvage. At Ashford police station, Salvage confessed to the crime almost immediately. He had lured the child into the house, he said, and had murdered her. He wrote an unequivocal admission of guilt, which he repeated to police officers the next day. But at his three-day trial at the Old Bailey, Salvage denied his guilt.

After a withdrawal of only thirty minutes, the jury returned a verdict of guilty and Salvage was condemned to death. This sentence was respited and Salvage was sent to Broadmoor from where he was never released.

Salvage was also suspected of several assaults and of the murder of Louisa Steele, whose nude, mutilated body was found at Blackheath in January 1931. He later confessed to this but there was never enough hard evidence to bring the case to court.

Front page of the *Illustrated Police News*. and page showing the discovery of the body.
(*Illustrated Police News*)

8 JULY 1904

The *Tonbridge and Sevenoaks Standard* reported a recent case at the Kent Assizes:

> George Williams, a 52-year-old labourer, serving two years at Borstal Prison, was accused of maliciously wounding a warder.
>
> Mr Justice Darling did not think that this case should have been brought before the Assize court. In his view, it was a simple matter for magistrates. The visiting justices should order him to be flogged, the judge said. 'It is absurd for me to send him to penal servitude again. Find out from the Home Secretary and let me know if he can be flogged.'
>
> The following day the judge was informed that, on account of his age and condition, it was impossible for Williams to be flogged and so the trial went ahead.
>
> A written statement from Williams explained that on 28 May there was one dinner short and he had to do without until later, when it was 'kicked into his cell.' He complained too that the potatoes were bad. In the afternoon, after exercise, he lost his temper when being searched and struck a warder. After this, Williams said, he was put in a cell where he was beaten for twenty minutes by four warders armed with staves. One of those who had beaten him was a civilian guard, kept in the prison for the sole purpose of beating prisoners.
>
> The deputy-governor of the prison and the warders denied all of this. Williams had never been heard to cry for mercy; no one had heard him call out 'Murder!' The prisoner had never been told that he should have a rope round his neck.
>
> The prison doctor said that Williams had complained to him that his arm was broken. But there was no injury, the doctor said, nor any sign of assault. He had given the prisoner a cold-water bandage.
>
> *Judge:* If there was nothing the matter why did you order the bandage?
> *Doctor:* To satisfy him.
> *Judge:* Why did you not say so and not order the bandage?
> *Doctor:* I thought there might be a substratum of truth.
> *Judge:* Have you had complaints from the prisoners as to the treatment by the warders?
> *Doctor:* Yes, but they have not been true.

At the conclusion of the case the judge repeated his view that the proper punishment would have been a flogging. In the circumstances, he thought it would not be right for Williams to go back to Borstal. Instead he ordered him to serve twelve months in Maidstone Prison and after that to complete his two-year sentence.

9 JULY 1940

In the orchard of Crittenden Cottage lay the bodies of Dorothy Fisher and her daughter Freda. On a path outside the house lay Charlotte Saunders, the housekeeper. All had been shot.

The door of the cottage had been left open and several rooms had been ransacked. But nothing valuable had been taken. Had there been a robbery? Or had someone deliberately made it seem so? And further, there were only three women in the house yet cups, saucers and plates had been laid for four. Had someone been expected? And what of the glove in the orchard? And the abandoned bicycle discovered not far from the cottage?

Above: Crittenden Cottage.
(Photograph by Sue Edwards)

Right: Dorothy Fisher and Freda in the early
1930s. *(True Detective magazine)*

The Fishers had only recently come to Matfield. Walter Fisher, a wealthy journalist, regularly visited the cottage though he lived on Carramore Farm near Bicester with the exotic widow, Florence Iris Ouida Ransom, who, despite three first names, was known as Julie. Of course, Dorothy Fisher, his wife, had her own particular male friend.

Detective Chief Inspector Beveridge visited Carramore Farm near Bicester where he met Julie, who looked after the farm, assisted by the Guilfords – a mother, a son and a daughter-in-law. The auburn-haired Julie, expensively dressed, her nails scarlet, frequently visited Matfield. The detective made further enquiries and then, on 12 July, arrested her in London. Witnesses at an identity parade held at Tonbridge police station identified her: a boy who saw a woman near the cottage; a taxi driver and a ticket operator at Tonbridge station who recalled seeing a red-headed woman carrying a long, narrow parcel. At Bicester, the Station Master had seen her joining the 8.56 a.m. London train. And the glove in the orchard was hers.

At her trial at the Old Bailey in November 1940 the court heard that two weeks before the murder, Julie had asked Fred Guilford to teach her to ride a cycle. She also asked him to teach her to use his shotgun, insisting that he did not tell Walter Fisher.

On 9 July, after Walter had gone to work in London, Julie told the Guilfords she was ill and would stay in bed all day. But when Walter came home at night she was not there and did not return until about 9 p.m. She made up a story but the truth was that she had gone to Matfield that day. She had found her way to the cottage, presumably telephoning the

Fishers to warn them of her arrival. The Fishers were in the garden. Miss Saunders, the housekeeper, was in the house preparing tea.

Julie had taken out the shotgun from her long, narrow parcel. She fired and reloaded six times. She first shot Freda in the back. Then she chased Dorothy, shooting her in the head and then as her quarry lay there, she shot her once more in the back. Miss Saunders was shot in the head. Two more rounds were pumped into Freda's back as she lay on the ground. Somewhere in the orchard, she dropped her glove. There was a cycle at the cottage, which Julie took but abandoned up the lane.

The truth soon came out. The Guilfords were not simply old friends of Julie. Mrs Guilford was her mother. Fred was her brother and Jessie her sister-in-law. And Walter Fisher had been unaware of this relationship. Difficult to credit but true

Why this fiction? Was Julie ashamed of her modest connections, yet rather than cut them out of her life, did she allow them into it with conditions?

As for the murders, they were very carefully planned: the shooting lessons, the cycle riding and the feigned illness.

Motive? Perhaps Julie felt her future with Walter was insecure. Or perhaps she was jealous of Dorothy Fisher.

In court, it was learnt that Julie Ransom had had a long history of mental instability. She was found guilty of triple murder, but the death sentence was commuted and she spent the rest of her days in Broadmoor.

10 JULY 1868

Mrs Caselton, a farmer's wife who lived at Barnes Cray Farm, Crayford, was on her way to visit a sick neighbour. As she was walking along Hop Lane, a man who had been lurking in the trees by the roadside jumped on her and pulled her to the ground. He snatched Mrs Caselton's purse and took out all of the money. But it was too little for him. Had she any more money? he asked her. As she struggled to stand up, Mrs Caselton told the man that that was all the money she had on her. Her assailant threw her down again but Mrs Caselton was not going to give up without a fight. She fought her attacker, screaming 'Murder!' Avery put his over her mouth and the other round her throat and she feared that he was intending to strangle her. She managed to tell him that if she had had more money she would willingly have given it to him. But now he was deaf to her pleas and he threw her into a dry ditch where he 'commenced taking gross liberties with her.' But Mrs Caselton was made of stout stuff and her resistance saved her. Remembering that there were workers in the nearby fields, she called out, 'Thank God, someone is coming!' at which the man got up and ran off.

Mrs Avery ran to the nearest house, which belonged to a magistrate, Mr Stoneham, and told him what had happened. He immediately enlisted the support of his field workers, sending them out in all directions to search for Mrs Caselton's attacker. But it was Mr Stoneham himself who on his horse came across his quarry on North Cray bridge. He immediately arrested him and handed him over to the police. Thirty-two-year-old William Avery was sent for trial at the Assizes.

11 JULY 1792

From the *Maidstone Journal*:

> Yesterday afternoon came to anchor in our Roads, the Lisbon packet, in a most shattered condition, having met with a storm of thunder and lightning on Monday evening, between 8 and 9 o'clock, near the Goodwin Sands, and about four leagues from the North Foreland.

The Captain related the following particulars of the storm and its effects: that about an hour before this sad calamity, not the least appearance of danger was apprehended, as the serenity of the atmosphere had invited two ladies, passengers, to divert themselves with fishing; that the first symptom of an approaching storm discovered itself at a distance by an uncommon agitation of the water, and a thick mist resembling a waterspout to leeward. He gave immediate orders for two of the crew to hand the fore-topgallant-sail, while the remainder were preparing everything necessary to guard against impending danger, but before those two unfortunate men could execute their purpose, in an instant they were hurled into the deep, with the mast, sails and rigging in the general wreck.

As soon as the horror and surprise of so sudden a disaster had subsided, they sought their missing companions but, shocking to relate, one had found a watery grave, and the other with difficulty was rescued though dreadfully bruised from the shattered sails and ropes with which he was entangled. The vessel received the shock in a diagonal direction; first it shivered the mizzen-topgallant sail to pieces, severed the main topmast from the shaft, broke the foremast in the middle, and carried away the bowsprit. A high wind, accompanied by rain, succeeded, and continued the remainder of the night.

It is not yet discovered that the cargo has been injured. She is laden with wine and cotton from Colchester; but from her present situation, will be under the necessity of putting into some neighbouring port to refit before she can proceed on her voyage.'

12 JULY 1805

At a Special Session of the Peace for the Liberties and Precincts of Romney Marsh, held at Dymchurch, four soldiers: John Wood, James Webber, Richard Cook and Peter Lambert, were charged with burglary and robbery. It was alleged that they had broken into John Buckhurst's house at St Mary's. A man staying in the house told the court that he recognised Lambert who had twice entered his room. Mr and Mrs Buckhurst, however, were unable to identify any of the other prisoners. Webb and Cook were acquitted and escorted back to their regiment, the East Kent Militia, by a sergeant. Wood, who had acted as a witness for the prosecution, was found not guilty but remanded to Romney Gaol. He was to appear as a witness at the Assizes trial of Cook's father, then held in Maidstone Gaol, charged with receiving some of the stolen property. Lambert was found guilty and sentenced to death but there was some dispute over whether the court was competent to pass a death sentence. In the event, Lambert did not hang.

13 JULY 1838

Over the years, common land at Woodchurch had been occupied by landless labourers, who had built cottages and fenced off sections for growing crops and grazing animals. While squatting was clearly against the law, it was nevertheless understandable. Throughout the country, for the past 150 years, the economic condition of agricultural labourers had seriously deteriorated. At one time many of them had lived under the farmer's roof or in tied cottages on farmland. They often had their own patch of land on which to grow food. This security had disappeared so that families no longer had accommodation provided and little opportunity to grow their own cheap food; hence an increase in squatting.

When William Deedes, the Lord of the Manor of Aldington, asserted his rights to the common and insisted that the trespassers remove all buildings and fences, they refused. William Sidders, with a writ from the Sheriff of Kent, next tried to persuade the squatters to comply. When again they refused, Sidders returned with a small group of bailiffs and entered the house of Aaron Daw. But while the eviction party was inside the house, a hundred-strong mob arrived. It was apparent to Sidders that if he persisted in his demands, there would be serious violence. As it was, he and his men retreated, showered with stones and other missiles and with threats of further violence ringing in their ears.

But in the end, the demands of the law defeated the trespassers.

14 JULY 1893

A mother, unable or unwilling to keep her child, placed an advertisement in a newspaper seeking a good home. She received a letter in reply from a Mrs Green. It read: 'We should love to adopt your little darling entirely as our own. It would have a mother's loving care, a good Christian home, and every possible comfort . . . Its future would be well provided for and it would be well clothed and educated. Premium £3. You could hear from baby every month, and every three months have his portrait.'

The mother met Mrs Green, who claimed to be the wife of an Eastbourne grocer. The transaction was completed; the baby and the £3 premium were exchanged. Instead of going to Eastbourne, however, Mrs Green went to Gravesend where she abandoned the child in a garden. She went off with the clothes and certain articles the mother had left with the child.

At Maidstone Assizes Mary Boyle (31) pleaded guilty to taking a child from his mother by fraud with the intention of stealing the clothing. Four similar offences were mentioned in court. In one case the baby had died. She was sentenced to seven years' penal servitude on two offences, the judge ruling that the terms should not be served concurrently.

15 JULY 1788

A visitor to Maidstone Gaol recorded his impressions: 'The debtors occupied the same rooms which are crowded with too little in. There is no bath in the Infirmary. Twenty-two prisoners have just died of gaol fever. Thick wooden boards in the windows of the Infirmary obstruct the light and air. Divine Service is performed on a staircase. Debtors and felons have an allowance of bread and beer and assize convicts two shillings and sixpence per week. Some of the prisoners desire to have their bread allowance increased [even] though they were to have less beer. Irons on the felons were very light and they could take exercise. On 15th July, 1788 there were 61 convicts and 84 felons serving short sentences, and 31 debtors.'

The same person visited the House of Correction. He observed: 'The prison is not clean; not whitewashed for some years; fowls in the court; no coverlets to the beds. Many prisoners in irons; employment [is] the beating and spinning of hemp and the picking of oakum. Food and quartern [4lb] loaf a day and water.'

16 JULY 1844

At the meeting of the Woolwich Board of Poor Law Commissioners, the chairman, Mr Morgan, brought up the matter of the Woolwich House of Refuge, which was the responsibility of the parish; a place for the 'unfortunate poor' to sleep at night. It was swarming with vermin, Mr Morgan said, so much so that they dropped down from the poor people's clothing by dozens. Another commissioner, Mr Joulson, said that only one truss of straw was provided for all the sleeping places for fourteen days. He had been to examine the House and had never seen such a dreadful place in his life. Mr Cohen, who had formerly been an overseer, urged the commissioners to make a further investigation. He had visited because some poor people, refused admission, had appealed to him and it was only through his intercession that they were allowed in. He had never seen such a deplorable place in his life, he said. It was decided that the House should be fumigated with sulphur and afterwards lime-washed.

This discussion arose due to the numbers of vagrants recently appearing before the magistrates at Woolwich for destroying their clothes while staying in the House. On one occasion so many had been charged that the dock would not hold them. Many pleaded that they had burnt or cut up their clothes because they were lousy but the magistrates had not proved sympathetic. Instead they had committed the prisoners to short periods of imprisonment with hard labour at the House of Correction at Maidstone Gaol.

17 July 1806

While Napoleon appeared invincible in Europe, British troops in barracks in Kent seem not to have been much of a threat to him. At Ashford a deadly contagious fever had taken so many lives that the 14th Foot (the Buckinghamshire Regiment) was reported unfit for service. In the same barracks, the 91st Foot (the Argyllshire Highlanders) also suffered grave losses from what was described as 'a pneumonic complaint accompanied with typhus.' The 2nd Battalion of the 52nd Regiment (the Oxfordshire Regiment) had been moved to Maidstone where for the past nine months the 'Egyptian ophthalmia' had raged 'in terrible degree,' leaving an enormous number of men blind.

18 July 1832

The *Kent Herald* reported the following outbreak: 'The cholera has at length made its appearance in this city [Canterbury]. By accounts from different parts of the county, we are sorry to announce that the cholera is increasing to an alarming degree. At Sittingbourne, Faversham and Broadstairs, several deaths have occurred. At the latter place, a gentleman arrived from London was taken ill and died, all in the short space of a few hours.'

19 July 1890

Henry Smith (51) and Henry Scott (39) were charged at Kent Assizes with burgling the home of Mr McAndrew at West Wycombe. During the night of 10 April, the two men had arrived at the house and waited in the garden, eating oranges, until it was clear that the occupants of the house had gone to bed. Scott had used a jemmy to open the dining-room window. In the dining room they had helped themselves to a silver biscuit tin and other items. But what they were really seeking was the collection of valuable coins, which Mr McAndrew kept in his study sideboard. The cabinet was opened with a centre-bit, that favourite tool of the housebreaker. The two men helped themselves to 1,200 coins valued at £3,800. These were taken to 'Old Mike', a fence, living in Petticoat Lane. He bought them for about £150.

Smith was arrested and, believing that he could help his case, he gave the police information about the burglary. He explained how the centre-bit had been thrown away and how the two men's wives had helped to change some £5 coins. He told the police about 'Old Mike' but remained resolutely ignorant of his address. Despite his assistance, Smith received the same sentence as Scott – eighteen years. Both men had had police records for burglary.

20 July 1888

Months after the murder of Bensley Cyrus Lawrence, police at Tunbridge Wells were nowhere near solving the case.

Lawrence had had a caller at his back door some time after 9.30 p.m. on the night of his death. He was told by his visitor that the foreman of the sawmill wanted him urgently. So Lawrence, the engine man, walked with the stranger to the nearby Baltic Sawmills.

Baltic Sawmills. *(Courtesy of Brian Woodgate)*

Witnesses later said that they saw the two men waiting in Goods Station Road for about an hour. Then, at 10.40 p.m., there was a gunshot. Lawrence was found shot in the head but he was still alive when he arrived at the General Hospital. He died the next day.

But who was the mystery man?

Then came an anonymous letter to the *Advertiser* betraying surprising knowledge of the murder. And it appeared to be cocking a snook at the police. 'Bang!' the letter read, 'and once more Tunbridge Wells was startled with another mystery which is never likely to be found out.'

But a young boy came forward, telling the police that he had been standing in Mount Pleasant Road when a young man asked him to take the letter to the *Advertiser* office. He would be able to recognise the man in an identity parade, the youngster said. But this information did not lead directly to the killers.

The murder at Tunbridge Wells.
(Illustrated Police News)

Then one night in October, at the Salvation Army Citadel, Captain Cotterill invited any who wished to be saved to come up to the penitent bench. Two young men stepped forward. Early the next day, one of the men, William Gower, turned up at the Captain's house. He wished to talk and eventually confessed that he and his pal, Charles Dobell, had murdered Lawrence.

'Me and my mate did it,' Gower told Captain Cotterill. 'We tossed up to see who should do it and the lot fell to my mate.' They were seeking revenge, he said.

The captain said that he would see both men that evening. But after seeking the advice of his superiors, he informed the police. Dobell and Gower were arrested.

But why were they seeking revenge? Dobell had had nothing to do with the mill. He did not know Lawrence. What grudge could he have had against Lawrence?

Gower provided the answer. 'Dobell is a mate of mine,' he told the police, 'and as true as steel.'

The murder weapon, found hidden in a rabbit hutch, was a nickel-plated revolver bought for about 4s. Gower had paid for it; Dobell, a plumber, had been frequently out of work that summer and could not afford to pay his share.

And the motive? Gower hated Lawrence who, in addition to being the engine man, was the timekeeper. Between September 1886 and July 1888, Gower had been late twenty-seven times. Each time, in accordance with company policy, he was fined a penny. Lawrence had also insulted him by calling him 'a fathead' over some minor matter at work.

So Bensley Cyrus Lawrence died for 2s 3d and what Gower conceived to be an insult. And Dobell was the one who called for him and it was he who, out of loyalty, fired the shot. So when the shot was fired, Gower was already at home in bed. And it was the braggart Dobell who sent the letter to the press.

At their trial, the jury found both men guilty but recommended mercy. But it was all in vain; William Gower and Charles Joseph Dobell hanged on 2 January 1889 at Maidstone Gaol. Gower was 18 years old, his mate, Dobell, 17.

21 JULY 1769

Susannah Lott was burned at the stake at Maidstone. Until 1789, this was judged to be the appropriate sentence for women who had committed Petty Treason, the term used to describe offences such as coining or the murder of husbands or their mistresses. Susannah had poisoned her husband. The only other woman similarly sentenced in Kent in the eighteenth century was Margaret Ryan who, in 1776, had stabbed her husband to death. On the other hand, husbands who murdered their wives were hanged on the gallows; the assumption being that, unlike women charged with murder, men at least had not committed an offence against a superior.

A woman is burned at the stake.
(*Courtesy of the Neil R. Storey Archive*)

On execution day, Sarah Lott was tied to a hurdle (similar to a gate) and then drawn by a horse to the place of execution. Once there, she was pinioned to the stake and faggots heaped round her. As with other women in this plight, she died either from smoke inhalation or from strangulation by the executioner before the flames reached her.

22 JULY 1880

MURDER – The leg of a child has just been picked up on the shore of the river at Greenwich. It now lies in Greenwich dead house. The foot had been cut off and the leg separated high up on the thigh. The police are of the opinion that a chopper was used and that the person who used it had no knowledge of anatomy.

23 JULY 1868

At Maidstone Assizes a man named Simmons was indicted for burglary at Lord Holmesdale's house at Linton. The court heard that the watchman outside the house saw a light inside and went to investigate. He climbed in through a window, which he found open. Two burglars in the pantry immediately set about him and beat him violently. Simmons fired a gun, which fortunately missed the watchman. The jury returned a guilty verdict and Simmons was sentenced to ten years' penal servitude.

In a second case a man was given five years' penal servitude for setting fire to a stack of hay.

24 JULY 1801

General order issued to the local volunteer forces from the Military District HQ at Dover Castle:

FROM the great force now collecting on the coast of France, it is probable that the Enemy may have a rashness to presume to attempt a Descent upon Kent and Sussex. The Yeomanry and Volunteer Corps in the Southern District, will hold themselves in constant readiness to assemble at their respective places of Parade, on the first Information of the Enemy's appearance on the Coast.

25 JULY 1799

The *Maidstone Journal* reported the following: 'A few minutes before one o'clock, Margaret Hughes, for poisoning her late husband, Thomas, was brought from Wellgate, Canterbury, to a room in the Gaoler's house, whence she was conducted by a gallery to the temporary gallows, erected upon a platform about 10ft from the ground on the North side of the gate, and executed according to her sentence. Her behaviour before leaving the gaol and during the awful ceremony was such as highly became her situation. She received the sacrament and joined in the devotions with the utmost fervency. The lever was then touched and instantly part of the platform under her feet dropped by which she descended 6 or 8 inches. After remaining suspended an hour, the body was taken down at night and delivered for dissection.'

26 JULY 1825

At Maidstone Assizes James Sadler was charged with bigamously marrying Ann Court, 'a handsome young woman of respectable parents' at Hythe on 17 April 1825. Theirs had been a whirlwind courtship of only four months.

Two weeks after the marriage, Sadler told his 'wife' that he had to go to London for two or three days to attend to urgent business affairs. When, after more than a week, he failed to return, she was worried and went off to London to find him. When she eventually tracked him down in Shoreditch, he was, as the newspapers reported, 'domesticated with his first wife and family.'

It transpired that Sadler, a former gentleman's servant, married his first wife in November 1816 and was the father of three children. The court heard that the first marriage was in a bad way but that did not save him from a guilty verdict, although there is no record of the sentence handed down.

27 July 1859

At Maidstone Assizes Jonas Mitchell, a 20-year-old soldier, pleaded guilty to starting fires on two farms. In passing sentence, Mr Justice Blackburn said that Mitchell was not acting out of a spirit of vengeance. In fact, the motive for the man's actions was obscure. The soldier had not even known the farmer. Nor was there any prospect of financial gain from the offence. The judge was quite at a loss to account for what had occurred, nevertheless, he said, arson was a crime of the most dreadful character and it was necessary, for the protection of the public, to pass a severe sentence. Mitchell was therefore sent to prison for ten years. Another soldier, 21-year-old James Woodger, pleaded guilty to a similar charge. In his case it seemed that he believed a prison sentence was a way of getting out of the army. But it was a high price to pay. He too was sentenced to ten years in prison.

28 July 1837

The coroner's jury, meeting for the second day at the Tiger at Lee, reached the following verdict: 'We find that the deceased, Robert Cocking, came to his death casually and by misfortune, in consequence of several injuries received by a fall out of a parachute of his own invention and contrivance, which had been appended to a balloon.'

Cocking, a professional landscape painter and amateur scientist, had spent many years developing his parachute. And now, at the age of 61, he had made what he imagined

Cocking's parachute which was suspended from Green and Spencer's balloon. (*Wikipedia*)

would be a foolproof invention. His parachute, 34ft in diameter, took the form of an inverted cone, not unlike an umbrella blown inside out. Three hoops connected the canvas; the outside one intended to stop the fabric closing up. A wicker basket in which Cocking rode was suspended below the parachute.

To get the parachute airborne Cocking enlisted the help of balloonists Charles Green and Edward Spencer, persuading them that it would be good publicity for their massive Nassau balloon. The parachute was suspended 40ft below the balloon.

To the band of the Surrey Yeomanry, the Nassau, with its passenger and his parachute suspended below, set off from Vauxhall Pleasure Gardens at 7.30 p.m. on 24 July. The aim was to reach 8,000ft and then Cocking was to cast off. But over Blackheath, at 5,000ft, the balloon could lift its cargo no higher as Green and Spencer were unable to throw out ballast because of the parachute below. The decision was made for Cocking to cut adrift immediately.

At once, losing its heavy burden, the Nassau shot upwards, attaining an altitude of 5 miles and causing its two-man crew great anxieties. They had to inhale oxygen through tubes leading to an airbag. Fortunately, Green, the pilot, resumed control and the balloon came to land in a field near Offham with neither man hurt.

But Cocking's parachute descended with a rush and a roar. It was extremely heavy – too heavy for what was intended. As it fell, it disintegrated. One witness reported: 'At first it came down like thunder, that is with respect to noise. It frightened all the sheep.' Two hundred feet from the ground, the basket with its occupant tore away from the rest of the contraption. It landed in a field at Lee where those quickly on the scene found Cocking close to death and fearfully mutilated.

29 July 1831

John Any Bird Bell (13) stood trial for the murder of 13-year-old Richard Taylor at Rochester. Taylor had walked from Rochester to Aylesford with his younger sister, 7-year-old Mary Ann, to collect his father's parish relief money of 9s. Although Mary Ann had reached home, Richard had stopped to play in woodland with John Bell and his younger brother James. The boy had been missing for nine weeks when his body, badly decomposed, was discovered in the wood. His throat had been cut.

Under questioning by the parish constable, 10-year-old James Bell admitted that his brother had murdered Richard for the money. Further questioning led to a confession by John Bell. He had used Richard's own knife to commit the deed, the very knife which Richard had taken from home on the day of his disappearance. And the knife was now, he admitted, in the grave with Richard – he had put it back in the dead boy's jacket pocket. The knife had to be retrieved for evidence at the trial and John Bell was made to climb down into the open grave to retrieve it from the corpse.

On 1 August, John Any Bird Bell hanged at Maidstone County Gaol in front of a crowd of 10,000. The *Kent and Essex Mercury* describes how the crowds began assembling at 5 a.m. in the expectation that the execution was to take place at 8 a.m. As it was, they had to wait yet another three hours before the spectacle. Then the boy appeared, 'but his eye did not quail, nor was his cheek blanched. After the rope was adjusted round his neck, he exclaimed in a firm and loud tone of voice, "Lord have mercy upon us. All the people before me take a warning by me." Having been asked if he had anything further to say, he repeated the same words, and added, "Lord have mercy upon my poor soul!" At the appointed signal, the bolt was withdrawn, and in a minute or two the wretched malefactor ceased to exist. The body is to be given to the Surgeons of Rochester for dissection.'

30 JULY 1763

The *Gentlemen's Magazine* related the following: 'At Maidstone 8 prisoners were capitally convicted, all for the highway; and the Rev. Mr B—, a baronet, was sentenced to stand twice in and upon the pillory at Sittingbourne for the detestable sin of sodomy.'

31 JULY 1857

At Kent Assizes, Charles Chumley, a 22-year-old bargee, faced a charge of attempting to murder Elizabeth Jones. Chumley and a friend, another bargee, had met Elizabeth and her sister, both described as 'girls of the town'. The men invited the girls to go aboard their separate barges. Chumley was accompanied by the sister while Chumley's friend went to his quarters with Elizabeth. At some point – it is uncertain at which stage of the transaction – Chumley and his companion began to argue. Perhaps the commercial arrangement seemed to him a trifle exorbitant though whether his complaint was about services rendered or those on offer is not clear. Or perhaps the girl had her own view about how her customer was comporting himself. In any event, she marched off Chumley's barge and onto the friend's to seek her sister's support. But when Chumley followed her onto his friend's barge, the arguing was renewed. It was when Elizabeth Jones joined in, taking her sister's part, that Chumley picked up a broom handle and hit Elizabeth with it on the back of the neck. She died three days later. The jury found Chumley guilty and he was sentenced to four years' imprisonment.

AUGUST

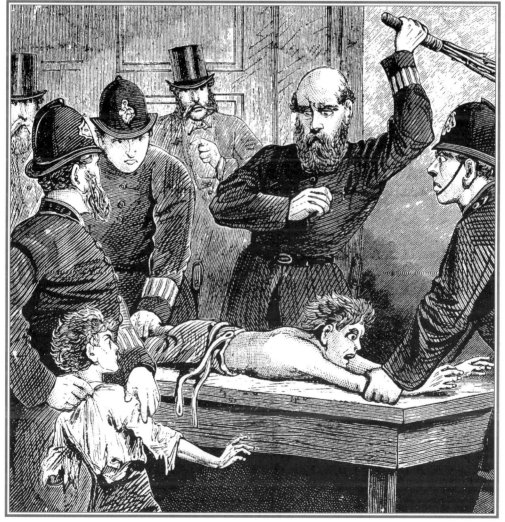

Minors were not infrequently birched by the police for their misdemeanours. Advice was sometimes given that the punishment of children under the age of 10 should be less severe than that meted out to older children. *(Courtesy of the Neil R. Storey Archive)*

1 AUGUST 1815

At 3 a.m. an eight-oared boat belonging to a Revenue cutter encountered a smuggler's boat. Thirteen smugglers, all of them armed, jumped aboard the Revenue boat and shot four of the crew. After throwing the corpses overboard, they left the rest of the crew, battered and injured, on the wreck of their own boat. The Prince Regent offered a pardon to anyone offering information leading to a conviction. In addition, the Commissioners of Excise offered a reward of £500.

2 AUGUST 1931

'Just a note. I am needing money very badly so I am writing to you. I happen to know about your affair in Herne Bay with a certain young man. I know what happened. Also I wonder if your husband would like to know about it. Shall I tell him? When you are with anybody don't drop your business cards in the grass. Well, Mrs X, is it worth money to you or shall I tell your husband? So if you don't want him to know, send the money to the GPO, Herne Bay by Tuesday. If you don't, you know. Send £4 and I will send back your business card and a letter. Don't fail.'

When Mrs X, as she was to be known in court, received this letter she took it to the police who sent a decoy letter to the post office as instructed. Twenty-seven-year-old Philip Tomkins was arrested and charged with sending a letter with menaces.

In fact Tomkins had met Mrs X in Herne Bay, claiming to be her brother's friend. At the time she was temporarily separated from her husband but she did not like Tomkins and cut short their acquaintance, which was never in any way physical.

Tomkins did not deny sending the letter but claimed that it was a joke. It was not seen as such when he appeared at Kent Assizes.

Herne Bay, where Philip Tomkins met Mrs X.

3 AUGUST 1905

An accident occurred at Ramsgate when a tram travelling down Madeira Road, 'a zigzag thoroughfare' leading from the East Cliff to the harbour, left the rails and crossed the road. It tore away the fence which bordered the road and toppled over the cliff, a distance of about 30ft. The tram driver and the conductor jumped from the tram as it fell and both were injured, the driver seriously. A young boy passenger was also seriously hurt, as were a lady visitor to the town who was bruised about the face and a man and wife who were staying at the Albion Hotel in Broadstairs.

The accident was attributed to the rainy weather, which had caused the rails to become slippery. The mayor said that the Board of Trade ought to hold a public inquiry into the frequent accidents on tramways. This was not the first serious accident on the town's tramways and he believed that had there been such an inquiry after the last accident this mishap might have been averted.

4 AUGUST 1922

'I admit I hit her on the head,' Albert Wiles, a farm labourer, told the court. He had hit a young woman with a stick as she walked along Crofton Lane, Orpington. 'This is caused,' he continued, 'through reading murder cases in the papers.'

5 AUGUST 1820

When Edward Best returned home from work at 9 p.m., his 13-year-old daughter Sarah and her younger sister were not in the house. Best was furious and even further enraged to see that on their return the younger girl was wearing her Sunday best. He called for a horsewhip and used it on the girls, although he later asserted that he had merely tapped them with it. But worse was to follow.

Best took the girls up to the attic where he tied the younger girl to a bedpost. Sarah's hands were tied behind her back and a rope put round her neck, the knot under her ear in true hangman fashion. He then threw the rope over a beam, pulling on it so that the girl's feet left the ground. He did this two or three times, threatening both girls that if they made any noise he would slit their throats.

Taken before the magistrates, Best was bailed on condition that he did not get in touch with his wife and was forced to live away from home. At Canterbury Quarter Sessions later in the year Best was charged with assaulting Sarah. In his defence, Best said that he had only tried to frighten them into behaving. He had raised his family by 'honest industry,' he said, and had never called on the parish for help. Any punishment he doled out was always for the girls' own good.

William Best said that his brother was a good man. He had visited Best's family home and tried to get a true account of what had occurred from the children but it was impossible because, as he said, Sarah suffered from 'an unfortunate malady' and was 'half an idiot.'

The recorder left it to the jury to decide whether Best had used appropriate punishment. He was found guilty and sentenced to fourteen days' imprisonment.

6 AUGUST 1805

At the Summer Assizes, Charles Stuart, a lieutenant in the Navy, prosecuted two men, Salmon and Parnell, for assault. Stuart explained how one bitterly cold night in February the chaise in which he and his wife were travelling broke down. They had been forced to abandon the vehicle and walked back towards Deal. It was half past eleven when, just outside the town, they had found a man lying in the road. At first they thought he was dead but then realised he was drunk and incapable of walking.

The lieutenant and his wife, anxious to seek help, called at a pub called the Walmer Castle. Salmon, the waiter to whom they spoke, was unsympathetic. But there was a heavy frost, and the lieutenant told the waiter that if the man was left where he was he might die of exposure. But the waiter was obdurate: drunken sailors were always a nuisance and he was going to do nothing to help.

Infuriated at the waiter's manner, Stuart told the waiter that if the man died he would let everyone know how help had been refused. At this point the landlord of the house, Mr Parnell – known to the local smugglers as 'Mr Spectacles' – appeared on the scene. He had heard the fracas and instantly took the waiter's side. 'You shall not come in here, sir,' he told the lieutenant. 'I am the landlord here.'

But the matter was not settled there for a bitter argument ensued between Salmon and Stuart. Then, according to Salmon, he saw that Stuart had had a knife in a sheath on his belt. There was pushing, shoving, wrestling, blows exchanged. In the struggle Salmon was said to have taken the knife out of the sheath and stabbed Stuart in the face, tearing one nostril.

More people arrived and Parnell, presumably emboldened by such support, seized the semi-conscious Stuart by the collar, lifting him up. Stuart's mouth filled with blood and he spat it out into Parnell's face. In return the landlord knocked the lieutenant to the ground. As he lay there, others joined in, kicking him and trampling on him. He was rescued only with difficulty after the frantic Mrs Stuart sought help.

The court heard several versions of the evening's events. The landlord and waiter claimed that Stuart's manner had annoyed them. It was his discourtesy that had led them to refuse assistance. The lieutenant had drawn his knife and had stabbed Salmon in the hand. Only then had the fight begun. Another waiter and a maid swore to this. But the jury accepted the account of Lieutenant Stuart and both defendants were found guilty.

7 AUGUST 1761

Convicts at Maidstone Gaol had their shackles removed prior to entering the chapel. But on this occasion, once the irons were taken off, the turnkey's sword was seized and he was stabbed and mortally wounded. The prison chaplain also underwent rough handling as the desperate men armed themselves with guns and cutlasses hanging on the walls. All of the cells were then opened and their occupants were released.

In the town it was obvious that something serious had occurred in the gaol and there was an exchange of gunfire in which a law-abiding onlooker was killed. Several of the convicts broke out. Some days later, soldiers traced them to Rove Wood where another gun battle took place. Two of the ringleaders were killed. Others were tried and hanged on Penenden Heath.

8 AUGUST 1790

When James Osborne, a customs official for the Canterbury district, overtook two Upchurch men driving asses, it may be that he recognised them, for both were known smugglers. On the other hand, he might just have queried why the asses they were leading were loaded with half-anker (5 gallon) spirit casks. In any event, Osborne called to the men to halt. He wanted to know how they had come by them. The inevitable verbal exchange followed and threats were levelled at the customs man and then, while one of the men hurried forward with the asses, the second, a man called Beavis, attempted to prevent Osborne from passing through a gate. There were more words, more threats and warnings from both sides of the gate but finally, outraged, Osborne drew his pistol and fired. Beavis fell immediately, the blood spurting from his mouth. In seconds he was dead. The dead man's companion ran off, leaving the asses which Osborne took with him to the Flying Horse at Wye. At the inquest, witnesses who had been working in the nearby fields and who saw the incident agreed that the officer had been seriously provoked and a verdict of manslaughter was returned.

Beavis, from Upchurch, left a wife and several small children.

9 August 1869

Defenceless, England was attacked by a succession of invaders, and it was the coast of Kent that withstood the first onslaught as the sun was blotted out and the air became so foul that it was difficult to breathe. Identified as aphids (greenfly), they were only the vanguard, for in the succeeding days followed swarms of ladybirds, yellow in colour and rather larger than the accustomed red variety. They came over from the Continent and deluged the towns of Kent – and elsewhere, of course – piling up in the streets, rattling like hail against the windows, seeming to turn whole towns yellow. Margate was overwhelmed and at Ramsgate, where the first swarms arrived, it was thought dangerous to be out of doors. So fierce was the onslaught that it drove outdoor workers, men and women accustomed to the harshest of weathers, indoors to shelter. Would this all lead to some dreaded outbreak of disease? In the emergency, men were employed to shovel up the mounds of ladybirds and throw them into the sewers or to burn them.

Then came another invader. A correspondent of *The Field*, writing in the last week of August, tells how he went to Ramsgate by steamboat. 'As we approached within five or six miles of Margate,' he writes, 'complaints of wasps began to be heard. I soon ascertained that that they were not wasps but a bee-like fly. As we neared Margate, they increased to millions and at Margate they were almost unendurable.' These were identified as Syphi. Poor Margate was confounded.

10 August 1796

The *Sussex Weekly Advertiser* recounted the following horrific accident:

Four persons who lost their lives by the explosion of the powder-mill at Dartford were literally blown to pieces. The shoulders and part of a body were thrown over a stream which turned the mill, above 150 yards; and part of a skull was found at a considerable distance; several other parts were also found, all of which were much scorched, and black with the fire; the timbers of the premises were thrown over the heath to the extent of half a mile; the trees in the neighbourhood were stripped of their bark; not a vestige even of the foundation of the mill is left, and the houses about Dartford, Crayford, and other places adjacent, experienced its effects in having their windows broken; the father of one of the sufferers had left the premises about half an hour before the explosion took place; and one of the persons lost was going into the mill with a rope as it blew up; the cause is not at present known.

11 August 1940

The Battle of Britain was at its height and this day was typical in the intensity of the German attacks with bombers supported by fighters. As early as 7.30 a.m. the first wave of enemy aircraft, targeting docks and convoys, was engaged by Spitfires, Hurricanes and anti-aircraft guns. The fight for supremacy, 20,000ft above Dover, lasted for several hours, with each repulsed formation of German aircraft replaced by newcomers. In all, there were 400 attackers over the south coast, among them the new Messerschmitt 110 Jaguar fighter-bombers. Ten of these were shot down by Spitfires and another three by anti-aircraft fire.

At about 11 a.m. there was a lull over Dover and the Spitfires were sent off to protect convoys off the east coast. But they were later recalled with news of yet another swarm.

Now battle was engaged over North Foreland, the Spitfire squadron going into battle for the fourth time that morning. Here, at 4,000ft, they met thirty Messerschmitt 109s. Dodging each other, playing a game of hide and seek through the clouds, the attack continued. On this occasion, two enemy planes were brought down.

At the day's end, the Air Ministry announced the loss of twenty-four British fighter pilots.

12 August 1926

Alfonso Francis Austin Smith was described as 'a bit erratic and of a highly volatile disposition', a spendthrift who had raced through three enormous legacies. In 1925 he had had a beautiful second wife, Kathleen, and three young children. Now, with a mere £10,000 to his name (about £400,000 at today's value), he could still enjoy a life of luxury.

While Kathleen was recuperating from an operation, the Smiths took a furnished house, Stella Maris, at Herne Bay. There they met dashing Jack Derham, now separated from his aristocratic

Kathleen Smith. (Isle of Thanet Gazette, *courtesy of Margate Library Local Studies Collection*)

wife. The men, both with Eton and Cambridge backgrounds, became friendly. But suddenly the friendship soured. Smith discovered that Derham and Kathleen had fallen deeply in love.

There followed months of recriminations, Smith finally leaving Kathleen. He began drinking heavily, his behaviour becoming increasingly erratic. When Kathleen started divorce proceedings, Smith made threats. 'This problem can only be solved in one way, the removal of your lover or myself,' he wrote to her.

For a brief spell there was hope of reconciliation, but Kathleen found she could not live without Derham.

Smith came on a visit to Tankerton and when the trio met there seemed the hope of a civilised resolution of the affair. Even so, Smith made it clear that he had a revolver. There was a scene in which Smith threatened suicide. Then everything calmed down and all three went off to dine at the Marine Hotel. On their return to Stella Maris, however, while upstairs, Smith raged at Kathleen. Derham, downstairs, was arranging playing cards on the table. Smith, his mood seemingly improved again, went down to join his rival. Were they going to play cards?

As Smith explained at his trial, 'It all happened in a flash. I went to get the chair and as I did so I put my hand to unbutton the back pocket of my trousers to take out the revolver.' He did not wish to sit on it, he said. 'The next thing that happened – all I know is that there was a terrific struggle. I was struck on the head, the revolver went off.'

Running downstairs, Lilian Wight, Kathleen's sister, claimed that she saw Smith on the floor with Derham on top of him, hitting him with the revolver butt. Eventually, the two men were separated. Derham, still carrying the revolver, wandered out of the house and into the street. On the pavement he staggered and fell. He had been shot in the stomach. He died the next day and Smith, despite the protestation that he was trying to commit suicide, was charged with murder.

The story of the decade's most glamorous murder came out at the three-day trial held at Maidstone. Most important was the question of what really happened in the few seconds before the gun went off. Premeditated or not? Well, the jury returned a 'not guilty' verdict.

Mr Justice Avory, however, was not satisfied with the verdict. He observed to Smith, 'The jury has taken upon your trial the most lenient view that was possible in this case. I have my own opinion on it.'

Smith was sentenced to twelve months' hard labour on a charge of possessing a firearm with intent to endanger life.

The shooting at Stella Maris was a mystery. In some senses it remains so, though many, like Mr Justice Avory, have their own opinion on it.

13 AUGUST 1799

The *Maidstone Journal* reported a theft: 'The following robbery was committed at the Red Lion public house on Charing Heath. Two women being alone in the house, on hearing somebody above stairs, one of them was induced to go up. When there, she found the drawers in one of the rooms all open. She then looked under the bed and saw a man lay, which so far alarmed her that she cried murder. The men immediately ran downstairs and got out of the house but one was stopped in the garden and secured by the Landlord. He had about his person 11 silver spoons, a gold watch, 4 gold rings and other articles. He was immediately taken before a Justice in the neighbourhood and committed to St Dunstan's Gaol.'

14 AUGUST 1867

In a week of blistering heat there were several serious sunstroke cases in different parts of the country. George Redwood began working in the fields at 5 a.m. in the morning, cutting wheat and tying up sheaves. At 11 a.m. he told his workmates that he felt unwell but went on working until finally he could do no more. He dragged himself over to a tree where he sat in the shade. Sometime later one of his workmates found him unconscious. Redwood was carried home but the doctor could do nothing for him. Twelve hours later he died. At an inquest at Birchington, 'death by sunstroke' was recorded.

15 AUGUST 1817

Twenty-nine-year-old William Morgan was found guilty at Kent Assizes for the violent robbery of an old woman in her home at Erith. Prior to his execution on 21 August 1817 at Penenden Heath, he wrote an account of his life; a restless but not untypical career of petty crime, which, given the age in which he lived, could have had only one outcome.

The account of his life in the *Maidstone Journal* is a simple catalogue of joining army regiments, desertions, minor thefts, spells at sea, highway robberies and intermittent periods as a brick-maker. It could have had no other ending for he lacks enterprise and intelligence. The narrative concludes with his running away from an employer in London:

I then went towards Chatham. Going over Shooter's Hill, I was stopped by a party of soldiers, and taken back to Woolwich, sworn in as a deserter, and received 300 lashes. I was sent to the hospital for twenty-four days and when I came out joined my troop, with which I remained seven days, when I deserted for the fourth time, and went to Southend. I remained there five months employed in brick-making and thieving. I there stole a fat hog near the brickfield and also broke into a gentleman's hall at Grays in Essex, and in the town of Grays stole another hog. After that I went to London and shipped myself on board the *Asia*, and went to sea for eighteen months, at the end of which period I was paid off at Chatham, and then went to Erith where I committed the robbery for which I am to suffer. Thirteen housebreakings, eight highway robberies, four desertions and a number of small offences that are not here inserted are the horrible crimes of the unfortunate William Morgan.

16 August 1940

The head teacher at Boughton Monchelsea wrote in the school logbook: 'In spite of letters from Hd Teacher, Managers and Parents, the K.E.C. have done nothing yet to the School to afford protection against air-raids. During air raids this week the fall of bombs and the rattle of machine guns could be heard distinctly. Many enemy aircraft have passed over the School.'

17 August 1838

Sixteen men who had taken part in the 'Battle of Bossenden Wood' appeared at Maidstone Assizes. Seven were acquitted, three were transported for life and another for ten years, and the remainder were sentenced to a year's imprisonment.

They had all been followers of John Nichols Thom, a Cornish wine merchant, the self-styled Sir William Courtenay. Since his release after five years from Barming Asylum, this dangerously deluded man, claiming to be the Messiah, promised to lead them to Paradise. 'He giv' 'em all the sacrament,' one of his disciples explained, 'and after that he anoints himself and all of 'em with oil, and tells 'em that then no bullet nor nothing could harm 'em . . . and they says to him, "Now do tell us if you be our blessed Saviour, the Lord Jesus Christ" and says he, "I am he" – and then he shows 'em the mark of the nails in his hands which was made when he was put on the cross.'

Concerned at his revolutionary aims, the magistrates sent a village constable, Nicholas Mears, to arrest Courtenay. When he arrived, Courtenay shot him. The military were now called out. On the afternoon of 31 May, Lieutenant Bennett's men surrounded Courtenay's

Murder of Nicholas Mears. (*From* The Life and Extraordinary Adventures of Sir William Courtenay, *1838*)

The Tragic Scene at Bossenden Wood. (*Drawn by an eyewitness for the* Penny Satirist)

position where his followers were armed with sticks, but when the lieutenant approached Courtenay, inviting him to surrender, he too was shot and killed by the madman. The soldiers began firing and nine of the labourers, including Courtenay, died in the space of a few minutes. Three others died of wounds later.

18 August 1773

Another sovereign cure for the gullible, Beaume de Vie, was advertised in the *Maidstone Journal* and newspapers in almost every county. Residents at Maidstone could buy this 'most admirable Family Medicine' for 3s a bottle at the premises of Mr Russell at Maidstone and Mr Baker at Tunbridge Wells.

BEAUME DE VIE
By the KING'S Patent

The great Number of extraordinary Cures daily performed by this most efficacious Medicine, accounts of which are sent from all Parts of the British Dominions, render it unnecessary to lavish Encomiums on its salutary Effects; suffice it therefore to say, that the Beaume, by its cordial, attenuating, and detergent Powers, fortifies the Stomach and Bowels, and by procuring a good Digestion, purifies the Blood and Juices, and gives Vigour to the whole Constitution. To these Qualities the Faculty attribute its having proved so eminently serviceable in Gouty, Rheumatic, Scorbutic, Languid, Nervous, and Hypochondriac Cases: and hence, also, they account for its being so particularly beneficial in Female Disorders.

CASE – A.C. Esq; of a gross, corpulent Habit, had been several Years so afflicted with ulcerated Legs, that he could not walk: The sedentary life he led had reduced him so low, that he was confined to his Chamber, with both Legs supported on a Stool; and, to add to his Misery, he was constantly tormented with the Gout. A Friend, who was Eye-Witness to the good Effects of the Beaume de Vie, in the Case of Mr S, which he thought similar, strongly recommended it to him: He, for a long time, declined it, from a Dislike to advertised Medicines, but his Case growing daily worse, he at last ventured. The good Effects were almost instantaneous; Sleep, which for a long Time had forsaken him, was restored: His Appetite which had been quite palled, returned; and his Digestion was good. In Six Weeks his Gout left him; and in two more, the Ulcers, which during the Course was dressed with a Dossel [bandage] of Lint dipped in the Beaume were perfectly cicatrised. It is nine Months since the Cure was completed, and he can walk eight or ten Miles at a Time. He has not had the least Return of any Complaint except once that he was threatened with an Attack of the Gout but which yielded to a few Spoonfuls of the Beaume.

19 August 1922

On their way home to Ashford from a day's coach outing through Kent and Sussex, the men from the British Saw Sharpening Works at Ashford must have been tired. Their two coaches, the front one carrying twenty-five passengers, the other nineteen, had set off early in the morning and doubtless by 10 p.m. they were all dozing. Everything seemed to be going smoothly despite the mist until they drove along the lonely, narrow, winding road towards Brookland. Here, at a sharp corner known as The Flots, where the bank on one side of the road fell away steeply to a water filled-ditch, the coach, travelling according to witnesses at almost walking pace, mounted the embankment and slipped downwards and then turned over on its side in 4ft of water. Immediately the water poured into the coach, one witness later reporting that it came up to his shoulders.

The men in the second coach jumped out to rescue their friends, grabbing whatever tools they could and borrowing a sledgehammer from a nearby cottage in an attempt to batter in the sides of the vehicle. The screams and cries for help from inside were agonising and progress was slow, even though locals, alerted by the commotion, came to lend a hand. Eventually, 150 people, tugging with ropes, righted the coach and heaved it back onto the road.

But there were eight dead inside. At the inquest, where a verdict of accidental death was returned, no blame was attached to the driver who had, it was suggested, mistaken the reeds at the side of the road for the road itself.

20 August 1787

A letter from Cranbrook to the *Maidstone Journal* reads:

On Sunday, the 19th instant, an amazing quantity of rain fell here at different times in the day. About two o'clock in the afternoon, the rain poured down like a torrent, and near ten minutes past two the inhabitants were alarmed with a vivid flash of lightning, which was instantaneously followed by a tremendous clap of thunder; the cloud that contained the fulminous matter was very low, as appears from the momentary interval between the flash and the stroke. I was standing at the time in a room paved with bricks and was almost thrown on the floor by the violent compression of the air; the electrical shock affected my right cheek and under jaw, so as to deprive them of sensation, and they remained nearly an hour in a benumbed state; when the torpor went off, a glowing heat and uncommon pain in the jaw ensued, attended with a small swelling. This effect I conjecture to have been produced by the sudden rushing of the circumambient air into the vacuum, which was occasioned by the electrical explosion, for there was no appearance of my having been touched by the lightning. Many other persons were strongly and strangely affected by the stroke.

At the same time, the weather-cock on Cranbrook church steeple was struck by the lightning, which (as it is highly probable) ran down the large iron bar that supported the vane, and then split into several pieces the timber through which the bar passed, as its fixture; those pieces were thrown to a great distance from the steeple but had no mark of being touched by a fiery body; from the iron bar it is supposed to have passed into the chime loft, and from thence through the door (in which were made many holes and one of them very large) down the stone steps, some of which were loosened by its force. The dial plate on the fourth side of the steeple was also much struck by the lightning, and many of the gilded hour figures were affected, while the stately image of Time, standing over the dial, was unhurt; it shook the windows at the east end of the church, and glanced on the shingles over the chancel. During this heavy rain, there was only one flash of lightning, and one stroke of thunder, and it was perfectly calm. Providentially the congregation was not assembled in the church when the explosion took place; if it had, great confusion and damage might have been the consequence.

21 AUGUST 1878

At Sittingbourne station the collision between a passenger train packed with day-trippers travelling to London from Ramsgate, and two goods trucks being shunted in error onto the main line, resulted in the death of six passengers and injury to more than thirty others. The fast train collided with the trucks 'with the force of an explosion whizzing far away' and the two front carriages were 'wrecked in a fearful manner.' At the inquest held the following day, Jacob Moden and Charles Clark, the two guards responsible for two sets of points, were charged with culpable negligence and committed for trial on a charge of manslaughter. They had, at the last minute, become aware of their error but could do nothing to avert the tragedy.

22 AUGUST 1917

During air raids, bombs were dropped on Ramsgate, Margate and Dover. Field-Marshal Lord French, Commander in Chief of Home Forces, issued the following communiques:

1.10 p.m.
Ten enemy aeroplanes approached the Kentish coast near Ramsgate at about 10.15 a.m.
Being met and heavily engaged by machines of the Royal Flying Corps and the Royal Naval Air Service, as well as by gunfire from anti-aircraft guns, the raiders were unable to penetrate inland.
A small party travelled west as far as Margate but then turned homeward. The remainder skirted the coast to the south as far as Dover.
Bombs were dropped at Dover and Margate.
Casualties reported at present are three persons killed and two injured. The material damage is slight.
Two of the enemy machines were brought down by anti-aircraft gunfire and our own aeroplanes.

3.35 p.m.
The latest police report shows that bombs were dropped by the raiding aeroplanes this morning at Dover, Margate and Ramsgate.
No casualties occurred at Margate but at Dover and Ramsgate 11 persons were killed and 13 injured. A hospital and a number of houses were damaged
One of the enemy pilots was rescued, having been only slightly injured.

The Secretary of the Admiralty issued the following announcements:

In amplification of Lord French's report issued earlier today, 10 enemy aeroplanes of the Gotha type were attacked by Naval aeroplanes in the vicinity of Ramsgate between 10 and 11 a.m. today

The enemy machines, which were flying at a height of between 11,000ft and 12,000ft, were closely engaged and in addition to the two mentioned by Lord French in his earlier communique, another was shot down by RNAS machines close to the coast. The remaining seven Gothas returned seaward, followed by numerous Naval aircraft.

The pilot of the RNAS aeroplane, which chased the raiders oversea, reports that after firing 300 rounds of ammunition into one of the enemy machines, both gunners appeared to be killed. There was no fire in reply, even at 20 yards distance.

23 August 1813

For the murder of his employers, Mr and Mrs Bonar, their footman Philip Nicholson was executed according to the customary ritual. In their fine house at Chislehurst, he had smashed their heads in with a poker. After being sentenced, he was lodged in the condemned cell at Maidstone Gaol.

At about noon on his last day Nicholson was taken to the gallows, erected on Penenden Heath about a mile and a half outside the town. At the door of the gaol, he was put into a horse-drawn sledge, with irons on his wrists and ankles. A rope was also fastened round his body and another rope, what the press called 'the fatal cord', was hung round his shoulders. Next to Nicholson on the sledge sat the executioner. Facing him were a clergyman and one of the Maidstone gaolers who carried a loaded blunderbuss.

The procession set off very slowly towards the execution ground where there was the usual large crowd. On arrival, Nicholson and the clergyman knelt in prayer and then they both climbed the ladder to the platform, raised about 7ft from the ground so that all could see what was happening. This platform had a trapdoor through which Nicholson would be, as the newspapers of the time usually said, 'launched into eternity.' This was 'the new drop': when the prisoner dropped down, it was hoped that his neck would be broken instantly. Under the old style, when the horse drew away from the cart on which the prisoner stood, he frequently strangled slowly.

After the rope was placed round Nicholson's neck, he was asked if he had had an accomplice. No, he told the clergyman, he had acted alone. And no, there was no real motive. The Bonar's murder had been 'a momentary thought'.

These were his last words before he fell through the trapdoor, though he was not instantly killed. Instead, he 'died hard, being greatly convulsed'.

24 August 1908

There was the sound of gunshots up in Fish Ponds Wood. Somebody after squirrels, one of the witnesses had thought. A woman in her garden heard the shots, too, and she had looked at her watch – 3.15 p.m. precisely. At least that would furnish proof that the old man had not shot his wife up in the wood because at that very time several other witnesses saw him a mile and a half away, bound for Wildernesse Golf Club at Godden Green. The coroner was able to dismiss any evidence to suggest that Major General Charles Luard was a murderer.

Earlier that afternoon, 69-year-old Luard and his wife, Caroline, had left their home, Ightham Knoll, for a walk with their dog. When they reached the village of Crown Point they separated, he making for the golf club and she for the summerhouse in Fish Ponds Wood. The general returned home at 4.30 p.m. expecting to find his wife entertaining a friend to tea. The friend was there: Caroline was not.

Right: Major General Charles Luard and Caroline Luard.

Below: Ightham Knoll, 1908.

After entertaining the guest, Luard went up to the wood and found his wife at the summerhouse. She had been shot twice in the head. The police thought that she had been killed by a tramp as her purse and rings were missing.

Despite all the evidence that the general could not have committed murder, he received an unprecedented number of poison-pen letters. These, with their unfounded insinuations, preyed on the old man's mind. On 18 September, he stepped in front of a train at Teston. The murderer was never found.

25 August 1867

Even before the search party had recovered the body of 11-year-old Louisa Kidder Staples from the ditch in which she had drowned, her stepmother, Frances Kidder, was under arrest. She was sentenced to death at Maidstone Assizes in March 1868.

While there were witnesses to the constant cruelty to which the child was subjected, no one had managed to stop it. What of Louisa's father, William Kidder, who only two years before had reluctantly married Frances when she was pregnant with his child, Emma? He seems not to have noticed the thrashings with sticks, the cuffs around the ear, the threats to murder the child. Frances had even been before the Hythe magistrates for ill-treating her stepdaughter. Another witness said: 'The child has been very badly used by her mother-in-law [*sic*]. I have frequently seen her with black eyes and bruises on her body.' Yet another told the court, 'I always feared Mrs Kidder would make away with the child.' Neighbours expressed similar sentiments. Even the parents and sister of Frances Kidder gave evidence at the trial of her unreasoned hatred of the girl.

On the evening of the last day of a stay with her parents at New Romney, Frances took Louisa for a walk. She returned without her, saying that she and Louisa had been frightened by rampaging horses and that the child had fallen into a water-filled ditch. Frances claimed that she was unable to rescue her. The jury could not accept such an explanation. On 2 April 1868, at Maidstone Prison, a crowd of 2,000, many of them women, witnessed the last public execution of a woman in the UK.

26 August 1898

The official report by local government inspectors into the Maidstone typhoid epidemic of the preceding year was published. The epidemic, which began in September, lasted four months. Up to the end of January 1898, there had been a total of 1,681 cases in the borough, excluding 107 cases at the Barming Lunatic Asylum and thirty at the workhouse. In their concluding comments the inspectors wrote: 'We have no hesitation in coming to the conclusion that the epidemic was caused by the pollution of the water by the Maidstone [Water] Company from their Farleigh sources . . . There is abundant testimony to show that grave sanitary defects exist in the construction of some of the sewers and of many house drains and water closets . . . But the responsibility for the existence of these insanitary conditions lies with the town council, whose duty it was to take steps that would lead to the effective remedy of these defects. This duty they have in a large measure neglected, notwithstanding that for many years the Medical Officer of Health has repeatedly warned them of the risk to which the inhabitants of the town were exposed by the continuance of these insanitary conditions.'

27 August 1818

Stageco.
(Luton
Museum
and Art
Gallery)

At a meeting held at Malling, the trustees of the Wrotham Heath turnpike road considered a recent accident when a coach, travelling 'at a furious rate', overturned and ten passengers travelling on the roof were thrown off and seriously injured. The trustees decided that if the tollgate keepers did not report reckless drivers, they should be immediately dismissed. In the above case, the owner was fined £40 and the stagecoach driver £10 for 'furiously driving'. The driver had not turned up in court and a warrant was issued to commit him to the county gaol for three months.

Dadd's Hole, Cobham Park.

28 AUGUST 1843

Richard Dadd was a hugely gifted artist. He was also fortunate that his father, Robert, encouraged him right from his early days at Rochester Cathedral Grammar School. After training as an artist he had several exhibitions, and commissions began to pour in to this most promising young artist.

In 1842 Richard toured the great classical sites of antiquity with his wealthy patron, Sir Thomas Phillips. It was at this time that he began to suffer from headaches and delusions. In Egypt he thought he heard Osiris, the ancient god of the Egyptians, telling him that he must oppose the Devil. Now convinced that the Devil could take on any shape or form, Richard believed the Pope to be the Devil and seriously considered an assassination attempt in Rome. In Paris, he attacked his patron. It was clearly time to go home.

On Richard's return his condition worsened and it was suggested that he should be confined in a mental institution. But his father desperately hoped to avoid this. The two men decided to go down to Kent where they might discuss Richard's difficulties in the quiet of the countryside.

On 28 August, arriving by gig at the Ship Inn, Cobham, they arranged to spend the night. Before dark, Richard and his father went for a walk. The following morning Robert's body was found in a field off Cobham Park Road. It lay on the edge of a deep hole, which

Richard Dadd at Bethlem Hospital, *c.* 1856.

came to be called Dadd's Hole. A stab to the left breast had penetrated a lung. Near the body was a spring-blade knife.

But where was Richard? Had he taken the gig as far as London? A search of his rooms revealed huge quantities of eggs and ale, his most recent obsessive diet. More disturbingly, there were also sketches of friends and acquaintances. Each one had a deep red gash across the throat.

Richard was finally arrested in France after an attempt to cut a man's throat. In his pockets was a list of 'people who must die'. These included the Emperor of Austria and other prominent figures.

In November 1844, Richard Dadd appeared at Maidstone Assizes and was found unfit to plead. He spent the rest of his life in Southwark Bethlem and Broadmoor Hospital for the Criminally Insane. Doctors in both hospitals encouraged him to continue painting and for the next forty years he had a successful artistic career. More recently, one of his paintings brought for valuation at the BBC's *Antiques Roadshow*, later sold for £105,000.

29 AUGUST 1830
Four hundred farm labourers gathered at Hardres and destroyed threshing machines at local farms. Anxious that there would be further disorder, special constables were drafted into the area of Hardres Court and these were later joined by Dragoons. The soldiers were ordered not to intervene until it was obvious that the civil powers were unable to contain the crowd. As it was, the labourers drifted away but for months – perhaps it might be more accurate to say years – general disorder was to continue throughout the southern counties.

The *Spectator* attributed this particular disturbance to a dispute between farmers about a threshing machine. In the course of this, a magistrate expressed his views about the machines, claiming that their introduction robbed men of work. When the labourers then began to destroy the machine, the magistrate remonstrated with them. In consequence the mob turned on him and burned his ricks. Another farmer, perhaps in jest, was understood to have said, when speaking of the plight of poor farm labourers, 'Ah, I should be well pleased if a plague were to break out among them and then I should have their carcases as manure and right good stuff it would make for my hops.' It was an ill-judged comment, for his stacks were also set on fire.

30 August 1927

Mr R.W. Honeywill of Chislehurst, the thirteenth victim of the Sevenoaks train crash, which occurred on 24 August, died. It was remarkable that so violent an accident did not result in the deaths of more of the 350 passengers.

At Riverhead, the eight-carriage train from Cannon Street left the rails, ploughing an 80-yard furrow as it zig-zagged its way to the railway bridge, tearing up the rails as it went. Finally it came to rest, jammed under the bridge, a mass of wreckage. The front coach was partially telescoped and the third crushed and twisted. 'The havoc wrought among passengers,' says one report, 'was terrible.'

At the inquest in November a jury returned a verdict of accidental death, exonerating the driver and fireman and questioning the suitability of this class of train – the River type – for fast traffic.

31 August 1760

From the *Whitehall Evening Post*: 'A Matross (artilleryman) belonging to Woolwich was last Week bit by a mad Dog, (between that place and Deptford) in his Leg, in such a Manner

A view near Woolwich, showing the employment of the convicts from the hulks. *(Courtesy of Greenwich Heritage Centre)*

that the Teeth of the Dog met together in the Wound. He was immediately ordered hither [Sheerness] to be dipt in the Salt Water; but by the Time that a place was got ready for his Reception, a Surgeon arrived Express with Directions to administer Sir George Cobb's Remedy of the Cinnabar and Musk, a Dose of which was given directly; soon after which very violent Symptoms appeared, and then another Dose was given; after which he became calm and reposed; a few Hours after a third Dose was given, which completed the Cure and yesterday he went from hence for Woolwich perfectly recovered.'

TEN GUINEAS REWARD.

STOLEN, on Monday the 10th inftant, from Maidftone, a fmall POINTER DOG, marked with a liver-coloured fpot on one eye, and alfo a fmall fpot near the tail, the reft of his body white—Anfwers to the name of CARLO.

Whoever will give Information of the offender or offenders, fo that the Dog may be had again, fhall, upon his or their conviction, receive a Reward of TEN GUINEAS, by applying to Mr. John Ruffell, of Maidftone.

A newspaper advertisement offering a ten guinea reward for the safe return of a dog. (*Maidstone and Kentish Gazette*)

SEPTEMBER

Top: The explosion of the rocket factory at Woolwich Arsenal, as seen from Plumstead Marshes.
Bottom: Sappers and miners repairing the embankment following the explosion.
(Illustrated London News, courtesy of Greenwich Heritage Centre)

1 SEPTEMBER 1850

The *Maidstone Gazette* recounted details of a fire: 'At about half past eight in the evening a fire broke out in a straw stack at a farm near Ford Mill at Wrotham. The fierce blaze ultimately engulfed 14 other stacks and destroyed two barns which contained all the year's harvest and about half of the previous year. Although the farmer, Mr Ledger, was insured, he had lost so much property that he still faced a seriously significant loss. The [fire] engine, which was on the road in less than quarter of an hour after the alarm had been given in Maidstone, arrived quickly at the farm. Fortunately there was enough water in the millpond for the firemen who concentrated their efforts on saving of the dwelling house and oast house, together with a haystack of about 30 tons. After 18 hours the fire was extinguished. 'The labouring people exerted themselves in the most praiseworthy manner,' said the *Gazette*. 'Mr Ledger bears the character of a good and respected master.'

No one was arrested for starting this fire but arson attacks on farms, which had long been a feature of country life, continued down the years.

2 SEPTEMBER 1823

The following notice was placed in newspapers as a consequence of an earlier robbery:

ROBBERY of the CRANBROOK BANK – Notice is hereby given, that in consequence of a Parcel of Notes of the Cranbrook Bank having been stolen, on 24th of April last, a NEW ISSUE of NOTES from the said Bank is now in circulation, distinguished from the old notes as follows, viz:- the words 'Cranbrook Bank,' on the top of the notes, are printed in blue ink, an oak tree is engraved on the left hand side of the notes, and they bear date in August 1823. It is particularly requested that the holders of the old notes will not circulate them, but immediately send them in for examination and exchange.

In the following year Henry Walsh was charged, tried and acquitted of the theft.

3 SEPTEMBER 1878

> About five hundred precious lives
> Women and children, men and wives
> In the midst of joy and pleasure's games
> They were all drowned in the River Thames.

These lines from the crudely written ballad, 'The Loss of the Princess Alice', tell of Britain's greatest river tragedy.

In Memoriam cards. (*Courtesy of Greenwich Heritage Centre*)

Photograph of the *Princess Alice*. *(Courtesy of Greenwich Heritage Centre)*

The *Princess Alice* was one of the most popular paddleboats on the Thames, taking hundreds of passengers each year from London Bridge on daytrips to Gravesend, Sheerness and Margate. On this dreadful day the return journey was almost completed and many were preparing to disembark at Woolwich North Pier. The brass band continued playing for those expecting to stay aboard until they reached London Bridge.

But further up river, Captain Harrison on board the collier *Bywell Castle* altered course thinking that the pleasure boat was crossing his path, making for the north side of the river. Accordingly, Harrison gave orders to alter course but so then did Captain Grinstead on the *Princess Alice*. Aware now of the emergency, Harrison put his engines into reverse but it was all too late and the bows of the collier, a much more substantial craft than the steamer, hit the *Princess Alice* forward of the starboard paddle box. The smaller boat was cut almost in two.

Some passengers, who for the most part had seemed unaware of what was to occur until the last moment, jumped or were thrown by the impact into the water. They found themselves trying to swim through polluted waste and raw sewage. Some are thought to have been poisoned. Others, waterlogged in their heavy Victorian clothing, drowned in a short time. In the saloons below decks, hundreds of passengers, hysterical and panicking, made for the staircases, but failed to reach the deck as the water washed in on them.

The boat sank within four minutes: only a few were rescued and it is suggested that about 640 people died. Over the next week several hundred bodies were retrieved but many were unidentified.

The collision between the *Bywell Castle* and the *Princess Alice* saloon-steamer near Woolwich. (*Courtesy of Greenwich Heritage Centre*)

At the subsequent inquiry, both Captain Grinstead and Captain Harrison were criticised for lack of judgement. But, at the time, despite centuries of heavy river traffic, there were no precise rules and regulations about how boats passing each other should conduct themselves. In consequence, rules were now formalised. In future, when vessels were to pass each other, they had to go 'on the port side'. Another consequence of this dreadful event was that sewage treatment plants were introduced along the river.

> Beneath the Thames their bodies lie,
> Both old and young were doomed to die.

4 SEPTEMBER 1823

The great acerbic political observer, William Cobbett, had just left Deal behind him, observing that it was 'a most villainous place . . . full of filthy-looking people.' In a hamlet just outside Margate he breakfasted poorly and grumbled that he could get no corn for his horse even though he was in rich corn country. 'All was corn around me. Barns, I should think, two hundred feet long; ricks of enormous size and most numerous; crops of wheat, five quarters to an acre, on the average; and a public house without bacon or corn! The labourers' houses all along through this island beggarly in the extreme. The people dirty, poor looking, ragged – but particularly dirty. The men and boys with dirty faces, and dirty smock-frocks, and dirty shirts; and good God, what a difference between the wife of a labouring man here and the wife of a labouring man in the forests and woodlands of

Hampshire and Sussex . . . The cause is this . . . every inch of land is appropriated by the rich. It is impossible to have an idea of anything more miserable than the state of the labourers in this part of the country.'

5 SEPTEMBER 1909

After morning service at Lympne church, the Prime Minister, Mr Asquith, was attacked by three women, one of whom struck him repeatedly, though their blows seem not to have been excessively hard. Later the same day, Mr Asquith, accompanied by four political colleagues, was about to enter the clubhouse at Littlestone golf club when the same three women rushed at him and, in the words of the Home Office report, 'molested him'. In the ensuing struggle the women were forced outside and prevented from re-entering the clubhouse. Later that night, at about 10 p.m., when the Asquiths were sitting in the dining room with their guests, two large stones were thrown through one of the windows. A woman shouted something through another open window and then she and her companions ran away.

6 SEPTEMBER 1894

The Maidstone Board of Guardians met to consider the alarming numbers of casuals that the workhouse was currently being called upon to help. In the past week these had reached an unprecedented height with 5,204 being admitted to the wards. In the identical period the previous year the figure was only 134. A considerable number of these casuals were unemployed skilled men from London, tramping the county seeking work. The Chairman of the Board said that these figures alone were evidence of the great economic distress among the poorest people in the country.

7 SEPTEMBER 1802

Yet another 'most melancholy scene' at Faversham, with another explosion at the powder mill. Houses shook to their foundations and every window in the district was broken. The bodies of five workmen were found, 'their limbs being scattered in all directions'. Only one man was found still alive, 'dreadfully torn and mangled'. He was unable to speak and died within an hour. It was thought that the grinding machine had been going too fast, causing sparks.

8 SEPTEMBER 1900

At Tonbridge an inquest was opened into the deaths of Charles Tattam and his three daughters aged 16, 12 and 6. All four were burned to death in a fire in the High Street shortly after midnight on the previous Thursday.

Gathering crowds saw the only two people to escape from the blaze – which was described as being like a furnace – Mrs Tattam and a boy, standing on the parapet, almost surrounded by flames.

Not without difficulty, the firemen, using a long ladder, rescued Mrs Tattam but the boy fell to the street below and was severely injured. And it was too late to save Mr Tattam and his three girls. He had been wakened by his wife and had straightaway sent her off with the boy while he went to the girls' room but the stairs fell in before he could return and he perished with his children.

There had been a rumour that the fire escape, which the local authority had purchased, was locked up in the castle grounds but this was denied at the inquest. If Captain Ferguson, the fire chief, had wished to use it, he could have done so within minutes, but by the time the brigade arrived on the scene it was too late for it to have been of any use.

What was possibly a more valid criticism was that there was no effective system of calling out the brigade members in times of emergency.

9 SEPTEMBER 1794

Errant wives, stolen horses, missing apprentices and absconding servants frequently figured in the pages of the press. This story appeared in the *Maidstone Journal*:

> Chatham, St Margarets
> Whereas my wife, Ann Lamb of the parish of St Margaret's, eloped from me, William Lamb, of the said parish on Tuesday morning last, without any just provocation whatever; now this is to caution the public but I will not be answerable for any debts contracted by the said Ann Lamb, (born Ann Barnes), of the parish aforesaid, from the date hereof. Witness my hand,
> Sept 7, 1794   WILLIAM LAMB

10 SEPTEMBER 1894

At Faversham Police Court Richard and Sarah Grant faced charges of neglect of four children at Ospringe brought by the NSPCC. One of the children belonged to the prisoners; another belonged to Richard Grant by a previous wife; the other two were illegitimate children whose mother paid the Grants £13 a year out of her £16 wages to look after them. The children were seen singing and begging in the street on a rainy day by an NSPCC inspector. The youngest 'nurse child', being carried by Sarah Grant, was drenched to the skin. Although 3½ years old, he was ill nourished, weighing only 12lb 11oz instead of the standard 28lb. He was suffering from whooping cough and rickets. The other children were also in a deplorable state, the elder 'nurse child' having no stockings. While the three

Kent County Constabulary, Faversham, 1899. (*Courtesy of Kent Police Museum*)

older children were not ill fed, witnesses brought from Basingstoke, where the Grants had formerly lived, told of their improper treatment. On occasion, neighbours had had to give the children food, which they had eaten ravenously.

11 SEPTEMBER 1903

The storm which broke over the Channel continued all day with hurricane-force winds. At Dover in the early hours of the morning a temporary viaduct, 600ft long, which was part of the building work on the breakwater, was carried away. Damage was estimated at about £7,000. Huge waves battered the sea wall and rebounded onto the parade, which was smashed to pieces. The new sea wall stood up to the pressure but the waves carried away thousands of tons of beach and weakened the wall's foundations.

The Hastings pleasure steamer *Britannia*, with 144 passengers aboard, finally reached the harbour after eighteen hours at sea. Then the steamer *Hesleden* arrived in the harbour and landed the body of the captain who had dropped dead during the gale. The lifeboat was called out but the waves were so ferocious that it could not be launched. It was decided to launch from the harbour and the lifeboat was therefore put on its carriage and wheeled round to the harbour. On the way, the fierce wind turned the carriage round. Inspector Nash of the Dover Borough Police and a sailor named Clark were knocked down. The lifeboat carriage passed over the inspector's body and he was killed on the spot.

At Sandgate, the promenade was smashed in many places. The sea swept through the Arthur Bevan Convalescent Home drenching 100 inmates as they lay in their beds.

At Deal, small boats on the beach were smashed and the South Sands lightship began to drift towards the Goodwin Sands. Distress signals were sent up and the Walmer lifeboat was launched but was forced to abandon its task because of the force of the gale.

12 SEPTEMBER 1830

The *Brighton Gazette* printed an extract from a letter from Sevenoaks, Kent, to a gentleman in Brighton:

I do not know how you are going on at Brighton in respect to fires but here they are terrible. Scarcely a night passes without some farmer having a corn-stack or barn set fire to. It is really dreadful. They began at Orpington by setting fire to a barn and stack which were very soon burnt down. Then they came to Love's at Shoreham and burnt several thorns [hedges], hurdles and faggots. Since then, Thompson's property at Henden has been set fire to – all his barns, stables, outbuildings and farming utensils and everything destroyed: and his house, which is a new one of his own building has been set fire to but that without the [fire] engine, they themselves extinguished. Mrs Minnett, last week, had five or seven stacks of different sorts set on fire and our town engine, as well as Lord Stanhope's and Mr Nourvalle's, was there but to very little purpose as the [hose] pipes were so cut they could not be used and from Mrs Minnett's to Jesson's, a distance of about half a mile, people stood in two rows to the amount of many hundreds, handing pails down and back. The expressions of the mob are dreadful; they said, 'D— it, let it burn. I wish it was a house. We can warm ourselves now. We only want some potatoes. There is a nice fire to cook them by.' It is really dreadful.

Since that time there has been another fire at a miller's near Brasted and one at Mr Harvey's at Cowden. A poor widow of the name of Huble, under Ide hill, said yesterday a letter had been dropped near her hands house, threatening to burn her property and to give her a rap on the head if she was out late in the day. Several people, it is said, have received these sort of letters and Mr Morphew is threatened to have his house burned down. Mr Nourvalle has, it is said, been threatened to have his house set on fire if he leaves home and to have his head broken if he goes to Mr Tong's fire so that no doubt he will soon have one. I have been told that Mr Nourvalle was gone to London to Sir Robert Peel to get a military force as he is afraid to move out without. It is not yet arrived.

13 September 1816

It was intended as another of those great days out, a late summer trip upriver, with tea at Wouldham, all to mark young Mr Gilbert's 21st birthday. And there was no doubt that the whole affair had been a huge success. As they made their way back downstream, the sun now just fading, the hymns rang out from the little party 'in the most melodious style'. If evidence was needed of how much these fourteen young chapel members had enjoyed themselves, it was their joyful singing. And then, just as the boat passed under Rochester Bridge, the hymn was cut short quite suddenly. There was one heart-rending scream and then more screams, cries, yells and then silence. Boats nearby were all too late. Every soul was lost in the fast running tide. A post intended to protect the piers of the bridge had somehow twisted out of place. Perhaps it was hidden under the surface for the evidence is not clear. But whatever occurred, as the small boat passed over it, the post forced up the head of the boat and the rear filled with water in seconds. That night not a single body was raised from the water. The next day, when the search started again, creepers were used. These long hooks attached to a bar further mangled the bodies.

But it is the death toll that so appals. In addition to the 'estimable young man,' the 21-year-old Mr Gilbert, there was his sister, 'a lovely girl of about 18 years of age.' Their married sister, Mrs Mills, perished along with her husband and her 2½-year-old baby, Eliza. Others, all girls, included three 12-year-olds, two 11-year-olds and a 10-, a 9-, a 7- and a 6-year-old. The boatman, Thomas Lear, left a wife and five children.

The Times suggested that the stricken relatives would have great consolation that 'from the general tenor of their lives, they were not unprepared to appear before their Maker.'

At the inquest questions were raised about the 'dangerous and neglected state of this scandalous bridge' and the lack of any safety equipment which had long been called for.

14 September 1816

At about 7 p.m. James Sharp and his brother were travelling from London to Wrotham in a one-horse chaise. Near the 23-mile stone, seven armed men, all on foot, stopped them. The robbers took two leather pocketbooks, a purse, a £5 note, three £1 notes, $2 and two watches. As soon as the brothers reached Wrotham they reported the robbery to the Revd Mr Moore, a magistrate. He immediately collected and dispatched a large posse of voluntary constables to search for the robbers (there was no police force in Kent at that time). At 6 a.m. the following morning, five of the footpads were overtaken at Grinstead Green but the constables were unable to detain them for they put up a fierce struggle and eventually escaped through woodland. During the fracas one of the thieves was shot in the back and a constable received a deep cut in the arm. Nevertheless, they did recover a leather pocketbook containing £6 and a bag with three loaded pistols and a powder flask. There is no record of any of the gang being arrested.

15 September 1826

With typical nineteenth-century relish for the most graphic descriptions, the *Kentish Chronicle* recorded the following incident:

It this day falls to our lot to relate one of the most melancholy accidents we ever recorded. On Sunday last, as a respectable man, named Court, landlord of The Bull at Adisham (accompanied by his wife and sister), was journeying to this city, in a one-horse chaise, when he had reached Guttridge-bottom, near Canterbury, the horse shied and instantly commenced kicking violently. In order to preserve his female companions from injury, Mr Court alighted, and the horse, finding himself released from the pressure of the rein, galloped off at full speed, drawing and kicking the driver, in consequence of his having become entangled with the harness until he reached the turnpike-gate; during which Mr and Mrs Court were clinging to the hinder part of the chaise. Mr Court was taken up as soon as some persons had collected on the spot; when it was found that the animal had kicked his face, from the chin, carrying away the entire part of his nose from the bridge, and rendering him a terrible object. His body was also severely injured. He was conveyed to the Kent and Canterbury Hospital, with little hope of recovery; and, even should he survive, his appearance cannot but excite the most heartfelt sympathy.

16 SEPTEMBER 1797

From the *Maidstone Journal*: 'About a fortnight ago as some labourers were digging by the side of an old road contiguous to the park paling of Lord Romney, they found a human skeleton laying with the face downwards. A Medical Gentleman happening to pass on its being first discovered, pronounced it to be that of a woman, supposed to have been buried 40 years. And yesterday se'nnight, within two rods of the same place, the said labourers in digging, discovered the skeleton of a man, supposed to have been interred the like number of years. There are various conjectures in the neighbourhood on the subject, but none that can lead to any discovery relating thereto.'

17 SEPTEMBER 1810

An inquest was held on the body of William Campbell of the 23rd Light Dragoons who had died in a military hospital the previous night. At one time Campbell had been a naval officer but for some unspecified reason had enlisted in the Dragoons. A week or so before his death he had deserted but was soon arrested at Boughton Monchelsea. As a punishment he had been given 400 lashes which, according to reports, 'very much affected his mind'.

A military flogging in 1838. (*Author's Collection*)

According to witnesses, all of them soldiers, Campbell appeared to be recovering well but he suddenly took a turn for the worse. Because the cause of his death might be misinterpreted, an inquest jury was convened to ascertain the facts. The staff surgeon who had attended him in hospital was certain that the punishment was not the cause of death. The body was opened up and the stomach and bowels were said to be in a perfect state. On examining the head, however, a blood clot was found on the brain. The surgeon was in no doubt that it was this which had led to an apoplectic fit. Accordingly, the jury returned the verdict – 'Died by the visitation of God'.

18 SEPTEMBER 1849

While cholera raged throughout the country – 5,000 deaths in one week – the *Maidstone and Kentish Journal* took 'much pleasure in stating that there have been no cases of cholera in Maidstone for the last week or ten days.' Nevertheless, elsewhere in the county and particularly at Court Lodge Farm in East Farleigh, there was cholera among the hundreds of hop-pickers. There were 300 sufferers at the farm of whom forty-five died, eight of them children under ten years of age. A cross in the churchyard carries the inscription: 'In memory of Forty-three Strangers who died of cholera Sepr 1849 RIP.'

Many of the 'strangers' were from London's East End, others were 'travellers' and itinerant workers. Some were Irish and others local Romanies. During that particularly hot summer, they lodged in crowded, ill-ventilated huts, barns and sheds. The cause of the outbreak was principally from water taken directly from the River Medway, contaminated by raw sewage, human and animal, coming down-river from Tonbridge.

19 SEPTEMBER 1904

A case considered by the magistrates at Bearsted Sessions certainly causes one to doubt any idea of the romance of hop-picking and the good-hearted folk who thronged to the hop gardens each summer. Before the court was an affray among the pickers in Mr White's hop-garden in Gallant's Lane at East Farleigh during which one of the pickers had been stabbed in the back. Where the truth lay was difficult to discern for there were so many versions of what happened.

What emerges is that it happened on a Sunday afternoon at about four o'clock. By that time all of those involved were drunk. There was a general melee involving half a dozen men and up to eight women. Alfy Squires ended up with two stab wounds in the shoulder although he was unable to say who had done it. He had lost a great deal of blood and had to be taken to Maidstone Hospital by a policeman called to the scene.

The difficulty of the case is not solely to work out the chronology but where to assign the blame. Somewhere in all of this, George Greenwood became involved. A bucket that he had been using fell on Wally Martin's baby's head. Greenwood claimed to have apologised but that did not stop Wally from coming out ready to do battle with him. According to Greenwood, Wally had armed himself with a knife. When Alfy Squires intervened there was a struggle involving several people and he was stabbed. At some point Amelia Martin, Wally's wife, said that Alfy hit her in the mouth which loosened all her teeth. For her part, Susannah Greenwood, George's sister, swore to having seen Wally Martin use the knife on Alfy.

Two witnesses said that even before the outbreak of hostilities, George Greenwood had stripped naked and was challenging people to fight. Wally Martin said that he had been attacked by five men and three or four of their wives and daughters who had armed themselves with knives and forks. He had locked himself in the hopper house fearing that they might kill him. While in there, George Greenwood tried unsuccessfully to break down the door and then tried to stab Wally through the window.

Wally Martin was committed to take his trial at the Quarter Sessions.

20 SEPTEMBER 1930

Margery Wren, an 82 year-old spinster, had run a general
dealer's shop in Ramsgate for over fifty years. It was a
typical corner shop, open all hours, and that was why
the young girl who went to the shop at 6 p.m. found it
odd that the door should be locked. The child went on
knocking at the door until Miss Wren eventually let
her in and served her. But when the girl went home
she mentioned to her parents that Miss Wren was
bleeding from the head. The parents went to the shop
to see what the trouble was and Miss Wren explained
that she had tripped over the fire-tongs. She gave the
doctor the same explanation.

At the hospital she was found to have several head
wounds as well as bruises on her face. There were bruises
on her neck too. Had someone attempted to strangle her?
Had someone attacked her with the tongs?

The remarkable feature of this case is that, until she
died five days later, the old lady made a number of
contradictory statements to the police. First, she said she

Margery Wren. *(Kentish Express)*

had been attacked by a man; then it was two men who had attacked her; at other times she
returned to the story about tripping over the tongs. Before she died, she made the cryptic
remark: 'I do not wish him to suffer. He must bear his sins. I do not wish to make a statement.'

Did the dying woman know her attacker? If so, why did she not identify whoever it was?
The mystery remains.

21 SEPTEMBER 1809

A man named Goldsmith, working in the stone quarry of Mr Bensted at Fant, near
Maidstone, was suddenly overwhelmed by falling stones in a minor avalanche. As he fell to
the ground, a crowbar which he had been carrying hit him on the neck. He was killed on
the spot. 'This is the fourth man who has met with a similar fate in the same quarry within
four years,' says the *Maidstone Journal*, though whether it is simply reporting the facts or is
breathing indignation is unclear.

22 SEPTEMBER 1809

The *Maidstone Journal* relates this sad story: 'A young woman who had been seduced by a
soldier to leave her service in London, and follow him to Maidstone where he deserted her,
in a fit of desperation threw herself into the River Medway, near the barrack field, and was
drowned. A coroner's inquest was taken on the body. Verdict – Lunacy.'

The verdict is interesting. Was it simply a kindness so that the girl, a suicide, should not
be buried at a crossroads rather than in a graveyard? Crossroad burials for suicides, seen as
self-murderers, continued until 1823.

23 SEPTEMBER 1881

September was the season for hop-picking, that month or five weeks when families went en
masse into Kent. September was also the season for newspaper correspondents horrified at
the intrusion. In 1881 the editorials and correspondence took up no more column inches
than other years. The following random lines come from a variety of newspaper sources in
the last week of September 1881:

The hop-picking draws from London and elsewhere an invasion reckoned at 20,000 and more, who do at their sweet will no small part of the mischief usually done by lawless soldiery.

As fast as they are paid they fill the public houses and soon fill the streets and lanes of Maidstone and of other towns with violence, horrible language and helpless intoxication.

Why is this state of things permitted? How is it possible that in a country which is not only professedly Christian but considers itself competent to send out missionaries to other countries, the high street of a considerable county town can be thronged with drunken men and women and the side streets and alleys blocked with human beings prostrate with drink?

Mothers come back drunkards or immoral; daughters, even at 14 or 15 years of age, debauched and ready for the streets; and little children glib-tongued in obscenity and blasphemy.

24 September 1785

Thomas Day wrote about the victims of gaol fever at Maidstone. The disease was typhus caused by bacteria spreading through bites from fleas and lice:

E.G. Discharged at the quarter-sessions went to Town-Malling about six miles distant and was there taken dangerously ill of the gaol distemper and died although every attention possible was paid him by the medical gentlemen of that town. The beadle, John Fowler, who attended him more frequently than any other person, caught the same fever and recovered, after having lain in a very dangerous condition for a long time. Robert Fowler, hairdresser, received the infection from the deceased and died. James Palmer was one of the persons who frequently visited the poor deceased prisoner. He was also taken with the fever and died. Mrs Field, who from motives of humanity attended the deceased in his illness, caught the fever but recovered as did likewise a servant man.

William Edmonds, a debtor, discharged, went to his home at Bredhurst and there fell ill of the fever and died. – Martin of Tovil frequently visited his brother while he lay dangerously ill of the fever in the prison. He also was taken with it and died. A publican's boy carrying beer to the prisoners in the pound of the court hall at the quarter-sessions caught the fever and recovered.

And nothing is more evident than that the prisons in most parts of England are in effect rather places of execution than places of confinement for trial.

25 September 1798

What is described as 'a melancholy circumstance' occurred at Dover. Some artillerymen, firing the great guns in Archcliff Fort, were badly out in their judgement of direction and distance for one of their cannon balls hit the sloop *Osprey*. Two men were killed on the spot and another man's arm was shattered so badly that he died shortly afterwards. Apparently the gun had been aimed for some hours before firing but the tide had changed and *Osprey* had moved from her original position into the direct line of fire. Nevertheless, this blunder occurred during daylight hours. It is remarkable that the artillerymen should have been so careless.

26 September 1816

Some young men, gathering nuts in the woods near the Old Upper Blue Bell on the Maidstone road, were alarmed to see a woman lying under a tree, for they had seen her in the same place, five days earlier. At that time they assumed her to be asleep, so they had passed without disturbing her.

One of the men went over to her and touched her hand. She was alive, 'but,' according to the *Kentish Gazette*, 'in such a situation, as excited the most shuddering sensations of horror and disgust, mixed with surprise, that a human being could retain any portion of animation under such complicated sufferings of want and wretchedness. She was almost in a state of putrefaction, large maggots were feeding on every part of her frame exposed to the attack of flies; her nostrils, and even her mouth, were infested by them; behind her ears, and between her toes, they were crawling in sickening quantities and her clothes were literally rotten from long exposure to the varying and humid atmosphere.'

The young men sought help and the latest report was that she was 'in a fair way of recovery.' Her name was Ann Martin, a Lewes woman, who had taken up with an artillery soldier and had gone to live with him at Chatham. Then she had left him but, tired and penniless, and in despair, she had lain down expecting to die. She had been in that hopeless situation for eleven days.

27 SEPTEMBER 1878

A gentleman signing himself 'Seaside Visitor' wrote a grim account to *The Times* of how he and his family at the end of September had come for a six-week stay at Ramsgate. All were in good health and were simply seeking a change of scene and sea air. Then suddenly in the course of a few days, the children began to feel ill. On the Friday before the letter was written, the doctor recommended that three of the children should go to a hospital. Then the distraught parent wrote: 'On the Saturday one of the remaining three died; on the following Monday, the second; and this morning the third – all of diphtheria.'

The doctor suggested that the cause of the deaths was drain fever. And this was not in some slum area. The family had stayed in what the father described as 'the healthiest quarter of the town.' When they arrived, he wrote, the children were 'the admiration of the neighbourhood.'

The writer had already taken his case to the local authority but complained that their efforts were simply confined to remedying the evil of the house in which he and his family had stayed. His concern was that the same thing might be going on elsewhere in Ramsgate and indeed in other towns. The law apparently did not permit private homes to be inspected. The writer begged that there ought to be closer supervision of all homes; otherwise families would be periodically destroyed, just as his had been, by the neglect of simple hygienic laws.

28 SEPTEMBER 1838

The master of the Greenwich Union Workhouse entered Thomas Robinson's name into the record book, indicating that he had absconded. There was nothing new in that: paupers often left parish workhouses and the master was to claim that Robinson's disappearance had not in any way surprised him. Yet it was curious for Robinson to go off like that: he had been chargeable to the parish for eighteen years and it

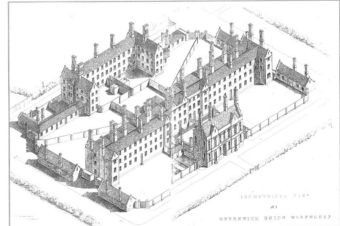

An isometrical view of Greenwich Union Workhouse. *(Courtesy of Greenwich Heritage Centre)*

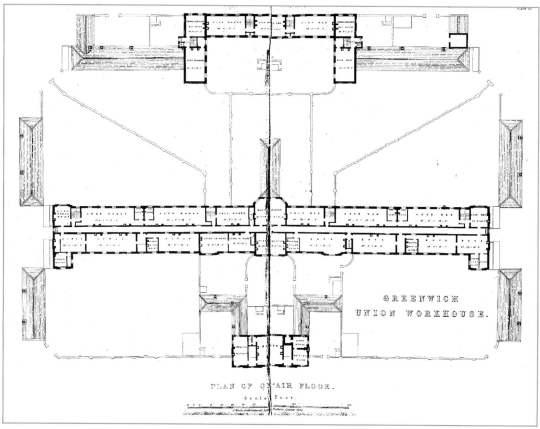

Plan of Greenwich Union Workhouse. *(Courtesy of Greenwich Heritage Centre)*

Greenwich Union House. *(Courtesy of Greenwich Heritage Centre)*

Old Workhouse, Greenwich. *(Courtesy of Greenwich Heritage Centre)*

was most unlikely that such a reliable man, now aged 63, would simply walk away. After all, he had had some responsibility within the institution, being in charge of the oakum room for which he was allowed 1s each week. The master might also have considered other reasons for such an odd occurrence. For example, Robinson had been dejected for several weeks; he had complained about headaches and had been seen by the workhouse surgeon. Some inmates spoke of having seen Robinson with his son at the workhouse gate: he had burst into tears when the young man told him he was going to sea. 'I shall never see you again,' Robinson had said tearfully.

It was three weeks later when his body, in a dreadful state of decomposition, was found under a staircase. The head was almost severed from the body and a razor lay nearby.

The inquest jury returned a verdict of 'temporary insanity'.

29 SEPTEMBER 1882

Two of the Marquis Conyngham's gamekeepers encountered a couple of poachers on the Bifrons estate near Canterbury. They had been patrolling the woodlands and spotted the men coming out of one of the coverts. When the gamekeepers called to them to stop, the poachers immediately took flight and the gamekeepers set off after them. The chase lasted for more than half an hour by which time the gamekeepers caught up with their quarry. The keepers each engaged a poacher who proved too strong for them. Littlewood, the head keeper, was butted in the chest; his head was thrust between fence wires; he was bitten on the neck and his face was savagely battered. Nor did the under-keeper fare any better. The poachers then made off, leaving some rabbits behind them.

30 September 1885

At an inquest held at the Two Brewers, Bromley, into the death of 5-year-old Edith Baldwin, the jury heard that a month earlier, while the girl was in the street, a small brown retriever dog which had been on the loose for several days, bit her on the left hand and then on the cheek. The animal had then gone into the town, snapping and snarling at other dogs as it went. It went into a chemist's shop where it bit a little girl behind the counter. The police were informed and the dog was tracked down and killed. A month after being bitten, Edith became poorly, shuddering after taking anything to drink. On the preceding Saturday, 26 September, her condition deteriorated and she screamed when any liquid was brought near her. On the Sunday she snapped and bit at everything within her reach. She died on the Sunday evening in intense agony.

OCTOBER

Remand prisoner Frank Alfred Brine, 1898.
(*Author's Collection*)

1 OCTOBER 1825

Mary Beckwith, described as a 'decent looking woman', sought the assistance of magistrates in London. She was desperate to recover her 13-year-old son whom she had been compelled to leave at Deal Workhouse. Recently she had been to the workhouse asking for his release but the Overseers there told her that he was no longer an inmate nor had they any idea where he had gone.

Eight years earlier, Mary's husband, a smuggler, fled the country, leaving her destitute and responsible for the maintenance of eight children. Eventually all the family had been admitted to the Deal Workhouse but later she scraped up enough money, working as a seamstress, to leave the workhouse with three of the children. She had continued to work hard and was able to take four more of the children out of the workhouse. Only the 13-year-old remained there. Her recent application to bring this boy home had been scornfully rejected by the overseers who had treated her application with indifference, intimating that although her child had been an inmate of the workhouse they could not now give her any account of him, and desiring her not to pester them with any more applications on the subject.

The magistrates in London were extremely sympathetic and gave her a letter addressed to the Recorder of Deal asking him to institute an inquiry.

2 OCTOBER 1864

The newspapers were full of accounts of the previous night's explosion at two gunpowder depots on Plumstead Marshes, which killed eleven people. What a scene of devastation. The gunpowder magazines were no more; barges, laden with hundreds of gunpowder barrels, no more; all around, a desolate scene, all flattened; huge fissures in the ground; the wall holding back the tides shattered for a hundred yards and threatening devastating floods until the speedy arrival of more than 2,000 soldiers and navvies; here, within a radius of half a mile, among the bricks of fallen walls, lay tables, bed-heads, cooking pots and armchairs, picture frames and fragments of modest suits and best dresses. A mile distant, Erith Church had its ceiling blown in and part of its roof lost. The explosion was heard thirty miles away at Uxbridge, heard throughout the capital and away down as far as the south coast. Fragments of powder kegs were found miles away. And so were charred and mutilated body parts.

The explosion had begun on one of the loaded barges and within seconds the landward magazines went up, perhaps 1,500 barrels in all.

At the inquest the jury could assign no cause to the catastrophe though a letter written by George Rayner, the storekeeper at the gunpowder mills, was found remarkably enough three or four miles away from the explosion. In it he warned of the hoops falling off the powder barrels which 'leaked to a very unpleasant degree.' Sadly, he was killed in his own house.

3 OCTOBER 1792

From the *Maidstone Journal*:

> At the General Quarter Sessions of the Peace held at the Court Hall for the Western Division of this county, prisoners took their respective trials for different acts of petit larceny, assaults and other misdemeanours, and were sentenced by the court to receive the following punishment,

> Maidstone Gaol Calendar:
> Aaron Lott alias Weaver – to be publicly whipt and imprisoned six months
> Thomas Hughes – imprisoned fourteen days

Mary Earl – six months Bridewell and kept to hard labour

George Aldridge and John Parker – publicly whipt and discharged, which punishment was inflicted on them in Maidstone last Thursday

John Sweeney – to remain till next assizes

Evan Evans – to be publicly whipt and imprisoned six months

Maidstone House of Correction Calendar:

John Angell – to be imprisoned six months and three times publicly whipt

John Young – publicly whipt last Thursday and discharged

At the Quarter Sessions for the Eastern part of the county, at Old Castle Yard, Canterbury the following persons were tried:

David Mimes for stealing six shirts from Mr J Reid of Chilham – whipt at the cart's tail on Saturday

Elizabeth Ramplen for stealing rags from Henry Pain of Buckland – to be privately whipt and discharged

Thomas Finnis for stealing fowls at Barham – remains for the assizes

William Clarke for stealing old rope from Mr Horn of Buckland – whipt on Saturday at the cart's tale

4 OCTOBER 1773

In the days when there were rough and ready methods for curing toothache, Mr Hamilton's very dubious cure, as advertised in the *Sussex Weekly Advertiser*, was frequently resorted to by those who could afford it:

The most violent TOOTH ACH [sic] cured in a few minutes without drawing, by a tincture, which gives immediate ease, and cures all disorders whatever in the mouth or gums, and in a few days using will fasten the teeth, if ever so loose; and, with a little continuance, will perfectly cure the scurvy in the gums; it preserves the teeth from rotting, keeping such as are decayed from becoming worse, and takes off all disagreeable smells from the breath. By applying this tincture outwardly, it will remove all kinds of swellings in the cheeks, or pain in the ears; and is an absolute cure for the head-ach, if ever so violent. This valuable tincture is sold by Mr Hamilton's appointment, at Mr Poyton's, Perfumer, No. 60, Newgate Street; W. Lee, Printer, at Lewes; Carnan, at Reading; Linden, Southampton; Cranston, Alton; and by Smiths, at Canterbury, in bottles at 2 shillings 6 pence each, signed with his name, to prevent counterfeits, that persons may be supply'd with his tooth ach tincture as prepar'd by him, and advertised in London for these twelve years past, with such uncommon success. Mr Hamilton having made it his peculiar study, to find out a tincture that is a sure preservative for the teeth and gums, as thousands have experienced and will testify.

N.B. Mr Hamilton returns his sincere thanks to the nobility, gentry, &c. for the great encouragement his tincture has met with, and is happy to find it has answered to their entire satisfaction.

5 OCTOBER 1866

James Wood, James Bartholomew and Martin Quittenden, ringleaders in an affray, appeared before the Sevenoaks magistrates charged with causing the death of 17-year-old Abraham Dobson on 29 September.

A party of hop-pickers, Dobson among them, had spent the Saturday night in a local beerhouse and at about 10 p.m. they moved on to the local public house, the Cock at Ide Hill. Here Dobson, a lively boy, began to entertain the customers, singing and dancing. And as he sang, he beat time with a stout stick he was carrying. Most customers, but not all, seemed pleased with his performance. Some of the local labourers drinking in the Cock resented the incomers and it might be that there was some muttering, threats even, for the landlord decided to close for the night before trouble broke out. Outside, Martin Quittenden began arguing with Dobson, warning him to keep his stick quiet in future.

In the struggle between the men, Quittenden managed to snatch the stick from Dobson's hands and then proceeded to beat him with it. Dobson fell to the ground and a general melee involving locals and hop-pickers broke out. Knives and sticks were freely used. Men on both sides suffered serious injuries.

And when it was all over, Dobson was dead. He had been brutally beaten about the head. There were five wounds on his forehead and three on the scalp, his right eye was closed, and there was a very severe wound under the right ear. His hair was matted with blood, mixed with gravel and small stones. At the Assizes each of the three men involved was sentenced to five years' imprisonment.

6 OCTOBER 1820

During the afternoon, a basket sent from Tunbridge Wells and addressed to a prisoner, William Greenstreet, was received at Maidstone Prison. Inside were some clothes, bacon, apples and onions and a plum pudding. Greenstreet and another prisoner, Hearn, ate the pudding and shortly afterwards both men became violently ill and died within hours. On analysis the pudding was found to contain an ounce of arsenic.

Some weeks earlier, Greenstreet and another man named Hughes had been committed to Maidstone Prison on a charge of horse stealing. As this was a capital offence, Greenstreet offered the magistrates a considerable amount of information about other thefts and in particular, about a gang of gipsy horse-stealers. Hughes, it seems, let his friends on the outside know what Greenstreet was up to. It was his betrayal which led to Greenstreet's being poisoned.

Knowing that he was dying, Greenstreet made further confessions, identifying a man named Proudly as the one who was behind the poisoning.

Despite their best efforts, the Maidstone magistrates were unable to find Proudly and his gang and on 17 October they applied to the Bow Street magistrates for assistance. Two runners, Bishop and the tireless Stephen Lavender, later the

A Bow Street Runner. (*Courtesy of Chatham Police Museum*)

Deputy Constable of Manchester, discovered that all the articles in the basket had been purchased at Tunbridge Wells by gipsy women and that a female servant living in the town had written the address on the basket at the request of a gipsy woman.

On 6 November Lavender went to Romsey fair, which he suspected Proudly might attend. But Proudly was not there. Late that night, in a dark lane outside the town, however – and was it pure chance? – Lavender, accompanied by a local constable, met Proudly and another man, the brother of the imprisoned Hughes, both on horseback. Lavender managed to unhorse Proudly and there was a violent struggle, the gipsy apparently trying to take off his clothes so that Lavender could less easily catch hold of him. But Lavender was skilled in tussles of this kind and he succeeded in handcuffing his quarry. Meanwhile, Proudly's companion had made his escape.

The gipsy ended up in Maidstone Prison and weeks later so did Mary Baker, tracked down to a gipsy encampment at Chesham, where she was arrested under suspicion of poisoning Greenstreet. There is no record of either of these people being executed.

7 October 1938

Police constable Thomas Phillips waited in an alley near the home of a 16-year-old Gillingham schoolboy whom he intended to arrest. The boy did not turn up until 4.30 a.m. and when the constable tried to detain him there was a struggle during which Phillips was stabbed four times.

At Kent Assizes the boy admitted to stealing fifteen motorcars and motorcycles in the five weeks prior to his arrest. He had also stolen a diamond ring and other property. From the proceeds of his robberies he had purchased a boat, a motorcycle and several other articles which he kept in a disused building. He was described as untruthful and cunning, one of the worst boys of his age to fall into police hands. His liking for 'indecent literature and lurid American crime books' was mentioned, perhaps to indicate a depraved nature or to suggest the causes of his criminal behaviour. The boy was sent to Borstal for three years.

8 October 1886

The newspapers were full of the renewed hostilities between English and French seamen, their mutual antipathy going back centuries. The most recent occurrence, one of several in recent weeks, had occurred two nights earlier and had led to the appearance in court of Louis Lemaire, the master of the St Esprit.

Twelve French fishing boats, all at least twice the size of the local smacks, had arrived in Ramsgate from Gravelines. Each boat was manned by a crew of up to fourteen men. They seemed overjoyed that they had had such a large catch but the appearance of so many Frenchmen in the town caused resentment. At about 11 p.m. Frederick French was one of a mob who went to the outer harbour. There is a dispute about what actually happened on this occasion and the following is only a best guess at events.

Louis Lamaire was on deck mending fishing nets. He was challenged by several of the bystanders; all of them ready to believe that he was working on stolen English nets. The French had a reputation for cutting nets, expensive equipment at £500 per net. Against that, it has to be recalled that similar charges about net-cutting were levied at English fishermen by the French.

There followed some stone throwing by the English – a fact denied by the English, by the way. French, the English fisherman – we need not be confused here if we are careful – is said to have taken off his sea boots and thrown one at a Frenchman after which he boarded the St Esprit. The Frenchman ran off, fearing what was to happen and armed himself with an axe. The Englishman was hit on the knee with the axe, which further enraged the crowd though the resentment seems to have transferred to the centre of the town where 150 Englishmen had a fierce set-to with 100 Frenchmen near the fish market.

When Lamaire appeared in court charged with assault, the case against him was dismissed. Had he wilfully and maliciously attacked the Englishman with an axe? Or had he been defending himself and his 9-year-old son who was aboard and who had been hit with a stone?

And why, asked the magistrates, was there so much ill feeling? Could the men from neighbouring nations not exist on friendly terms? There was enough fish for all, wasn't there?

9 OCTOBER 1942

The body of Mrs Ellen Symes was found in Brompton Farm Road, Strood, at 9.30 p.m. She had been stabbed in the neck. Her 4-year-old son, however, was unharmed and he was able to tell police that his mother had been attacked by a soldier.

The following day the police picked up an army deserter, Gunner Reginald Buckfield, who, the previous night, had been sleeping rough in a barn near the murder site. After three days Buckfield was released from custody at Rochester police station and handed over to the military police. There was no evidence that he had committed the murder. But as he left, Buckfield gave a detective thirteen sheets of handwritten paper. 'Read them very, very carefully,' he said. 'You'll find them very interesting.' During his time in the cell, the soldier had been writing a story entitled, 'The Mystery of Brompton Road'.

The police certainly found the work of fiction fascinating. It contained references to a woman who, with her child, visited her parents every Friday night; on these occasions her

parents used to see her part of the way home which she usually reached at about 9.30 p.m.; the woman's husband worked night shifts. The story ends with strong indications that the husband was the murderer. It was a bizarre piece of writing. During his time in the cells, police had told Buckfield very little about the murder yet here was a man showing detailed knowledge of the victim's habits, her family life and the roads in the area. Ellen Symes, wife of a shift worker, and her son, regularly visited her parents on Friday nights; her parents always took her part of the way home which she reached at about 9.30 p.m. This was the pattern followed on the night of her death.

The coincidences in the writing were too much for the jury to accept. At the Central Criminal Court in January 1943 Buckfield was found guilty of the crime and condemned to death. He was later reprieved and committed to Broadmoor.

Reginald Sidney Buckfield. (*Sunday Dispatch*)

10 OCTOBER 1829

A few jokes and pranks lighten long days of tedious labour. Perhaps that is why the women working in Mr Selby's hop garden at Tovil decided to cheer themselves up with a bit of horseplay. Their chosen victim was the bin man, the man responsible for the hopper. Doubtless there was much laughter and shouting as they seized him by the arms and legs and carried him struggling and swearing towards the hopper. It was all such great fun and there he was, the bin man, snatching up the dog (a heavy, metal tool) from the ground and now threatening the ladies in mock anger with what was going to happen to them when he was free. One flourish of the dog and down it came, the bin man laughing. Sadly, the woman who got in the way was hit on the head and was killed immediately.

11 OCTOBER 1914

Four boats arrived from Ostend carrying more than 4,000 Belgian refugees and a boat from Flushing brought another 900 to Folkestone. Most were well dressed, although every one of the 1,000 passengers in one of the boats was destitute, each one carrying all he possessed in a small bundle. In recent days more than 10,000 refugees had landed at Folkestone, telling tales of German bombardments and destroyed homes. Most of these people had gone on to London. A considerable number were not destitute and were able to pay their rail fares to London and it was thought that they had enough money to last for the immediate future. Most of them were from Antwerp. The number of the refugees appeared to be increasing daily.

War-wounded were also expected from Ostend where there were serious difficulties in dealing with the numbers of casualties owing to a lack of bandages, chloroform and medical necessities. There was already accommodation prepared for 600 wounded at Folkestone.

12 OCTOBER 1802

Lieutenant Fraser of the 1st Regiment of Life Guards, accompanied by his groom, left Canterbury for Margate in his chaise. In a sandy lane, just beyond Sturry, Fraser tried to overtake a slow-moving waggon but, perhaps because of the surface, Fraser drove against a post, which overturned the chaise. He and the groom were thrown out but while the groom was uninjured, the lieutenant went under one of the front wheels of the waggon. Eventually the groom and the waggoner managed to lift Fraser into the chaise. They returned to the King's Head at Canterbury. When they arrived at the inn Fraser called out, 'You cannot take me out of the chaise alive,' but eventually they did so and the officer was carried upstairs into a bedroom. 'Lay me on the bed,' Fraser said. 'I shall soon be dead.' He died within two hours.

13 OCTOBER 1924

At Ashford Police Court, Harry Sabini, Pasquale Papa, Antonio Mancini and Thomas Mack were charged with assaulting two bookmakers at Wye's tiny racecourse a fortnight earlier. The charge against Sabini was dismissed but the other three men were each sentenced to one month's imprisonment with hard labour.

The Sabini gang from Little Italy (Clerkenwell and Soho) were still in the process of taking over control of the southern racecourses. Led by Darby Sabini, on whom Graham Greene would base his gangster Colleoni in *Brighton Rock*, many of the gang were of Italian extraction although, despite their names, few spoke any words of the old language. Darby Sabini was cunning and violent and his son, Harry Boy, was his lieutenant. The Sabinis controlled the bookmakers on the racecourses using the roughest methods to ensure their position. So they were always, like the opposition when it dared to face them, armed with guns, axes, knuckledusters and bludgeons. It is likely that, despite the light sentences 'for lack of evidence,' such weapons were used at Wye. On occasion those who had displeased the gang – for example, jockeys who had won instead of losing or bookmakers who had had the temerity to take a pitch on a course without paying 'protection' – were thrown out of moving trains.

In 1935 the Great Croydon Airport Robbery, which netted a never-recovered haul of £11,000,000 at today's value, is thought to have been carried out by Harry Sabini, Pasquale Papa (who boxed professionally as Bert Marsh), and Silvio Mazzarda. Although one man was imprisoned, he was not a full-time member of the gang.

14 OCTOBER 1881

What could be starker or more heart-rending than the following announcement which appeared in national and local newspapers: 'THE FISHING DISASTER AT RAMSGATE – A Subscription has been commenced at Ramsgate to meet the terrible distress caused by the loss of six fishing vessels, with all their crews, numbering 30 hands, who perished during the fearful hurricane of the 14th October, leaving 13 widows, 42 children and several aged relatives.'

15 OCTOBER 1805

We are accustomed to think of this period as one of severe punishment and at the time there were more than 200 capital offences. Sometimes men and women, sometimes even very young boys and girls, were hanged for offences which today might merit community service or an ASBO. But there was considerable inconsistency in sentencing. In our more enlightened time, how would the man found guilty in this case have fared?

Two soldiers of the Herefordshire Militia, stationed at Dover, were playing cards at the Carpenter's Arms in Dover. There was a disagreement and the two men, Privates Richard Butler and George Farr, began fighting in the pub. Even so, this seems to have been a formally conducted fight because in court there was a reference to rounds. Richard Butler not only hit Farr but also kicked him – the rules of boxing at the time allowed for more variety of attack than today. In the third round, both men fell and Butler claimed that as he fell, his left knee had sunk deeply into Farr's stomach. Farr had cried out and presumably the onlookers assumed that he was badly winded. Farr insisted that he must be allowed to go outside to pass water and then, after failing to urinate, he asked to be laid on his back on the table. Butler had killed him, he said. After a week, he died.

The assistant surgeon of the regiment said that Farr had died of an inflammation of the bladder, the result of external violence. Richard Butler was found guilty of manslaughter and sentenced to six months' imprisonment.

16 OCTOBER 1829

The *Annual Register* gave an account of an attempt by convicts to scuttle the hulk *Dolphin* at Chatham.

Before any alarm was given, the lower deck was covered with two feet of water and at that moment two hundred human beings, buried in profound sleep, were locked in, totally unconscious of their perilous situation. There were nearly two hundred more convicts on the second deck and, in all, the vessel contained nearly five hundred persons. It was precisely 1 a.m. on Friday morning when the Dolphin fell upon her beam ends . . . In a few minutes the alarm was given that the vessel was sinking; a gun was fired as a signal of distress, the bells of the dockyard and garrison were rung, and blue lights were hung out on the mast of every vessel in the river. The troops of the garrison – in all, about 200 – were mustered in about twenty minutes on the beach in the dockyard; and during that period Captain George Lloyd of the *Dolphin*, the Quarter Master, and the boatswain were actively engaged in using all their efforts to save the lives of the convicts.

About 150 convicts had by that time escaped from the lower deck, many having been pulled through the portholes and others having escaped up the gangway. Holes were also cut in the top of the deck and also in the sides of the vessel; and through one aperture thirty-five men were taken out almost dead. They had kept their heads above water for nearly an hour by holding to the tops of their hammocks. Before two o'clock nearly 380 convicts, many of them perfectly naked, and none having more clothing than a shirt, were taken from the vessel and marched along the beach by the military to a place about a quarter of a mile distant from the ship and contiguous to the hospital ship *Canada*.

There is no record of any inquiry into this affair. There is no indication of how many lives were lost. There is no explanation why no one came with keys to release the men on the lower decks.

17 OCTOBER 1838

Richard Butler, one of the guards on the Dover mail coach, appeared before the Dover magistrates charged with smuggling a quantity of lace. William Edds, a customs officer, told the court that he had had information about Butler's intentions and that he had challenged the guard when the coach had halted at the post office. Butler was uncooperative, denying that he was carrying smuggled goods but Edds insisted that he open the boot. Butler searched through the boot, the passengers identifying which were their bags. Finally two unclaimed carpetbags were left. 'Is that what you want?' Butler asked, throwing them into the street. Certainly they were, for Edds found that they contained the lace.

The magistrates fined Butler £18 7s. As he was unable to pay, Butler was taken off to gaol. The magistrates, taking into account his previous good character, promised to recommend a reduction of the penalty and further said that they would ask that he should not be dismissed from his employment by the Post Office. Was there some softening of hearts here? Or were there other reasons for such consideration on the part of the members of the Bench?

18 OCTOBER 1838

The Victorians and their predecessors enjoyed the gloomy and sad intimate details of deaths and accidents, the more unexpected and bizarre, the better. Yet, there are occasions when the tone of their reportage does not quite accord with what we are accustomed to. Take the following paragraph from an unidentified Canterbury newspaper. It is the inclusion of the herring in one of these cases which robs it of complete seriousness, and how do we tend to respond to men who fall down holes? And is there such a condition as 'not so fatal'?

Broadstairs, within the last few days, has been the scene of several serious and fatal accidents. On Thursday week John Clarke, employed in pitching some straw, wounded his toe with a fork, a lockjaw ensued, and on a following Saturday he expired. On Saturday morning last Mrs Massared suddenly expired. The deceased, who was 70 years of age, had been eating a herring and while in the act of asking for another she ceased to exist. In addition to these we may mention another case which, though not so fatal, is of a serious nature. Mr Stevens, a tinman, while closing his shop on Thursday evening, fell through into the area beneath his shop and fractured his leg.

19 OCTOBER 1930

Irene Burnside, the 21-year-old daughter of Canon Burnside, headmaster of St Edmund's School, Canterbury, was killed and the pilot, Edward Read, a physician, seriously injured when the aircraft in which they were flying crashed in the grounds at East Sutton Park, near Detling.

Eyewitnesses said that on a dark and misty evening the pilot circled round and round for some minutes as if looking for somewhere to make an emergency landing. Coming in, he was trying to rise above a belt of fir trees which surrounded the park. But one of the wings was shorn off as it hit a tree. The aircraft then went into a sudden descent and crashed into a sycamore. Such was the impact that the propeller and part of the engine were buried in the tree trunk.

20 OCTOBER 1853

The working day over, the hop-pickers at Thomson's Farm at Golden Green left for their lodgings at Tudeley. As several days of incessant rain had flooded the area, their employer, Mr Cox, provided them with a horse-drawn wagon. A first wagon-load of perhaps forty men, women and children, gypsies for the most part, some local, others from Ireland, completed the journey, twice crossing the wooden bridge over the swollen Medway at Hartlake. But when the second group of passengers reached the middle of the bridge, one of the horses stumbled, causing the wheels to go through the rotten side boards. Unbalanced, the wagon toppled, throwing all of the passengers into the river.

Above: Hartlake Bridge. *(Reproduced with permission from Frank Chapman's* Book of Tonbridge, *Barracuda, 1976)*

Left: Monument in St Mary's Church, Hadlow where thirty hop-pickers are buried. *(Kent Registration Service)*

In the dark, only eleven people managed to scramble to safety. The *Kentish and South-Eastern Advertiser* painted a graphic picture: 'The screams and shouts of those who were not immediately taken below the surface – the fierce struggles of the horses – the momentary struggles and bubbling cries of the drowning – the efforts of those who were safe to rescue the others – and then, in a few seconds, when the eleven survivors stood again upon the bridge, their blank dismay at the utter disappearance beneath the surrounding waste of waters of so large a body of their friends, who a few moments before were as hale and lifelike as themselves.'

Two days later, the inquest jury visited the scene. 'We found groups of the bereaved friends and relatives standing about in mute despair – others with animated gesticulations were describing the terrible catastrophe – some with long poles were probing the eddies and backwaters of the river for those that were lost. A little bareheaded shoeless girl was pointed out to us as having lost father and mother and infant brother. One man (Hearn) had lost fourteen relatives – another whose face and mien were the personification of grief itself, threw a piece of wood to direct the men with poles to the spot where he had last caught a glimpse of his drowning wife. Only six of the bodies had been found; and thirty more it was believed were then to be discovered. It is scarcely possible to perceive a more distressing sight.'

In all thirty-five lives were lost, the oldest a 69-year-old-woman, the youngest a 2-year-old child. Despite evidence from witnesses that the bridge was dangerously defective, the inquest jury returned a verdict of accidental death, which absolved the Medway Navigation Company of all responsibility, and none of the victims' families received any recompense.

21 OCTOBER 1837

The activities of the 'swell mob' – rather elegant and well-dressed professional criminals – were described at Maidstone Assizes. Two 'dashing young fellows,' Jones and Moore, had arrived at the Three Compasses and after handing their horse and chaise over to the ostler, they went to a private room where they stayed the night. After breakfast the next morning they went to work.

In court, Joseph Kingsnorth, a wealthy farmer from Ospringe, gave evidence. Between 11 and 12 o'clock on Tuesday morning, he had left the fair and walked into the very busy High Street. He was carrying a £10 Bank of England note and a £5 Canterbury Bank note in the breast pocket of his coat. A man came up the street on horseback and suddenly the horse appeared to be out of control. In the confusion, with people dashing for safety, Jones picked his pocket but Farmer Kingsnorth was aware of what was happening and he grabbed hold of the culprit and wrestled him to the ground. But in the violent struggle that followed Jones managed to escape.

Afterwards, Jones and his colleague Moore were arrested. The superintendent of Maidstone police sent them to the Quarter Sessions. Despite evidence from witnesses who said that the behaviour of the men at the fair was noticeably suspicious, both men were acquitted, probably because they could afford to employ Sir Walter Riddell as defence lawyer. He was able to cast enough doubt on the exact identity of the man that Farmer Kingsnorth had struggled with.

The two men then returned to the Three Compasses to retrieve their chaise. They stayed for a drink, handed the landlady a sixpence (smirking, they advised her to ensure that it was not counterfeit), paid for the upkeep for the horse and 'drove off in the most audacious manner.'

Masked convicts exercising at Pentonville Prison. (*Illustrated London News*)

22 October 1887

A correspondent to *The Times* expressed concern about 'the very objectionable conditions at Maidstone gaol.' While it was one of the finest prisons in the country from an architectural and scenic point of view, because of its internal arrangements it was also a breeding place for crime. 'What is the purpose of imprisonment?' the writer asks. 'How might that purpose be achieved?' By not allowing prisoners to congregate and talk to each other. He cites the Prisons Act of 1865, confirmed by the Act of 1887: 'In a prison where criminal prisoners are confined such prisoners shall be prevented from holding any communication with each other, either by every prisoner being kept in a separate cell by day and by night, except when he is at chapel or taking exercise, or by every prisoner being confined by night to his cell and being subjected to such superintendence during the day as will consistently with the provisions of this Act prevent his communicating with any other prisoner.'

But at Maidstone 'the comparatively uncontaminated have been habitually congregated with some of the vilest and most bestial specimens of fallen humanity.'

At Pentonville, years earlier, prisoners had worn masks in the exercise yard so that they could not even recognise each other. Imagine it. Total silence. For years. No friendships. No kindnesses.

23 OCTOBER 1929

At 11.40 p.m. the fire alarm was raised at the Hotel Metropole in Margate. Sixty-three-year-old Mrs Rosaline Fox was eventually carried out of her smoke-filled room but died soon afterwards. Her grief-stricken son, Sidney, who had always seemed so caring, raised suspicions when he pestered the insurance company for the payout. After all, he had only recently increased his mother's insurance against accidental death to £3,000. After his arrest on suspicion of murder, the body was exhumed and the conclusion of the celebrated pathologist, Sir Bernard Spilsbury, was that Mrs Fox had been strangled before the fire started. At his trial, the prosecution showed that Fox had plied his mother with port and then strangled her before setting off a fire under her chair, using petrol and paper.

Sidney Fox, a con man recently released from prison, often posed as an Old Etonian or an RAF officer. In recent months, he and his mother had travelled from hotel to hotel, leaving a trail of unpaid bills behind them. But increasingly anxious about his financial situation, Fox hit on a monstrous solution. He hanged at Maidstone on 8 April 1929.

Above: Mrs Rosaline Fox, the victim. *(Daily Mirror)*

Above, right: Sidney Harry Fox. *(Daily Mirror)*

Right: Mrs Fox's bedroom and the chair in which she sat. *(Daily Mirror)*

24 OCTOBER 1786

Here's something for hypochondriacs and innocents. It is a newspaper advertisement which made frequent appearances, this time in the *Maidstone Journal*. Not that the ailments described were not serious but the cures were frequently prescribed by quacks.

To our READERS
We have inserted very extraordinary cures performed by
Mr SPILSBURY'S DROPS – Here is another proof of the powers of his medicine.
SCURVY, GOUT, RHEUMATISM, &c.

To Mr SPILSBURY

SIR,
The wonderful relief experienced by your Anticorbutic Drops, on a person 76 years of age claims an acknowledgement for public benefit. My case in August 1782, I had a virulent Scurvy, which affected my body, more particularly my legs; my right leg so bad having three wounds laid open; dreading a mortification, which was apparently coming on, I sent for a surgeon, under whose care I received not the desired effect, and by his recommendation I began to take your Drops; in November my wound had a better appearance, yet the Scurvy continued very bad; about August, 1783, my body was free from the Scurvy, but the wounds in the leg were now spread into one; in September, my foot swelled to an enormous size, and broke out into five holes; at Christmas, 1783, all my wounds healed up, leaving no appearance of the Scurvy, and I have since continued well.

Witness my hand   JOHN STURT
                                   14th December, 1785

Mr Spilsbury's Drops are vended in bottles of 5s at his Dispensary in Soho Square, London.

NB: The Proprietor's excellent Treatise on the Scurvy, Gout, and Diet, third edition, with a selection of eighty cures, may be had, with his Drops, at Mr Blake's, Printer, Bookseller, and Stationer, at the King's Arms Printing Office, Maidstone; and of the Newsmen; where the Compound Balsam, now raised to one shilling a bottle may be had. This is an excellent medicine for Coughs, Colds, &c.

25 OCTOBER 1792

In the early hours of the morning, after they had filed off their leg irons, five convicts in Maidstone Gaol, led by the noted escaper William Terry, broke out of their cells and, after picking three locks, found their way into the prison yard. Here, using cords made from their bedding, they tied two benches together, and one of them scrambled up this makeshift ladder to the top of the wall where he fixed a rope so that the others could clamber up. At the same time some of his companions were trying to open the other cells to release their fellow prisoners. Unfortunately for the escapers, there was too much noise and this alerted the prison governor, who presumably had no staff on night-time duty. He sounded the alarm in time to restore order and return the escapers to their cells. The convicts gave up without any resistance.

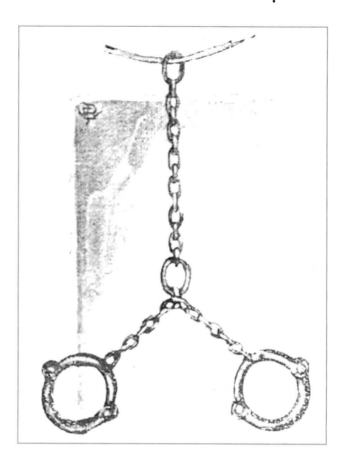

Leg irons.

It transpired that the files with which the convicts removed their irons had been smuggled into prison by Terry's 2-year-old child. Mrs Terry had been forbidden to come into the prison, presumably because of her husband's earlier escape attempt from Maidstone the previous summer. But the baby, well, that was a different matter, for what could a dear little child do to help effect an escape? It seems that Mrs Terry's cunning matched that of her husband for she sewed the files into the baby's clothes. While Mrs Terry went off shopping, she left the baby in her husband's arms.

26 OCTOBER 1945

A furious gale had raged along the Channel for some days and Folkestone, like many other coastal towns, suffered severely. Two days earlier, three houses in May Terrace had been flooded and severely damaged when parts of the sea wall were breached. The towering seas inundated the seafront and esplanade and sections of the main road were carried away.

And as if such misfortune were not enough, at about midnight, a mine, which earlier in the day had been spotted in Dungeness Bay, exploded west of the Victoria Pier. The whole of the town was violently shaken and there was scarcely a plate-glass window left in the large hotels and boarding houses along the Leas. In Sandgate Road, the main shopping centre, windows were reduced almost to powder by the monstrous blast which shrieked through from the Leas.

Police were called out to guard the displays in some of the now vulnerable shop windows.

27 OCTOBER 1794

A young man described as having a 'genteel appearance and a becoming address' called at a watchmaker's shop in Chatham. He was interested in a silver watch and chain and discussed its merits with the watchmaker. Yes, he rather liked it but he was not too certain. He weighed it in his hand, slipped it into his waistcoat to see what it was like. What did the watchmaker think? Did it suit him? Did he think it was a reliable timepiece? Were there others that he might look at? And so on. Then, when the watchmaker was distracted by another customer – a perfectly innocent person according to all accounts – and showing him his wares in another room, the young man ran off with the watch. He was later found on Chatham Hill and the stolen watch was recovered, but the young man, a genuine artful dodger, managed to make his escape.

28 OCTOBER 1861

In the evening, George Gibbs and Thomas Sanders were drinking at the Bald Faced Stag in Ashford when a coach driven by Edwin Waghorne pulled up at the door. Waghorne and his passenger went into the taproom and joined the others. Gibbs, who lodged at the Stag, knew the landlady Mrs Taylor well, and after some time he followed her into the passage for a confidential word. He told her about the passenger. He knew a lot about him. His name was George Monckton and, Gibbs said, he was a perfect gentleman. And of course, Gibbs went on, he was very wealthy. In fact he had four or five houses on the Plain at Tunbridge Wells.

Mrs Taylor appears not to have been particularly impressed by the wealthy so-called 'perfect gentleman'. She told Gibbs that he did not look much like one. 'Ah,' Gibbs answered, 'Never mind his clothes. He often changes them.' In any case, that was not the point. What Gibbs was anxious that Mrs Taylor should know, just in confidence – and here you can imagine the lowered tones – was that Mr Monckton tended not to carry any cash. 'They don't do that, these rich people,' Gibbs might have said. 'You see, they tend to carry cheques. Anyway, Mr Monckton may just ask you to cash a cheque for him later this evening and if he does, you know, remember he is a wealthy man so don't refuse him.'

And thus it came to pass. Later on, Mr Monckton came to Mrs Taylor and asked if she could cash a cheque for £6 10s. Mrs Taylor duly handed over the money. After all, she knew Gibbs and Sanders well and had no need to doubt them.

But George Monckton had no cash and no houses in Tunbridge Wells, and pretty well nothing at all anywhere else. He had pulled the same trick before, and had already served a prison sentence for doing so. That was taken into account by the judge who rewarded him with a twelve-month sentence with hard labour. His companions, Gibbs and Waghorne, each collected three months with hard labour. Thomas Sanders was acquitted, there being no evidence against him, though how could he have spent the evening in total ignorance while his companions played out this farcical fraud?

29 OCTOBER 1877

In a letter to *The Times*, Dr Samuel Prall from West Malling relates how, only three days earlier, he had been asked to visit a 17-year-old farm worker who was said to be suffering from severe symptoms of hydrophobia. He had been bitten on the thumb and the palm of the hand. Apparently, the signs had first shown up a day or two earlier but had not been recognised. Now the spasms were severe and the young man, 'a fine, strong fellow,' could swallow neither solids nor liquids. Although he was delirious, there were occasions when he was lucid and able to respond to questions, but he died within two hours of the doctor's visit.

30 October 1830

From the *Kent Herald*: 'We fear it cannot be denied that a considerable portion of the peasantry of Kent is in a state of reckless insubordination. Outrages on property of the most alarming description are manifestly on the increase. Bodies of men almost nightly, and of late, even by day, assemble and proceed from one farmhouse to another, destroying in the most open and daring manner the agricultural machinery on the premises and, far worse, the secret incendiary plies his dreadful occupation with a frequency and success that must, if continued, ere long desolate the whole country. Alarm naturally prevails all around. No man who possesses and dwells amid property of this description, can lay his head on his pillow without the frightful anticipation of being roused to witness its destruction, and endeavour to rescue his dwelling and his family from the flames.'

31 October 1871

At Tonbridge Petty Sessions William Chittenden, a plumber, was committed to trial at the Assizes on a charge of the attempted murder of his wife, Amelia. Theirs had been an unhappy marriage and in August 1871 they were divorced on the grounds of Chittenden's cruelty to his wife, and adultery.

Chittenden had left for the United States but returned, demanding that his wife come back to him. What was not later contested was that he threatened to murder her if she did not live with him again. But the reconciliation did not last and the couple again separated, though not without Chittenden's renewed threats.

On 16 October, Chittenden had gone to a barber's shop in Ashford and purchased a false beard and whiskers. He then went to Tonbridge where Amelia was now living. He lurked outside the house until the lights were out at about 11.30 p.m. and he was sure that Amelia had gone to bed. He broke the kitchen window and, before climbing through, left his boots and overcoat outside. Once in the kitchen he found the passage doorway was chained, but undeterred he smashed it down.

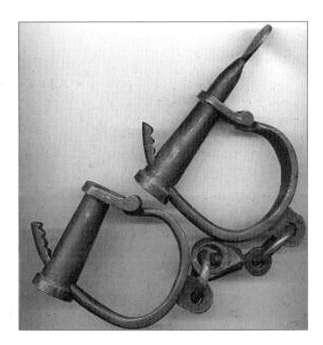

A pair of Hiatt's adjustable ratchet Derbys, introduced in the early nineteenth century. This a very rare pair exhibited at the Kent Police Museum.
(Courtesy of Kent Police Museum)

Upstairs Amelia and Mary Cox, a friend who was sleeping with her in the same bed – nothing untoward or unusual about this, incidentally – trembled, having no doubt about who had smashed down the door and who was now tiptoeing up the stairs.

Chittenden entered the bedroom, brandishing a cut-throat razor. Mary Cox struggled out of bed and had her hands severely cut as she went past him screaming 'Murder!' Amelia, terrified, hid under the bedclothes as Chittenden tried to cut her throat. 'I have done for you now!' he shouted at her, 'You'll never move again!' His thrusts at the shape under the bedclothes were savage, one of them nearly severing an ear and two others cutting the back of her neck.

But now two policemen were in the house, running up the stairs. Fortuitously, they had been passing the house and had heard Mary Cox's screams. Chittenden left off the assault on Amelia and now turned the razor on himself, hacking deep cuts into his own neck. But the policemen disarmed him and soon two surgeons arrived to patch up Amelia's wounds, which were less serious than might have been expected. They also stitched up the life-threatening wounds that Chittenden had inflicted upon himself.

At the Assizes the following December, William Chittenden was found guilty of attempted murder.

NOVEMBER

Dover police station was damaged by a medium-sized bomb in November 1940.
(Kent Police Museum)

1 NOVEMBER 1796

The *Maidstone Journal* reported the following:

RUN AWAY – With his Master's property, in the last year of his apprenticeship, WILLIAM FEATHERSTONE, a native of Rodmersham, near Sittingbourne, in Kent, apprentice to Stephen Rouse, Carpenter and Wheelwright, of Minster, Sheppy [*sic*], Kent.

Whoever will apprehend him, or give notice by a line or two where he may be found, shall receive all reasonable satisfaction, and thankfully rewarded by the said Master; whoever employs or harbours him after this notice given, will be prosecuted as the law directs.

Two sober country-bred Carpenters, (with tools) may have constant work and good wages; as also may a pair of sawyers, by applying to Stephen, or Richard Rouse, at Minster aforesaid.

N.B. Featherstone is about 5 feet 7 inches high, dark hair, and not a pleasant countenance.

2 NOVEMBER 1827

From the *Kentish Chronicle*:

On Wednesday last, the coast of this county was visited by an influx of sea which threatened the most awful consequences. The principal damage appears to have been done at Margate, at which town the bathing-machines are kept on the sands under the new wall and near the walk designed for the recreation of visitors. Not only was the walk in question destroyed, but the side of it [a mass of chalk, the natural soil that part of the shore] deeply indented by the action of the water. Several bathing machines were also dashed to pieces and the fragments scattered in every direction on the surface of the sea which flooded the promenade in front of the beautiful row of houses at this spot. A large collier, coal laden, lying opposite Wright's hotel, with its bowsprit extending over the walk, knocked down a great part of the parapet wall; a portion of the lower pier was inundated; and the steam-vessels prevented making their usual trip. On Thursday morning tide again was very high. Two steamers from London were obliged to run for Ramsgate harbour in the evening, whither they arrived. At Ramsgate and Broadstairs, the like effects were experienced; at the former town, scarcely a vestige of the pier was seen from the height of water, which, assisted by a northerly wind, presented the most awful appearance. At Herne Bay, the sea rose to a height of several feet in the marshes, and the greatest difficulty was experienced in preventing the vessels in the offing going ashore. At Reculver, the spray dashed over the wall and flooded the land to a considerable distance.

3 NOVEMBER 1825

From the *Kentish Chronicle*: 'Deal, – 3 Nov – About the daylight this morning, blowing a violent gale from about WSW, a ship [apparently about 400 tons], with a poop and figurehead, painted yellow sides and ports, was observed under her topsails in a direction towards the South Sand Head, standing in on the larboard tack; almost immediately afterwards [half past six in the morning] she struck on the Goodwin, with a tremendous sea going over her; the mast soon fell, and the crew assembled on the poop, from which every succeeding sea lessened their numbers. Seven Deal boats went out to their assistance, but such was the violence of the wind and sea, that none of them could get near enough even to obtain her name. The whole of the crew and all on board perished. She was under English colours, having, when she was first struck, hoisted her ensign, union downwards; the ship broke up entirely about noon and disappeared.'

Betteshanger Colliery, near Deal. (*Courtesy of Deal Library*)

4 NOVEMBER 1927

Two coal miners, Henry Marlow of River and Frank Jenkins of Northbourne, were killed in an accident at Betteshanger Colliery. They were working on scaffolding in Number 1 shaft, removing ventilation piping. They had just sent up a fifth load of material in the cradle to the top of the shaft. They were awaiting the descent of the cradle for the sixth time when suddenly it came down without warning, crashing onto the scaffolding and landing on top of them. The coroner said that the man in charge of the winding gear had taken his eyes off the indicator dial in the engine house for a minute or two.

5 NOVEMBER 1857

Bonfire Night was customarily disorderly in very many towns throughout the country, and Faversham was no exception. Here, as elsewhere, local magistrates were regularly anxious that the high spirits of large crowds should not develop into something worse. On this occasion, the magistrates decided during the course of the evening that matters were getting out of hand and called in special constables to assist the police in maintaining order. At one point, when police were struggling with some of the rowdier elements, a firework was thrown. For this offence, a man was arrested and taken to the lock-up. As news of the arrest spread, and especially as it appeared that the police had taken the wrong man, the mob broke into the lock-up and the prisoner was released. After this, three empty tar barrels were set alight in Court Street. The mayor attempted to read the Riot Act but was forced into retreat. A menacing mob had overcome the law.

Four days later was Mayor-Making Day, another traditionally boisterous occasion. To ensure that there would not be another such humiliating occasion, a hundred special constables joined by constables from surrounding areas and Horse Guards from Canterbury barracks, were drafted into the town. At one stage, two haystacks in the town centre were set alight. The crowd was hostile and many were ready for serious trouble. But after the reading of the Riot Act, the streets were cleared with few serious disturbances.

6 NOVEMBER 1897

The number of people suffering from the typhoid epidemic at Maidstone was reported to be 1,795, an increase of two since the previous day. Earlier in the week, the fresh cases notified reached double figures for the first time in a fortnight and this was the cause of considerable anxiety. Since the epidemic began seventy-five people had died in west Maidstone and forty in east Maidstone. A local relief fund had been established and £17,500 had been collected.

7 NOVEMBER 1849

Report of the Registrar General's Quarterly Return of Births, Deaths and Marriages in England:

In Kent, the districts on the Thames, the Medway, and coast from Gravesend, Milton, Rochester and Chatham, to the Isle of Thanet, including Margate and Ramsgate, suffered severely. The deaths in Gravesend are on an average 127 in this quarter: they were in the last quarter 340, of which 193 were by cholera. There are no available sewers, and the drainage falls into rudely constructed cesspools. The mortality of Margate, Ramsgate and the Isle of Thanet were more than double the average . . . Maidstone, on the Medway, suffered; but of 43 deaths from cholera in Loose, one of its sub-districts, all except two or three were among vagrants, chiefly Irish, who came into the parish of East Farleigh to pick hops.

This cross in St Mary's churchyard, East Farleigh, was erected to commemorate the deaths of forty-three itinerant hop-pickers in September 1849. *(Kent Registration Service)*

8 NOVEMBER 1803

Extracts from a letter from an unidentified correspondent in Margate:

> Last night a naval officer landed on the Pier about ten o'clock with a press gang, and having exercised his authority in a manner deemed improper by the High Constable and another peace officer of this port, they interfered and informed the naval officer that the persons he had impressed were not objects of the Impress Act. In consequence of this interference, the gang seized the two constables and sent them with several others on board the ship.

Thus was it ensured that the ships of His Majesty's Navy had sufficient numbers of men.

9 NOVEMBER 1841

An inquest took place at Margate on the death of Mr and Mrs Brown. They had been driving a pony-drawn chaise from Spreading Street towards the Sandwich turnpike road. They had just cut across a turnip field – presumably there was a pathway – and, quite suddenly it seems, the horse plunged into Green Sole Pond, taking with it the chaise and its occupants.

Witnesses saw both Mr and Mrs Brown struggle in the water for a brief time but no one had the opportunity to save them.

The pond was not more than 15ft across and about 8ft deep. It was thought that the pony slipped on the bank.

Chaise. *(Courtesy of Luton Museum and Art Gallery)*

St Peter and St Paul's Church, Bromley. *(Courtesy of Bromley Libraries)*

10 November 1843

The inquest jury into the death of 23-year-old Harriet Monkton, whose body had been found three days earlier in the water closet adjoining Bromley Church, heard further revelations. The young woman, described as of 'exemplary character' and as 'a very religious person,' was, to the surprise of the inquest jury, five months pregnant. Furthermore, she had died of prussic acid poisoning.

So who was her lover? Few had seen her with young men. There had been a man some months earlier of whom she had been fond but he had explained to her that he was engaged to another woman. But who was he? At this stage no one had any idea.

As for the poison, how had she come by it? There was no record of her having bought any and her mother explained to the court that there had been none in the house. More mysterious still, there was neither phial nor any kind of container in the water closet or in the grounds of the church. Neither was there any sign of a cork. Yet so great a quantity of the poison had been ingested that death would have been almost instantaneous. She would have had no time to dispose of whatever had contained the poison.

And further, how had she managed to get into the church? There was a suggestion that on the day of her death, when the organist went inside to collect his music, she had taken advantage of the unlocked gates to gain access to the water closet.

So was it suicide, or was it a murder? The matter was never resolved. But if it was murder, how did two people manage to get into the church? Did both go in stealthily after the organist? But would a murderer devise so complex a manner of disposing of his victim?

The most likely solutions are either that Harriet committed suicide or that she was attempting an abortion. Suicide is a strong possibility. A letter posted to a friend the day before she died contained phrases suggestive of a worried woman, perhaps even a deeply disturbed woman. 'I am rather unsettled,' she wrote. 'I shall hope to see you if I am spared . . . I have a great deal to tell you when I see you.'

11 November 1844

Butcher and James, aged 16 and 17 years, applied for assistance to the relieving officer at Shoreditch. They had neither hats, shoes nor shirts and were, so the reports say, 'literally covered with rags'. Both boys were famished, wet through and wretched. When they undid their clothing, the relieving officer had no doubt about their claims. Their bones were so visible that they seemed little better than skeletons.

In making their application, the boys said that they were both natives of Canterbury and had neither father nor mother. Because they had been unable to find work in their own area – Butcher was a plasterer and James a farm labourer – they had left Canterbury about four months earlier and had travelled the country looking for jobs. At Leicester they were both seized with fever – James's head, recently shaved, suggested that he had had some basic medical care – and after both had recovered they had gone on from town to town, still in search of work. They had been so unsuccessful that they had often gone without food. Now, they did not think they had the strength to walk back to Canterbury.

The relieving officer took them to a ready-made clothes workhouse and fitted them out with clothing. They were given money from the poor box to pay for their passage to Gravesend by steamer and 2s to tide them over as far as Canterbury. They were also furnished with a letter addressed to the Superintendent of Police at Canterbury, asking him to place them in the workhouse on their arrival.

12 November 1897

The presence of hop-pickers and fruit-pickers in Kent was often a source of contention. They were, of course, of huge economic importance. Nevertheless, thousands of people descending annually on the county for several months angered and frightened many who disapproved of their disorderly lives and their potential for spreading diseases.

A letter from a reader of *The Times* expressed the distaste that some felt for the visitors. He told how, one Sunday in the previous September, he had been out cycling and between Tonbridge and Wrotham had found the whole countryside given over to 'a horde of low-type savages commonly known as hoppers'. He had seen them half-naked, both men and women, fighting and generally behaving badly. Outside an inn at Mereworth, he had seen a young boy sitting on a bench, stark naked, drying himself in the sunshine, his clothes spread all around him. Beyond that dreadful sight he had come across women stripped to the waist, 'washing or performing their toilets in full view'.

13 November 1933

Alfred Crofton, a 29-year-old labourer, set fire to three haystacks at St Margaret's Bay near Dover. He had been released from prison only two weeks earlier having served three years for a similar offence. In fact, since 1925, Crofton had been found guilty four times for firing haystacks. At Kent Assizes later in the month, Superintendent Webb said that Crofton committed the offences out of spite although today such an analysis might be considered somewhat simplistic. Nevertheless, Mr Justice Charles appears to have been sympathetic to the policeman's view, sentencing Crofton to five years.

14 November 1938

At Kent Assizes George Stangroom, a Chatham labourer, pleaded guilty to demanding money with menaces from a young man, Mr Y. The prosecution said that the offences had lasted for a considerable period. Stangroom had accused Mr Y of slandering him but said that he would accept £4 not to institute proceedings. At a later stage, there was an allegation that an improper act with a girl had occurred, Stangroom saying that he had had photographs taken and threatening to tell Mr Y's and the girl's parents. Altogether Mr Y paid Stangroom £130.

Mr Justice Atkinson, condemning the case as one of the most wicked he had ever come across, said, 'For two years you have been making this young man's life miserable and you have been getting money out of him by threats of the vilest description.' He passed a sentence of five years.

15 November 1935

At Kent Assizes, Jack Lorraine, a 33-year-old ship's cook, was sentenced to twelve months' imprisonment with hard labour. After breaking into a bungalow at Alkham near Dover and finding nothing there to steal, he had set it alight and burned it to the ground. His idea, he told the police, was to divert them so that he could then commit a smash-and-grab raid in Folkestone. This seems a likely story. Lorraine, who was already serving a sentence of three years for shop-breaking, appealed to the judge to give him a longer sentence so that he could be sent away to another prison. If he did not move away from his present prison associates, he said, he would have no chance of reformation. Mr Justice Humphreys said that he would get in touch with the appropriate authorities.

16 November 1847

The newspapers reported that a huge seizure of smuggled goods was made by the revenue cutter, *Vigilant*. At about 8.30 p.m. some days earlier, the *Hannah* was seen off the Little Nore approaching the *Vigilant*. Suddenly the boat changed tack, speeding off in the opposite direction. The revenue boat set off in pursuit, the chase lasting twenty minutes. Several shots were fired at the smugglers' boat, which eventually hove to, the crew surrendering.

When searched, the *Hannah* was found to be carrying 6,000lb of tobacco and 500lb of snuff.

The *Hannah* was taken into the Custom House at Rochester and the following day the prisoners, John Rigden, Henry Brown, Sampson Burford and Robert Osborn were taken before the Rochester magistrates for examination. The prisoners pleaded guilty to the charge of being found on board with contraband goods. Rigden, from Whitstable, pleaded that he had been unaware that the *Hannah* was carrying contraband goods. He had been lying off the Little Nore in a fishing boat when the crew of the *Hannah* called to him, asking him to pilot them up the river. He had agreed to do this but until he had heard the guns firing he had not suspected anything.

The four men were all convicted and fined £100 and, as this was not forthcoming, they were sent to Maidstone Gaol and ordered to stay there until the fine was paid. As they left Rochester for Maidstone they were loudly cheered by a large party of supporters assembled to wave them off.

17 November 1866

An inmate at Blean Workhouse gave an indication of how power was abused in some workhouses: 'The Master came and caut three of us in bed after the appointed time to get up, the man Pattenden he did not punish; Blackman he stopt his food for one day and Martin he gave the full extent of his punishment forty-eight hours on Bread and Warter . . . the Master is very cruel to the young Men and Women, for he first took the milk of that was allowed wen he came here and gave us the washings of the old peoples tea leaves . . . the Poor old men go out for a walk on Wensday they go out [at] one O'clock and if they come home before a quarter to five they will not be aloud to go to their Hall, they have to stand shivering in the cold till the bell Rings.'

18 NOVEMBER 1941

At Maidstone Assizes Mr Justice Charles passed sentences of five years on two coalminers, guilty of five cases of looting from unoccupied houses in Deal. Two of the men's female relatives were sentenced to twelve months' imprisonment.

The judge condemned looting as a particularly foul crime. He said that people engaged in looting were taking advantage of the misery of others. The houses on the coast had been evacuated because of bombing, aerial combat and the threat of invasion and it was important that they should not become prey to looters. 'It is as well that everyone should know that the law in its wisdom has prescribed the sentence of death for this offence,' he told the men, adding, 'One day, in an appropriate case, that sentence will be imposed.'

A police constable said that there had been 159 similar cases in the Deal area in the course of the year.

19 NOVEMBER 1793

A press-gang tried to get aboard the *Camden* East Indiaman in port at Gravesend. But the crew resolutely opposed their invasion, swearing to cut any who dared to set foot on deck. One crew member, an Irishman, raised a grindstone which he found on deck over his head and threatened to throw it if the 'gangers' would not leave. At this point the attackers rowed away but returned at 4 a.m. the following morning when they were again sent packing.

Impressing men in this fashion was common in the eighteenth and early nineteenth centuries and was a form of government-licensed kidnapping, carried out to furnish the Navy with sailors. As in this case, even sailors aboard merchant ships were vulnerable. The Impress Service, an official body, was represented in each seaport and local roughs were employed to seize likely candidates – not always men with experience of sea-going – between the ages of 18 and 55. Life aboard a navy ship might mean facing the dangers of battle, being absent from home for years, putting up with atrocious living conditions below deck and frequently being unpaid for months.

20 NOVEMBER 1802

At the Court of King's Bench, Thomas Winter was convicted of the theft of naval stores which he must have known were illegally come by. The Chairman made the general point that 'bad men, in the employment of his Majesty in his Dock-Yards, make a constant practice of embezzling such articles, . . . others, equally bad, encourage them by receiving the articles stolen, is as true.'

Recently, because former penalties had proved inadequate, the sentence for this offence had been raised to fourteen years and Winter, a builder, must have feared the worst. He had been buying nails from children, knowing them to have been stolen, presumably by family members, from the dockyard. The court decided in the circumstances, however, not to impose all the severity of the law. Instead, he was to be imprisoned for six months at Maidstone. He was also to stand at the pillory outside Chatham Dockyard for an hour.

The Pillory.

Aimed at destroying whatever reputation a man or woman still had, an hour in the pillory might turn out to be highly dangerous. On the one hand, the crowd who were attracted to the scene might simply throw rotten fruit or eggs at their defenceless target: they might hurl guts from the slaughter-house or excrement or dead cats or rats. On the other hand, depending upon the public view of the offence, stones or pieces of wood might be thrown. There were even deaths at the pillory. It is unlikely, however, that Winter suffered too extreme a punishment. After all, far too many must have benefited from his payments.

21 NOVEMBER 1799

From the *Maidstone Journal*: 'A sergeant belonging to the 2nd Regiment of Foot, which had marched into Chatham this same day, and lately come from the Helder Point*, was drinking at a public house. A quarrel arose between him and a corporal belonging to the 4th Regiment, lying here, about a girl that the sergeant wanted to have away from the corporal. A battle ensued when the sergeant received a blow that gave him a fall from which he never rose again. The coroner's inquest sat on the body and it appeared from the evidence that the sergeant was the aggressor and from the opinion of the surgeon who had attended, that the fall might be the cause of his death for want of immediate medical assistance. The jury found a verdict of accidental death.'

* British and Russian forces had recently fought a successful battle at Helder Point off the Dutch coast against a Franco-Dutch army.

22 NOVEMBER 1791

The rates burden fell on a relatively small number of people and the authorities were therefore always anxious to find absconding husbands whose families ended up in the local workhouse. The *Maidstone Journal* of this date carried the following notice:

Run away from the parish of Horsemonden, and have left their families chargeable to the said parish of Horsemonden:

Richard Cheesman, by trade a Blacksmith, about forty years of age, about five feet six inches high, light complexion, he has at times resided at a place called Ore, near Faversham, and has carried on the business for a widow woman there, and since for her daughter, with whom he went some years ago and took the Salutation Tavern at Deptford, where he continued about six months, and has since been seen about his former residence at Ore.

Also John Mace, by business a Sawyer, about forty years of age, about five feet six inches high, of a dark complexion, pale faced, and is very deaf, has been about Deptford following the business of sawing.

Also Abraham Ashdown, by business a labourer, about thirty-five years of age, about five feet three inches high, of a light complexion, and is a very thin person.

Whoever will bring the above-named persons to the parish officers at Horsemonden, so that they may be dealt with according to law, shall receive the following rewards from the Churchwardens and Overseers of said parish of Horsemonden.

For Richard Cheesman, Five Guineas.
For John Mace, One Guinea.
For Abraham Ashdown, One Guinea.

As witness our hands, this 15th day of November 1791

Wm.Lavender
Andrew Froming } Churchwardens
Daniel Richardson
John Ashdown } Overseers

23 NOVEMBER 1811

A court martial was held on board the Raisonnable in Sheerness Harbour. Thomas O'Hara, formerly a seaman on HMS *Nereide*, was charged with being connected with the murder of Mr Daley, the ship's mate, and running away with a prize-brig, *L'Agile*, which was being towed into an English port.

When in 1809 British forces attacked and captured the Isle de Bourbon (Reunion Island in the Indian Ocean), O'Hara was found to be fighting for the French. While there was inadequate proof that he had any part in Daley's murder, he was found guilty of mutiny and treason. He was hanged at Sheerness.

24 NOVEMBER 1931

Mr Justice Rowlatt sentenced Fred Smith, a 27-year-old labourer, to three months' hard labour for stealing a horse from a field at Hunton near Maidstone. 'People were hanged for this 100 years ago,' the judge told Smith.

25 NOVEMBER 1845

James Garden, a 24-year-old apothecary's assistant, appeared at the Assizes indicted for bigamously marrying Caroline Anne Smith during the lifetime of his wife, Elizabeth Garden from whom he had separated after a three-year marriage.

James Garden had been working for several months as assistant to Elizabeth's father and they had begun walking out together. But it seems that an 'improper intimacy' before marriage occurred between them and when the 'effect of that intimacy became apparent' the father insisted on the couple marrying.

Garden was sentenced to transportation for seven years.

26 NOVEMBER 1888

Miss Martha Foster, living at Homewood House in Chislehurst, had placed her very expensive gold watch and chain on her bedroom dressing table. Later in the evening when she returned to the bedroom she found the gas burning, the blind raised and the window open. And there, in the very act, was a man climbing out of the window. Bravely, she took hold of him by the arm but was unable to prevent his escape. He ran along the roof of the conservatory, then made his way down to the ground and ran off.

Inspector Silver came to examine the crime scene. He found two ladders lashed together with rope by which means the burglar got into the first floor bedroom. He had used a jemmy to force back the window latch. The inspector also found a pair of socks on the grass which had been used to cover the possibly telltale soles of his boots. Cords used by burglars as tripwires to hinder pursuit were also found on the lawn.

Some weeks later William Barker, alias Bright, was arrested in Walworth on suspicion of burglary in London and the provinces. At his house, police found strings of coral, diamond earrings and brooches, diamond rings, bracelets and numerous other valuable articles. Some of this came from Homewood House.

When George Bowen, alias Fraser, was arrested later, he was found to have £14 in gold in his possession. He refused to give the police any information about himself.

Weeks later both men were released by the court for lack of evidence and immediately re-arrested for other burglaries in Bournemouth and elsewhere.

27 NOVEMBER 1920

At Kent Assizes three men appeared, charged with conspiring to defraud Captain Crawford Kennedy at Ramsgate and other persons at Brighton and elsewhere between 1 January and 29 September.

Charles Mansfield, an optician, John Burns, a commission agent, and the unemployed Edward Firth were relatively successful fraudsters. Burns and Firth, a Cambridge graduate, met Captain Kennedy at the Granville Hotel in Ramsgate. At that time Captain Kennedy, who was commandant of a military rest camp at Southampton, probably thought that he had something in common with Firth, the former public schoolboy and army officer, who persuaded him to join their syndicate. Firth explained that he and Burns and a third man, who just happened to be a director of the Bank of England, ran a gambling syndicate. The three of them controlled a stable of 105 horses, he said, and had first-class information on the capabilities of runners.

Sometimes, Firth told Kennedy, they heard of a horse, an unknown perhaps or at least one who was not highly rated, but who had a good chance of winning a particular race. And, of course, they backed such horses at long odds and made a tidy profit. And there were occasions, Captain Kennedy was assured, even when the horses did not win or when the odds suddenly shortened, but they still profited by judicious placing of the money. It must have seemed very attractive to Captain Kennedy and these two fellows seemed decent enough types. Yes, count me in, he had said, handing over a cheque for £200.

Only days later police arrested Mansfield and Burns at the Grand Hotel in Brighton, pulling the same stroke. Firth was later picked up.

In court evidence was given of another man, a Belgian artist who was painting Firth's portrait, who had been similarly gulled to the tune of £500.

Mansfield, described as one of this country's most expert card sharps and con men, had, like Burns, been repeatedly convicted for similar offences. They appear to have persuaded Firth to join them because he added a touch of class to the enterprise.

Mansfield was sentenced to twenty-two months', Burns to eighteen months' and Firth to five months' imprisonment, all with hard labour.

28 NOVEMBER 1796

Another of the frequent notices printed in the *Maidstone Journal* about army deserters. It ought to be recalled that conditions for soldiers were atrocious, not only when they were campaigning but also when they were based in Britain:

Deserted, from his Majesty's EAST KENT Regiment of Militia, now quartered at Liverpool, on 21st of October, JOHN TURMAINE, private, about 5 feet 8 inches high, swarthy complexion, hazel eyes, dark brown hair, about 21 years of age, born in Canterbury, by occupation a labourer.

Likewise on 29th October,
DAVID MILTON and JAMES DENNIS, privates.

The said David Milton is about 6ft high, swarthy complexion, very much freckled, grey eyes, light brown hair, 21 years of age, by occupation a labourer, but follows the employment of a Rat-catcher, is well known in and about Canterbury.

The said James Dennis is about 5ft 9 inches and a half high, fresh complexion, hazel eyes, dark brown hair, 26 years of age, born in the parish of Bursted, by occupation a labourer but likewise follows the employment of a Rat-catcher, with the aforesaid David Milton, they being confederates, and have lately been suspected of thefts.

Whoever will apprehend either of the above mentioned Deserters or give Information to the Commanding Officer, so as to cause them to be apprehended, shall receive a Reward of ONE GUINEA for each of them, over and above the Reward allowed by Government, by applying to the Commanding Officer, or to William Tustin, Esq, Agent, No. 8 Findyer-street, Whitehall, London.

By order of the Commanding Officer,
JOHNSON MACAREE, Capt.and Adj.

29 NOVEMBER 1922

Four hounds belonging to the East Kent Hunt died from strychnine poisoning at Acrise near Folkestone. The poison was thought to have been deliberately administered.

30 NOVEMBER 1922

At Maidstone Assizes, William Balpin, a dentist, was found guilty of criminally assaulting a nurse at Leigh near Tonbridge and robbing her with violence. Balpin threw her to the ground. When she screamed he pointed a revolver at her and then committed the assault, afterwards robbing her. He was sentenced to five years' penal servitude and ordered to receive twenty strokes of 'the cat'.

DECEMBER

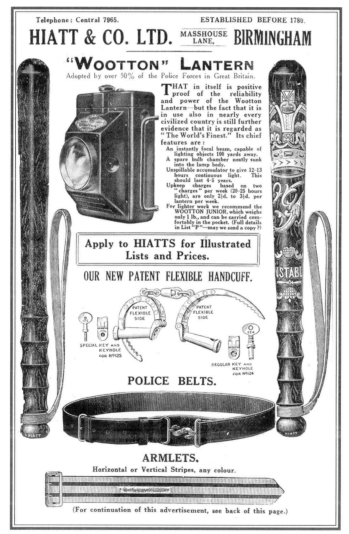

A poster advertising Hiatt & Co. Ltd products. Note their 'own product' truncheons and handcuffs.
(Courtesy of Kent Police Museum)

1 DECEMBER 1836

The *Kentish Observer* reported the following: 'CANTERBURY – this place presents a spectacle of the most saddening description from the gale on Tuesday. The number of tiles which every minute were detached from the roofs of the opposite houses, and which, driven by the force of the wind, in many instances damaged the windows to a great extent, was immense. The Cathedral braved the storm well for, with the exception of a building on the summit of the Oxford steeple (covering the great St Dunstan Bell) being moved from its position and a window blown in the western side of the south entrance, this noble edifice has sustained little injury. We regret to say that a boy named May was killed at St Peter's, Thanet, by slate falling on his head. The Canterbury Union coach was blown over on Rochester bridge. The coachman and coach were slightly injured, but the passengers were fortunately unhurt.'

2 DECEMBER 1873

At his trial at Maidstone, Thomas Atkins was accused of murdering PC Israel May. The court heard how, early in the evening of 23 August, the two men had had an altercation outside the Bull at Malling, the constable being concerned about Atkins' drunkenness. In the early hours of the following day, May's bloodied corpse was found in the middle of the Snodland to Malling road. Atkins, after an attempted flight, was arrested and charged with murder.

The attack on PC May at Snodland. *(Illustrated Police News)*

Atkins told the court: 'I was lying along by the road and the constable came and shook me. I got up and the constable then struck me on the head with his staff ... We struggled together . . . and I took the constable's staff from him and hit him about the head . . . I should not have done it if the constable had not interfered with me.'

Summing up, Mr Baron Pigott directed the jury to concentrate on two questions: did the accused set out with the deliberate intention of taking the life of PC May? He had used the constable's staff against him which might indicate that there was no premeditation. The judge also directed the jury to consider whether PC May had struck the first blow. If the accused was telling the truth, then the constable had committed an unlawful act.

The jury returned a verdict of guilty of aggravated manslaughter and Atkins was sentenced to twenty years' penal servitude.

3 December 1893

The Medical Officer of Health reported to the Maidstone Town Council on Bonny's Yard, a group of houses opening out of the south side of King Street and occupying the slope between it and the river.

Bonny's Yard comprised two rows of back-to-back houses. In one row each house had three floors, with a room on each floor measuring 9ft 9in × 8ft 9in. The rooms had sash windows, only the lower half of which could be opened for ventilation. Each cottage had its own closet but no water laid on. In the yard there was a communal bin used by all the people. The common water hydrant was also located there.

The eight houses at the bottom of the yard had one room on each of the two floors. These ground floor and first-floor rooms were subdivided into two by partitions. The front partitions measured 10 × 10ft and the rear 8 × 8ft. They too had separate closets but no water laid on. They shared the communal dustbin and water hydrant.

'They are all of a most miserable order of dwellings,' says the report. In the twenty houses there were eighty-eight people, an average of 4.4 occupants per house although in three dwellings there were eight people and in a fourth there were seven. 'The occupation of the inhabitants is very various and includes besides general labourers, hawkers, mill hands, gas stokers, sale porters, rag sorters, etc. . . . Viewed as a whole, these dwellings are relics of the past, such as nowadays would not be allowed to be constructed; from a moral and social point of view, without hesitation they must be condemned as not fit for human habitation.'

On the grounds of overcrowding and the effects of ill health from bad ventilation, the author thought they ought to be pulled down.

4 December 1862

After four months awaiting trial for a serious offence, George Dennis of Cranbrook was acquitted at Maidstone Assizes. It was bad enough being imprisoned for such a time but he also had worries about his wife and children.

Only a day or so before his arrest his wife had borne their third child. What most immediately concerned her was how to provide for the children. She feared she might have to go to the workhouse. 'I cannot bear to go there,' she said. 'They have taken George away and if I go there my poor children will be separated from me too.' She knew that if the guardians offered her some financial relief she would be able to keep the family together. But the guardians were adamant: she must go into the workhouse. If she refused she would have no help from them. Her father, a farm worker, now offered to take his daughter and her three children into his house and provide for them on condition that the guardians would allow them two gallons of flour and 2s a week. One morning, after having had a small piece of bread and a little weak tea for breakfast, Mrs Dennis, carrying her baby, went to the workhouse to hear the decision on this latest proposal. After waiting for some hours she was told that the guardians' decision was unaltered. She must enter the workhouse or do without. By the time she reached home it was 6 p.m. and she had had nothing to eat since breakfast time. No one had thought of giving her or her child anything during the long hours in which she had waited. One of the guardians said that he was aware that Mrs Dennis would starve but that the remedy was in her own hands.

When George Dennis returned home after his acquittal he found his wife in a state of semi-starvation and his children in rags. His watch, his furniture, even the bed, had been sold partly to procure bread and partly to provide a counsel to assist him in proving his innocence of the crime of which he was accused.

5 December 1878

The body of Arthur Gillow, manager of his father's farms, was found in the road at Woodnesborough early in the morning. He had left Sandwich at about 11 p.m. the previous night intending to go home. His head had been battered and his throat cut. On the ground nearby were two sticks: one, which was bloodied, was Gillow's and another, broken in two, belonged to a 28-year-old waggoner, Stephen Gambrill.

Gambrill, an employee of Gillow, was questioned and eventually arrested and charged. He was already under suspicion for recently damaging the steam threshing machine belonging

Above: William Marwood.
(Master Detective magazine)

Left: 'The Life and Career of Marwood' Like other hangmen, he became a celebrity in his time.

to Captain William Gillow who owned three farms in the locality. At nights, Arthur Gillow had been keeping an eye open for the saboteur and perhaps on the night of his murder he arrived on the scene at the same time as his murderer.

At Sandwich police station, Gambrill attempted to cut his own throat but was prevented and the wound was stitched up in time for him to appear before the magistrates at St Augustine's Sessions House on Christmas Eve. He was committed for trial at the Assizes but even before he came to trial he was confident that he would go 'to meet old Marwood,' the public executioner.

And meet him he did. Stephen Gambrill was the sixth murderer despatched by Marwood.

6 December 1827

A farm labourer called Joiner lived at Nackington near Canterbury. It being Saturday evening, Joiner and his wife had left their cottage at about 6 p.m. to go to the market. They had secured the doors and shutters but on their return, found the wash-house door open. Upstairs, they found a large chest had been broken into. All the money they possessed – 14 sovereigns and a £1 note – were gone. Then they discovered in the next room that two boxes belonging to two other men, Jordan and Hinds, had also been tampered with and Jordan's wages for the year – £5 – and another £2 savings had also been taken. In all, Jordan had lost a sum worth about £500 at today's value. Downstairs, from Mrs Joiner's father's bureau, another sum of money had gone.

The thieves had climbed onto the washhouse roof, used a stick to force an upstairs window and then, their mission complete, they had escaped through the wash-house door.

7 December 1915

Two men were killed and two others injured at Snowdown Colliery between Canterbury and Dover. The men were working 2,100ft below ground when a hopper containing about 30cwt of debris broke away from the pit-head and careered down the shaft among them. Both men were crushed to death and another had his arm so badly injured that it was amputated immediately on reaching hospital.

As it fell, the hopper struck against the sides of the shaft, breaking pipes and destroying electric light gear so that the pit was in darkness. When after two hours the rescue party reached the scene, they found floodwater 10ft deep and the man with the injured arm being held above water by his comrades.

8 December 1841

An inquiry into the treatment of the inmates at the workhouses of the Sevenoaks Union – Sevenoaks, Riverhead, Seal, Kemsing, Sundridge, Westerham and Brasted – revealed a catalogue of neglect, greed and indifference which outraged people living in the area.

For instance, from May until November 1840, it transpired that the children were never properly washed. In the winter, seventy-eight boys and ninety-four girls were found to have glandular swellings around the neck. In order to improve the health of the children, 105 gallons of milk had been ordered each morning but the master and his wife, the matron, skimmed off the cream for themselves and their family, just as they misappropriated clothing intended for the inmates.

One inspection revealed that seventy-five boys shared sixteen beds and eighty-six girls shared nineteen. There were fifty-seven men in thirty-one beds and forty women in twenty.

It was said that the women in the lying-in room did not receive the attention that they might have expected at home in their own poor cottages.

9 DECEMBER 1831

At Maidstone Assizes, Lucy Baxter, 'a wretched-looking woman, aged 27, but apparently of double that age,' was accused of killing her 20-month-old daughter, Elizabeth Amelia Baxter.

The wife of Joseph How, the master of Bexley Workhouse, gave evidence saying that Lucy Dexter had been in the workhouse with Elizabeth whom she agreed was a sickly child. During the morning of 21 September, Mrs How had heard Lucy swearing at the little girl and threatening her. 'You young bitch, I will kill you,' she had heard her say. 'You young devil, I will kill you.' Mrs How then heard Elizabeth crying out and then a noise like something falling. 'I went into the room, and saw the child lying on her back upon the floor. The mother was a few yards from it, wiping up the floor. She denied having ill-used the child . . . I afterwards saw her bring the child downstairs. She said the child had been very ill ever since she had beaten it.'

Mrs How was concerned at the infant's appearance and sent for Mr Payne, the surgeon. On the following Sunday Elizabeth died and, about eight hours afterwards, her mother left the workhouse. Mrs How used the word 'escaped' when describing the mother's departure.

The surgeon, George Payne, said that he had visited Elizabeth from 21 September until she had died four days later. During this period she vomited constantly. She also had bruises on her body. The mother admitted to having slapped her daughter, 'a cross, passionate child,' on her back and across the arms with a rod but denied ever having thrown her onto the floor. After a post-mortem, Payne was of the opinion that Elizabeth had died from inflammation of the bowels and was sure that she could not have received such bruising by falling on a flat surface. She had certainly received a blow of some kind 'but it might have been received in a fall against a corner of a stool.' He said that the child had been cutting her teeth. 'Sometimes,' he said, 'when cutting teeth, children have disordered bowels.'

Lucy Dexter was acquitted.

10 DECEMBER 1869

The *Maidstone and Kentish Journal* reported the following. 'VAGRANCY – George Jones, a sickly looking lad, was charged with begging in St Mary Cray. He told the Bench that he had travelled from High Wycombe, that he was out of work, and that he was endeavouring to find employment. Police Sergeant Higgins said that Jones had been to three or four cottages where he had been given the bread found on him. The Chairman said the Bench was determined to stamp out begging in Kent. Jones was given 14 days' hard labour.'

11 DECEMBER 1855

A bare-fist prizefight at Long Reach, Dartford, ended with the death of one of the combatants. Mike Madden and John Jones, both middleweights, each weighing about 10 stone, fought for a £100 purse in front of 3,000 spectators. Jones had previously been beaten by Madden but his recent successes in the ring now led to a rematch. At the beginning of the contest, Jones, the 5–4 favourite, had much the best of it but in the twenty-third round, Madden broke through his opponent's defence and felled him with a tremendous blow to the head. Jones, unconscious, was carried from the ring to a nearby tavern where he died within hours.

12 DECEMBER 1898

Five years earlier a report to Maidstone Town Council by the Medical Officer of Health, Matthew A. Adams, had expressed the view that the houses known as Bonny's Yard ought to be pulled down. But nothing had been done and Mr Adams had to return once more to the same theme.

Grove Court and Bonny's Yard were among the oldest buildings in the town. They were both greatly overcrowded and lacking through ventilation. Mr Adams observed that in Grove Court:

. . . there are nine closets about 12ft in front of the houses with very foul hopper pans, unprovided with any means for flushing. The service channelling and pavement are defective and water finds its way readily into the basements of the dwellings. The wall and ceiling plaster of the interior is broken away in places and the rooms are damp. In one instance, at No. 3, there are six inhabitants of whom four children aged 13, 11, nine and two years, sleep in an attic affording only 127 cubic feet of air space per head.

At Number 10 is a broken chimney that is dangerous, a leaky roof and the tenant complains of a bad smell from a drain which is said to be beneath the floor of his living room.

The interiors are in most cases dirty, having damp walls, with, in many places, broken and defective plaster; of the windows only the bottom sashes admit of being opened.

Mr Adams goes on to describe conditions at No. 40 in Ebenezer Place where the roof leaks, and continues:

the rain water pipe is broken, the wall is green from constant wet; then again, as respect the sanitary accommodation, the closets are wooden structures, very dark, out of repair, ceilings broken, pans very foul and unflushed.

Socially, as one might naturally expect, they are occupied by the lowest class of the people, day labourers and costers for the most part. Sometimes bargemen and waterside loafers: such people as belong to a distinct class and who as a matter of choice gravitate to the most squalid slums they can find, they seldom have any ties of occupation that bind them to a given spot, if turned out from one place as a matter of course they emigrate to the next dirtiest and cheapest they can discover, with little regard to locality.

Mr Adams then turns to mortality rates:

I find that during the 10 years from 1st July, 1888, to the last of June, 1898, there have been 52 deaths upon this area, constituting a death rate 25.2 per 1,000 per annum, which is little short of double the rate for the town generally. The mean age at death I find to be 17 years, which is just about half of the average length of life in the town generally.

Thirty-nine of the fifty-two deaths were of people below the age of 20. In other words 75 per cent never reached adult life. Without doubt the damp, dirt and squalor are accountable.

13 December 1935

Margaret Beer was surprised to find her former fiancé, Hugh Williams, a 22-year-old schoolmaster, outside the scullery window. Ever since she had broken off their engagement he had continually pestered her. But this time he was different. 'I'm going to kill you,' he told her. There was a sudden deafening bang and she was showered with window glass. She ran off in search of her parents. By the time they came on the scene, Williams had gone. When later the police picked him up, he said that he had thrown his weapon away. He was a humane killer. The bullet had narrowly missed Margaret. At the Maidstone Assizes Williams was sentenced to five years' imprisonment.

14 December 1833

The acquittal of 'Young John' Bodle, accused of the murder of his grandfather, the wealthy 81-year-old Plumstead farmer, George Bodle, was greeted with universal joy. At the inquest and later at the trial, witnesses had sworn that they had heard him speaking to his mother, admitting that he had poisoned the old man. And the two witnesses against him? His own

Contemporary sketch of John Bodle's farm at Plumstead. *(Courtesy of Greenwich Heritage Centre)*

On first being arrested, John Bodle spent the night in the 'cage' at Greenwich. *(Courtesy of Greenwich Heritage Centre)*

father, also called John, and his servant-woman. But at the two-day trial, serious doubts emerged about this evidence, particularly when it was learnt that the father of 'Young John' was a reckless philanderer and notorious womaniser, recently banned from his own father, George's farmhouse. Despite his respectable origins, it also turned out that this witness, who accused his own son of murder, had served time in Maidstone Gaol. Other witnesses spoke warmly in the young man's favour, describing him as kind and considerate, not the sort of man who would ever contemplate murdering his grandfather and endangering the lives of others.

One morning in November 'Young John', who lived with his parents in a cottage on the farm, had gone up to the house to collect the milk. While he was there the breakfast coffee was made. Later in the day everyone in the household – old George and his wife, another female relative and two servants – fell violently ill and after some days, George died. Tests proved that he had been poisoned with arsenic. Whether the poison was put in the kettle or in the coffee grounds was never established. In that respect the trial was inconclusive. With the acquittal the case was dropped and no one else was ever charged with the crime, though many harboured suspicions that George had been murdered by his son, John, who was after the old man's fortune.

In February 1844 came a bombshell in the newspaper: 'During the past week much interest has been manifested in the localities of Plumstead, Charlton and Woolwich, in consequence of a report that John Bodle, who was tried and acquitted 11 years ago for the murder of his grandfather, had confessed to being the individual who perpetrated the atrocious deed.'

At this time, the once much-admired 'Young John' Bodle had been found guilty of endeavouring to extort money from Lord Abingdon's butler, threatening to have him charged with an unnatural crime which would have carried the death penalty. As it was, 'Young John' was sentenced to twenty years' transportation.

15 December 1860

The *Maidstone and Kentish Journal* printed the following statement from the seven-man crew of the Margate lugger *Lively*, giving particulars of their rescue of four sailors from a wreck on Kentish Knock sand the previous day.

Being at sea on Friday morning, 14th inst, in the vicinity of the Kentish Knock sand, at about daylight, we discovered a sunken wreck with one mast standing, the wind being about E.S.E, blowing a little fresh, with a heavy swell. We, after trying with all sail to reach the wreck, found it impossible to get towards it, being too strong: but, as we neared it we fancied we discovered a flag on the masthead, which we took for a signal of distress, and seeing the dangerous situation of the crew, should they possibly have survived, in order to lose no time we immediately got our boat out, fully manned her and proceeded, rowing with all speed towards the spot which we reached with great difficulty, having been obliged to cross the sand in our skiff through a heavy surf. We found four of the crew of the sunken galliot *Hillechina*, from Hull for Bilbao, clinging to the top in a perishing condition (having been there since Tuesday night). We succeeded in getting them on board our boat and with all speed rowed back to the lugger, where, on reaching, we provided them with such refreshment as we had, and after getting them a little round, we learnt that Captain Schweing had perished from his long exposure. We then made all sail and proceeded to Margate Harbour where we arrived about half past 11 at night. Signed by Samuel Davis, William Davis, T. Pritchard, R. Robins, John Gilbert, R. Gilbert, J. Brookman. Margate, December 15.

16 December 1944

A southerly gale blew up in the Straits of Dover during the early hours. Torrential rain fell continuously and great seas were running. The storm was fiercest during the hours before dawn, gusts reaching nearly 90mph. At least two vessels went aground on the Goodwins. The Walmer lifeboat was called out just after dawn and succeeded in re-floating a stranded steamer. Dr James Hall of Deal had a busy weekend afloat. Among other emergency calls, he visited another vessel aground on the Goodwins, two of the crew of which had been injured.

17 December 1877

Lifeboat crews around the country had been extremely busy in recent weeks. The North Deal lifeboat had saved the crews from the Swedish brig *Hedwig Sophia* and the French brig *D'Artagnan*, both of which boats were wrecked in Pegwell Bay. On a subsequent occasion the lifeboat had brought ashore twenty-two crewmembers from *Crusader*, wrecked on the Goodwin Sands.

The Ramsgate lifeboat had saved five men from a French schooner, *George Valentine*, and had assisted in rescuing the twenty crew of a Dutch boat. A Ramsgate fishing boat, *Success*,

The Walmer lifeboat, *c.* 1870.
(Courtesy of Deal Library)

and the schooner *Starling* with a crew of five had been rescued, as had the brigs *Happy Return* and *Reward*, each with eight crew members.

The Margate lifeboat saved fifteen men from *Hero*, sailing from North Shields, and had helped the distressed schooner *Louisa* out of Weymouth into harbour.

Five men had been rescued from the schooner *Jane Cameron* by the Broadstairs lifeboat that had also helped rescue a cruiser, a brigantine and a second schooner.

In general recognition of his service and in particular for his courage on 11 November, Robert Wilds, coxswain of the North Deal lifeboat, was awarded a silver medal by the National Lifeboat Institution. The work of William Grant, coxswain of the Margate lifeboat, was similarly acknowledged and on 25 November he and his crew were commended for their arduous and gallant services.

18 December 1828

Early in the morning Josiah Paine stole six sheep from a farmer at Appledore. He led them way from the common where they customarily grazed and took them to his home four miles away. He decided to go a long way round rather than take the turnpike with its tollgates and farm carts, horsemen and stagecoaches. This, he believed, would be safer. But he took no notice of the one man who passed him in that narrow, usually unfrequented lane he chose to go by. He refused to acknowledge him in any way. He did not look at the passer-by, did not reply to his greeting, and did not agree that it was a very muddy lane to choose to take six sheep along. It must have seemed extraordinarily rude. These folk were countrymen. They were not sophisticated. They were not high society. But they knew the generally accepted courtesies. If somebody gave you the time of day, you answered. It was enough for the offended man in the lane to take a good look at this uncouth shepherd. He would remember him all right.

When he reached home Paine decided to have the animals slaughtered. Many sheep stealers, of course, did a rough butchering on site. They caught their animal, cut its throat, cut off the head, legs, coat, took out the lights. They were able to carry off a crudely butchered carcass in a sack. But that was when they worked in pairs. Paine, working alone, had no partner and presumably no time for any on-the-spot butchery. So he went to a man named Carter and asked him to kill and prepare the animals for market. Carter was surprised that Paine wanted to slaughter the sheep as they were all with lamb. Perhaps Paine felt that he could not afford to risk keeping the sheep too long in case their owner spotted them. And so the sheep were slaughtered and taken to market. Paine now had money in his pocket and the evidence had disappeared. Or, at least, most of the evidence had gone.

But people talk. How was it that Josiah Paine had come by six sheep, they wondered? When challenged by local farmers, he explained that he had bought them. Unconvinced, they asked whom he bought them from. Just a farmer. Which farmer? Produce this farmer, he was told, and there is £5 for you. Paine replied that he would certainly produce the farmer. But the three men he asked to pretend to be the missing farmer all refused to take part in the deception. They knew something was amiss.

In the end, it all led to the magistrates court and then to the Assizes where the man he had ignored in the lane identified him, and the constable who searched his cottage discovered a sheep's head. And finally it led to Maidstone Gaol where on 2 April 1829, the incompetent sheep stealer, Josiah Paine, was hanged.

19 December 1865

In Tonbridge Wells, a 49-year-old watchmaker, Richard Hawkins, was arrested for selling an obscene paper, *Peter Spy*. Hawkins claimed that it was satirical, intended to point out vice or folly where it existed. But Hawkins' prints were not simply satires on people's dress or manners: that might have been within the bounds of decency. But the matter was stronger than that, cruel and offensively personal, often based, so it seems, on unverified rumour. The consequence was that marriages had been sorely damaged by Hawkins' charges and the lives of individuals made desperately unhappy. The paper was full of passages intended to wound the honour and insult the integrity of private families. Not that the victims were named directly. Their names would be printed with two or three letters missing. Nor would there be any specific indication of where they lived. Readers would learn only that Mr J.n.s or Mrs R.b.n .o., guilty of some or other offence, 'lived not 100 miles from such-and-such a place.' It was always obvious who was meant. When, in the following January, the case came up at the West Kent Quarter Sessions, it was apparent that the jury considered the material to be not solely mischievous but filthy in both conception and design. Hawkins was sentenced to six months' hard labour.

20 December 1823

James Crouch was indicted at Maidstone Assizes for stealing the body of the recently buried John Dickenson from Beckenham churchyard. The day after his father's burial, Dickenson's son noted that the grave had been disturbed. Alarmed at what he had found, he had the grave opened and discovered that the now empty coffin had been forced open. Dickenson had information which led him to St Thomas's Hospital where he found his father's partly dissected body. Surgeons had bought it for twelve guineas. The principal witnesses against Crouch came from 'two persons in his own vocation' who apparently had not had any share of the proceedings, and who therefore had come forward to help the law. As the late Mr Dickenson was extremely fat, it is likely these two had helped Crouch raise him from the grave and transport him to the hospital. Crouch was sentenced to twelve months' imprisonment.

21 December 1868

At the Assizes the court heard of a grim occurrence at Malling Workhouse. One of the inmates in the tramp ward was a man named Brown who was lodging there with his two children. Waking suddenly one day, Brown found a fire burning dangerously close to him. Coming to, he realised that his clothing was on top of the fire. He called out 'Fire!' at which point another inmate, Henry Clark raged at Brown, threatening to knock his brains out with a stick. Finally, Clark calmed down and the police were called. He said to the police that he 'meant to burn the ****** place down because the Master would not give him his clothes.'

In court, Clark's demeanour suggested that he was not sane – he had in fact already been an inmate of the County Lunatic Asylum. As there was no fireplace in the ward, he had broken a wooden bed-guard, brought it into the ward and, placing the wood near Brown's bed, had set light to it. By the time Brown had raised the alarm the floor was charred and the wood had burnt through.

Clark's motive for starting the fire changed in court where he claimed that Brown had given him his clothes to burn because they were teeming with insect life. Clark said some of the insects 'stuck so close to the floor that, of course, the floor was burnt too.' He claimed the ward was infested with lice and fleas and that instead of prosecuting him, the Guardians ought to have rewarded him with £100 for what he had done for them.

Directing the jury, the judge, Mr Baron Channell, said that they might acquit the prisoner on the grounds of insanity if they thought it proper to do so. Clark was found guilty but recommended to mercy 'having regard to his apparent infirmity of mind.'

Before sentence was passed, Clark said that he had been uneasy in his mind for some time and that perhaps prison would do him good. Seven years' imprisonment would probably be just right, he told the court. Passing that sentence, the judge said that he would communicate with the authorities and have Clark's state of mind further inquired into.

22 DECEMBER 1802

The parish officers at Cranbrook, acting upon information, found a child's body floating in the stream and made further investigations. Mary Levett, servant at the house of the miller, Mr Bonnick, was arrested and charged with the murder of her bastard child. Miss Bonnick, who acted as her brother's housekeeper, had noticed that Mary was growing very fat but did not suspect a pregnancy. Then, on 30 November, she became aware that the girl had gone to the privy and stayed there an exceptionally long time. Then, she had gone a second time. Later in the day, Mary appeared to be very distressed. After some discussion with her mistress, she confessed that she had miscarried and that the body had gone into the stream which ran under the privy.

The following March, at Mary's trial at the Kent Assizes, the judge cut the case short, saying that as the surgeon could not determine that the child had been alive, the jury should acquit her.

23 DECEMBER 1818

Midshipman Robinson, who was stationed at Broadstairs, was out on the cliffs on a very dark night looking for smugglers. He fell over the cliff somewhere near the area known as 'Botany Bay'. His body was recovered floating in the water, his head 'literally dashed to pieces.' Another seaman, James Stewart, was also on duty with Robinson and, in a separate incident, also fell over the cliff. He was alive when picked up but was not expected to survive.

24 DECEMBER 1830

The last executions on Penenden Heath attracted a huge crowd. Because of fears of disorder and even of a rescue attempt, there was a very strong military presence which escorted the wagon carrying the prisoners, sitting on their coffins, from Maidstone Gaol to the place of execution.

The brothers William and Henry Packman, aged 18 and 19 respectively, had been found guilty of firing a farmer's barn. In his summing-up, the judge had observed that their accomplice, Bishop, who had turned King's Evidence, was 'according to the jury, more guilty than you' but that did not save them. Another man, John Dyke, found guilty of setting fire to a barn at Bearsted, suffered a similar fate.

On the scaffold, invited by the chaplain to admit his guilt, Dyke stubbornly refused. Others had perjured themselves, he said. The Packmans were likewise steadfast, shaking hands before, in the last seconds, William, whose wrists seem not to have been bound behind him, tore the hood off his face, declaring that he wished to see the crowd. After the bodies had hung for the usual hour, they were cut down. The father of the Packman brothers took his sons to Canterbury for burial.

25 DECEMBER 1819

In the early afternoon of Christmas Day, the house of William Chainey at Benenden was broken into, the robber making off with more than £20 in notes, sovereigns and 7s pieces. The thief also took several initialled shirts, a red waistcoat, several silk handkerchiefs and a velveteen jacket. He also stole two pistols. A young boy saw the man, describing him as youngish and tall, wearing a short round frock and long trousers. He looked to be carrying something in his shirt-front. The boy described him as looking rather like a millwright. But the thief seems not to have been caught.

26 DECEMBER 1839

The Times carried an extensive and detailed report on crime and vagrancy throughout the country. At the time, counties and towns were preparing for the first time to establish police forces. Part of the report referred to matters in Northbourne, near Deal. Here the principal felony was sheep-stealing. Such thefts occurred weekly and rarely was anyone caught. The animals were usually slaughtered in the fields at night. There were other minor thefts of poultry and honey from hives. Fruit, when in season, was taken as well as all kinds of garden produce and sacks of corn and barley. Farm tools went missing, even the wheels from barrows; in fact anything 'not under lock and key'.

27 DECEMBER 1927

For days, throughout the county, there had been freezing gale-force winds and the heaviest snowfalls for some years. Roads were blocked by huge snowdrifts and then, almost unexpectedly, as in many others parts of the country this winter, there was the slightest of thaws and consequent flooding. The London to Folkestone road was impassable at Maidstone where the approach roads to the bridge were under 3ft of water. The Weald suffered badly as did Dartford and Dymchurch, but few places in Kent escaped this spell of appalling weather.

Three hundred families were made homeless when large areas of Canterbury flooded when the Stour burst its banks. St Peter's Place, Black Griffin Lane, St Peter's Lane, Mill Lane, the Friars and other parts of the city were converted into fast-flowing rivers. In some areas the floodwater was 6ft deep.

Boats and rowing boats, some brought from Whitstable, and corporation carts and lorries delivered food, fuel and letters to stranded householders, and others were rescued from the upper floors of their homes. For the homeless, halls were commandeered and volunteers rushed to help the stricken. Many of the poorest families lost all of their possessions.

Within a couple of days the waters began to subside, leaving behind the strange sight of ice floes, 2ft deep. Workmen cleared the sluices where perambulators, wheelbarrows, furniture and the carcasses of sixty-four pigs blocked the escape of water.

As the waters fell, a large area of low-lying country in the north of Canterbury which had been a temporary lake, was, within two days, more like a vast ice-field.

28 DECEMBER 1824

Two days before his execution on Penenden Heath, John Ingram, convicted for burglary, wrote from Maidstone Gaol to the son of one of his victims. Ingram knew the house well enough. He had worked there as a footman. The letter, published in *The Times*, is interesting not solely because it is from a man soon to be executed but because it includes some thieves' cant, though its use here is probably an affectation or bravado, in the sense that it was probably more easily used by those who had been immersed in criminality over long years. Ingram certainly had not. Some of his terms, however, are simply current slang.

He begins: 'Sir, It appears to me that you are desirous of knowing who robbed your father's house in Northamptonshire; you, being a lattan scolar, I make no doubt but I can give you the wished-for information.' Ingram then goes on to say how he and Little Davy, two good 'ferrits' [burglars], broke into the 'crib' [house]. They made an incision in 'the jump' [drawing room window] with a centre-bit and made their way through that room into the 'back slums' or 'slaveys apartments' [the servants' quarters]. Here, while Little Davy, armed with a poker, stood at the foot of the 'Jacob' [the staircase], Ingram unscrewed the pantry door. Then they collected as much 'wedy' [plate] as they could take away. Little Davy also helped himself to a pair of 'crabs shells' [shoes]. They left the house and packed their 'lob' [booty] properly though they 'dinged' [threw] several things into the pond before setting out for Thrapston.

The letter goes on to say how they stopped for a cup of 'slop' [tea]; how at one point they paid out 'half a bull' [half a crown] to someone; how pleased they were with such a fine 'swag' [haul]; and how they went to see the 'iron-face man' [the receiver]. Ingram concludes rather defiantly: 'I have robbed nearly all I ever lived with, and many others, and had I lived longer, I should have robbed many more, no doubt. In fact, I felt a pleasure in so doing.'

29 DECEMBER 1936

Early in the afternoon an earth tremor was felt in several east Kent villages including Elvington, Nonington, Snowdown and Adisham. People ran into the streets fearful that an explosion had occurred. The tremor lasted for about thirty seconds and was accompanied by a rumbling noise. Only a mile from Elvington, nothing was felt or heard underground or on the surface at Tilmanstone Colliery. At Snowdown, though, halfway between Dover and Canterbury, the tremor was felt on the surface. It is thought that the disturbance was caused by heavy rains and the shrinkage of the earth underground.

30 DECEMBER 1911

At the fortnightly meeting of the Tonbridge Board of Guardians held at Pembury Workhouse, Mr A.K. Baldwin drew attention to the question of allowing old age pensions to pensioners who fell sick and were sent to the infirmary. It was wrong in his view that such people should continue to draw the pension when they were being fed and housed at ratepayers' expense. In his view the Act ought to be amended. There was a case at Tunbridge Wells, he told his fellow guardians, where a man spent all of his pension in a public house and then went a few yards to the relieving officer asking for admission to the workhouse. Once admitted, he still received his pension. Why was the man's pension not stopped? 'Why on earth,' he asked, 'should they take the money, get beastly drunk and then come into the workhouse?'

31 DECEMBER 1880

It was announced that after 4 January, strict regulations relating to foot and mouth disease within the county of Kent and in most towns were to be adhered to. No market, fair, exhibition or sale of animals could be held unless authorised by the local authority. The situation was serious as the returns of infected animals for the previous week showed: Ashford 15, Bromley 1, Cranbrook 28, Dartford 31, Faversham 221, Malling 22, Rochester 10, Tonbridge 29 and Wingham 58. This was an increase of 252 in one week. The number of affected beasts was increasing daily.

Bibliography

Books

Aspin, John, *Frances Kidder: The Last Woman to be Hanged in Public*, self-published, 1990

Branch, Johnson W., *The English Prison Hulks*, Phillimore, 1970

Chapman, Frank, *The Book of Tonbridge*, Barracuda Books, 1976

Cobbett, William, *Rural Rides Vol 2*, Dent, 1925

Cox, Dorothy, *Book of Orpington*, Barracuda Books, 1983

Crowther, M.A., *The Workhouse System 1834–1929*, Batsford, 1981

George, Michael and George, Martin, *Coast of Conflict*, SB Publications, 2004

Hammond, J.L. and Barbara, *The Village Labourer 1760–1832*, Alan Sutton, 1987

Hufton, Geoffrey and Baird, Elaine, *The Scarecrow's Legion*, Rochester Press, 1983

Johnson, W.H., *Kent Murder Casebook*, Countryside Books, 1998

——, *Kent Stories of the Supernatural*, Countryside Books, 2000

——, *Kent Tales of Mystery and Murder*, Countryside Books, 2003

——, *Kent: True Cases from the Past*, Countryside Books, 2005

Lansberry, Frederick (ed.), *Government and Politics in Kent 1640–1914*, Boydell Press, 2001

Mathews, Mike, *Captain Swing in Sussex and Kent*, The Hastings Press, 2006

Paine, Brian and Sturgess, Trevor, *Unexplained Kent*, Breedon Books, 1997

Parkin, A.M., *The Seal Chart Murder*, self-published, 1995

Price, Harry, *Poltergeist over England*, Country Life, 1945

Roberts, C.B.E., *The Trial of Reginald Sidney Buckfield*, Jarrolds, 1944

Rogers, P.G., *The Battle in Bossenden Wood*, OUP, 1961

Tye, D., *Boughton Monchelsea School: Log-book extracts 1863–1963*, Boughton Monchelsea P.A., 1973

Vincent, W.T., *The Records of the Woolwich District* Vol. 2, Virtue, *c.* 1880

Newspapers

Bromley and Beckenham Times

Chatham and Rochester News

Daily Graphic

Daily Mail

Daily Mirror

Eltham and District Times

Faversham News

Folkestone Chronicle

Folkestone, Hythe and District Herald

Folkestone Observer

Kent Chronicle

Kent and Essex Mercury

Kent Herald

Kent Messenger

Kent and Sussex Courier

Kentish Express

Kentish Gazette

Kentish Mercury

Kentish Observer

Kentish and South Eastern Advertiser

Kentish Times

Maidstone Gazette

Maidstone Journal

Maidstone and Kentish Journal

Maidstone Telegraph

Rochester and Chatham Observer

Sevenoaks Chronicle

South Eastern Gazette

Sussex Agricultural Express

The Star

The Times

Tonbridge Chronicle

Tonbridge Free Press

Tonbridge and Sevenoaks Standard

Tunbridge Wells Advertiser

Tunbridge Wells Gazette

Tunbridge Wells Journal

Tunbridge Wells Weekly Express

Whitehall Evening Post

Magazines

Bygone Kent
Family Tree Magazine
Gentleman's Magazine
Illustrated London News
Illustrated Police News
Master Detective
Murder Most Foul
North West Kent Family History Society Magazine
Police History Society Journal
The Spectator
True Crime

Official Reports

Report upon Bonny's Yard & Some Adjacent Properties, Medical Officer of Health
    Maidstone, 1893 and 1898
Some Considerations on the different ways of removing confined and infectious air . . . in
    Maidstone Gaol, Thomas Day, 1785
Thirty-Second Report – The Prisons of Great Britain, HMSO, 1868
Well Waters: Special Report on Well supplying Water to 14 and 15 Paradise Row,
    Maidstone, by MOH, 1891

Internet

www.ourworld.compuserve.com/homepages/Jill_M_Chambers Jill's Black Sheep Search:
    Convict & Criminal Research 1780–1900
www.kentishpeople.com
www.smuggling.co.uk